THE
JOURNALIST'S
CRAFT

A Guide to Writing Better Stories

THE JOURNALIST'S CRAFT

A Guide to Writing Better Stories

Edited by
Dennis Jackson & John Sweeney

ALLWORTH PRESS
NEW YORK

07   06   05   04   03   02   5   4   3   2   1

Published by Allworth Press
An imprint of Allworth Communications
10 East 23rd Street, New York, NY 10010

Cover and interior design by Jeannie Jackson, Newark, Delaware
Page composition and typography by SR Desktop Services, Ridge, NY

Library of Congress Cataloging-in-Publication Data
The journalist's craft : a guide to writing better stories / edited by
Dennis Jackson and John Sweeney.
        p.   cm.
Includes bibliographical references and index.
ISBN 1-58115-222-1
1. Journalism—Authorship.   2. Reporters and reporting.
I. Jackson, Dennis, 1945-   .   II. Sweeney, Dennis, 1947-   .
PN4775.J57   2002
808'.06607—dc21   2001007895

Printed in Canada

Contents

PREFACE

Creative Insecurity
By Jim Naughton

[Naughton is President of the Poynter Institute for Media Studies. After years of notable work as a *New York Times* political reporter, he became a major editor at the *Philadelphia Inquirer* and helped that paper win more than a dozen Pulitzer Prizes for reporting during the 1980s.]

I just wrung my hands. Again. I've already gotten up and walked around. Read a chapter in David Guterson's new novel. Worked a crossword puzzle, in ink. Told a few war stories to some pals who are in town. Like the time we put the camel in Gene Roberts' office at the *Philadelphia Inquirer*. Want to hear it? I should tell that. No. No. Not today. I'm supposed to be writing this preface, introducing you to the joys of writing for publication.

Okay, okay, I'm writing. Donald Murray says that's what you do. Get it down. Write a line a day. Live down to your expectations. Just write. Polish later. Write.

Here I sit, writing.

I'm describing this process of fits and starts to you because I know what you are thinking. You've bought this book, or are considering buying it. You've got it in your hands and are wondering if maybe it will give you the secret, the recipe for successful writing. Because every time you try to write, you do things like wring your hands, or stare at the screen, or get up and go out to prune the hollyhocks—anything to put off being daunted by sitting at the keyboard and trying to make words sing.

Guess what? This book is not likely to tell you the secret of making words sing. There is no secret. But it's perfectly okay—it's normal to be daunted by this work. It's called creative insecurity. There, I've said it. *Insecurity.*

You think you're the only one who is insecure at the keyboard? Listen to this:

> Most of us are unbelievably insecure. I don't know about Dave, who's just been described as the funniest man on earth, but I bet you every time he starts [writing] he's saying, "Oh God, is this funny or is this not funny?" There's terrible insecurity. You're out there. You've got your byline on whatever follows. There's always a feeling of, Did I get it right? Did I say it right? Does anybody understand?

That was Ellen Goodman of the *Boston Globe* talking—talking about, among others, Dave Barry of the *Miami Herald.* Renowned writers. They were on a panel at the 1998 convention of the American Society of Newspaper Editors with Donna Britt of the *Washington Post* and Rick Bragg of the *New York Times* and film critic Roger Ebert, all supposedly answering the question: "What is Good Writing?"

That's the same question you're asking . . . or you wouldn't have your nose in this book. What is good writing? Here's the answer: Good writing is what works. Now, what works for Donald Drake isn't the same as what works for Jon Franklin. What works for Lynn Franklin is separable from what works for Richard Aregood. What works for you is what it takes to tell the story.

Tell the story.

Don't "relate an article." Don't "communicate with an audience." Don't "portray an event."

Tell the story.

That means that you, the writer, reach someone. You connect with, you intrigue, you grip a reader.

There is no one single way. No best way. No absolutely, definitely, certifiably surefire way. There is only what works.

Oddly, that's the glory of it. You, yes you, can figure out a way to tell the story that Hugh Mulligan, Carl Stepp, Dennis Jackson, Tom Silvestri, Lucille deView, John Sweeney, Jeanne Murray Walker, even Mark Bowden, haven't. Pay attention to what these writers in this collection of essays say about writing. Follow their tips. Learn from their experiences. Just don't try to be them. Be you.

It is daunting, isn't it?

This may help: Every single one of the writers in this book is daunted. They're all insecure. It's the nature of the process. Read about lyricists, or portrait artists, or dramatists, or sculptors. They're all nuts. Ravaged by doubt. Driven to achieve. Writing news is no different. It is a creative act. Every journalist I've ever known, ever worked with, ever admired, comes to work every single day secretly thinking, but usually not saying, *Today's the day they're going to catch on.* We live in fear that we're about to be fired. We start our workdays convinced we won't rise, this time, to the occasion. We will. We must. We do. Somehow. But it is never easy.

That's why newsrooms should be environments that nurture, full of editors and colleagues who collaborate, who assist, who abet, who talk us through the whim-whams. We thrive when a neighboring writer looks over our shoulder and says, "Wow." Or when an editor wanders by and says how nicely phrased that third paragraph was. Uptight newsrooms—cauldrons of conformity—squash writers and deprive readers. Editors have to enforce rules, but the best editors know when the rule should be ignored or flat broken.

That's what Ken Fuson and his editor did in 1995 at the *Des Moines Register,* when Fuson got one of those dreaded assignments: Cover the first warm day of spring. Oh, great, a story that maybe 197 people already had written in Des Moines before Ken Fuson had to make it sing.

What Ken Fuson did was write it his way. He reported what it looked, sounded, felt, and smelled like on the first warm day of the year. He went back to the newsroom and told Randy Essex, his editor, that he planned to try something different. Essex didn't roll his eyes or jump up and down and demand an inverted pyramid or grab the stylebook and turn to the entry for First Day of Spring. He gave Fuson encouragement to try.

Try.

What Ken Fuson tried was so good that the *Des Moines Register* put it on page one the next morning in its entirety. What Ken Fuson did was to tell that story in 290 words constructed as a single sentence, like this:

Oh, what a day

MARCH 16, 1995

Here's how Iowa celebrates a 70-degree day in the middle of March: By washing the car and scooping the loop and taking a walk; by day-dreaming in school and playing hooky at work and shutting off the furnace at home; by skateboarding and flying

kites and digging through closets for baseball gloves; by riding
that new bike you got for Christmas and drawing hopscotch
boxes in chalk on the sidewalk and not caring if the kids lost
their mittens again; by looking for robins and noticing swimsuits
on department store mannequins and shooting hoops in the
park; by sticking the ice scraper in the trunk and the antifreeze
in the garage and leaving the car parked outside overnight; by
cleaning the barbecue and stuffing the parka in storage and just
standing outside and letting that friendly sun kiss your face; by
wondering where you're going to go on summer vacation and
getting reacquainted with neighbors on the front porch and
telling the boys that—yes! yes!—they can run outside and play
without a jacket; by holding hands with a lover and jogging in
shorts and picking up the extra branches in the yard; by eating
an ice cream cone outside and (if you're a farmer or gardener)
feeling that first twinge that says it's time to plant and (if you're
a high school senior) feeling that first twinge that says it's time to
leave; by wondering if in all of history there has ever been a day
so glorious and concluding that there hasn't and being afraid to
even stop and take a breath (or begin a new paragraph) for fear
that winter would return, leaving Wednesday in our memory as
nothing more than a sweet and too-short dream.[1]

I don't doubt that Ken Fuson was insecure when he wrote those 290 words,
or that the insecurity drove him to be better than he thought he was capable of being as a writer. That's what we do. I know. It took me the longest
time, a decade into a career as a writer at the Cleveland *Plain Dealer* and
the *New York Times,* to understand that the insecurity was natural, perhaps beneficial. I wrote about it, years later, at a Poynter Institute writing
seminar. Here is what I wrote:

Death of a Demigod

He was the most gifted professional I knew. A consummate
reporter. A nurturing boss. A compleat bureaucrat. A caring colleague.

It was easy to be in awe of him, and I was. Now it was going
to become difficult to live with.

The editor was about to join me, for several days, in coverage
of the political campaign I was following. He would be sitting

---

1. © 1995, reprinted with permission by the *Des Moines Register.*

next to me on the press plane, eating the same sterile airline food, reading the same handouts—and watching me write. Oh, God. How could I possibly get through the week?

As luck would have it—and if nothing else, I have been greatly fortunate—it was he who had to write first. He joined the campaign with a notebook full of some Washington development or other and had to write about it, typewriter perched on his knees, before we hit the next campaign stop, aboard the plane.

So he rolled the paper into the typewriter, just as I would. He sat motionless for several minutes, just as I would. He typed a bit and rolled the platen up and mulled, just as I would. He *xxxx*ed and *mmmm*ed with ferocity, just as I would. He anguished, just as I would.

And then he did an astonishing thing. He asked me to read, over his shoulder, his raw copy.

Dumbly, I read. He had a word in the second paragraph that was not quite correct. I meekly suggested a replacement. His eyes lit up and he rolled the copy back down to that spot and inserted my word. *My* word!

The experience recurred several times before he was finished. And when he had completed the story, he sighed. I looked at him—quizzically, I'm sure. And he said something that, in my naïveté, I thought he had coined at that very moment and that I realized only years later had been a citation of Dorothy Parker:

"I hate to write, but I love having written."

It summed up my whole existence. And I loved Max Frankel for having let me see, for the first time in my life, that I was not uniquely insecure as a writer.

The demigod was merely human. Thank God.

INTRODUCTION

A "Few Words" for Fellow Writers
By Dennis Jackson and John Sweeney

Some of the writers you will read in this collection of essays have won the Pulitzer Prize or similarly notable awards for their reporting. Other contributors have published acclaimed books of poetry; or watched their plays being staged by professional theater companies; or experienced the thrill of seeing their newspaper stories transformed into movies or published as best-selling books.

These writers have worked, variously, as editors of newspapers, magazines, or books; as columnists or editorialists; as general assignment, investigative, or business reporters; as magazine freelancers; as science writers; as college professors; as international correspondents.

In their diverse posts they've covered wars; the White House; Watergate hearings; funerals of popes, princesses, and presidents; Wall Street; space shuttle launches; Arkansas Razorback sports; the spread of AIDS; astonishing medical advances; preparations for a high school's spring musical; and the misfortunes of a jobless longshoreman who happened onto $1.2 million in cash after it toppled from an armored car. That's not to mention the thousands of daily stories most of these writers have filed while covering city hall, school boards, courts, cops, and seepage in the city sewer system.

Their jobs and their genres have been divergent. But these veterans have one thing in common: Every time they face a keyboard, they suffer anxiety.

Jim Naughton swears, in the preface to this collection, that that's true for him. And he is—in the opinion of the legendary editor Gene Roberts—

"a guy who could report with anybody and write with anybody." Naughton distinguished himself as a *New York Times* political reporter in the 1970s and then as an inspiring editor for the *Philadelphia Inquirer* reporters who collected more than a dozen Pulitzers during the 1980s. Roberts insists that Naughton is "one of the most brilliant journalists of his generation."[1]

Yet here he is, in this volume, telling us he feels daunted and insecure every time he starts to write. Further, he claims that "every journalist [he's] ever known, ever worked with, ever admired comes to work every single day secretly thinking" that, on this day, her (or his) inadequacies as a writer will be plain for all to see.

Naughton wouldn't have to look far in this collection to find supporting testimony for his sweeping declaration. Hugh Mulligan—a celebrated wire service reporter who spent four decades covering news events in 142 countries—recalls the stage fright he felt when he faced writing his first story. "It looms firmly in memory," he declares, "because it is still there, quivering, leaking stomach acids, whenever I sit down to write."

No wonder Richard Aregood complains, later in this volume, that writing well is brutally hard work.

———

Most unnerving of all, perhaps, is the way writing comes with no operating instructions. No rules, secrets, or magic bullets can guarantee that your prose will sing and lift off the page into readers' minds. All the contributors to *The Journalist's Craft* insist on that. No one here assumes that good writing can be taught. They understand that it can only be learned—in the heat of an individual's private jousts with words. They understand that there's an unconscious aspect of good writing that can result only from years of reading and countless hours spent tapping a keyboard.

So . . . what good is any workshop or collection of essays where other writers tell you how *they* work? What good does it do, for instance, to have someone encourage you to add more rhythm or cadence to your prose? Isn't that person talking about something magical or spontaneous that happens (or not) as you write, something you cannot consciously generate in your writing, no matter how much "workshopping" you've done?

---

1. Marc Duvoisin, "James N. Naughton to step down as Inquirer executive editor," *Philadelphia Inquirer,* Nov. 30, 1995, p. A-4.

How *do* you transfer something your conscious mind has learned into something your unconscious can translate into action?

—

Michael Jordan's career might provide a clue here. Who would deny the magic and spontaneity he displayed while zipping past screens and hitting those exquisite fall-away jump shots that led the Chicago Bulls to NBA titles? And wasn't it amazing to hear occasionally some broadcaster saying, "Michael talked during practice this morning about his low shooting percentage in recent games. Some of his shots have been hitting the front of the rim. He says he's tired, his rhythm is off. So he's been working during shoot-arounds to get his legs under his shots better, and to work on his follow-through." That is, when things weren't working instinctively, Jordan went *back to basics,* back to focusing on the mechanical things that made him the planet's best player. Two nights later, you'd see him zip around screens scoring basket after basket. And you know his conscious mind wasn't reminding him to "get your legs under your shot . . . follow-through." Jordan just flicked the ball into the net.

Shoot-arounds matter to writers, too. You'll find frequent insistence throughout this book that writers can make a conscious return to the fundamentals of our craft, can break down the steps in the *process* of how we do what we do, so that we can later put what we've discovered into play, instinctively, as we write new, better stories.

Gerard Manley Hopkins says in one of his poems that "sheer plod makes plough down sillion / Shine"—that if you walk back and forth over ploughed earth enough times, it becomes polished, beautiful.[2] If we can do that with dirt, then we should be able to do that with our prose. Practice. Write. Analyze. Revise. More practice. More writing . . . until the words do indeed begin to shine.

Writing is part magic, part craft. If you learn all you can about the craft, you enhance your chances of achieving magic at the keyboard.

—

The finest writers often seem the most willing to believe this is so. Notice as you read Hugh Mulligan's essay how he soaked up advice given him by

---

2. Gerard Manley Hopkins, "The Windhover," in *Poetry: An Introduction,* 2nd Ed., ed. Michael Meyer (Boston: Bedford, 1998), p. 422.

writers such as Vladimir Nabokov and James Jones (whom he met in Saigon). Notice, as you read all of *The Journalist's Craft,* how persistently the essayists mention or quote other writers from whom they've learned. A theme stressed throughout this volume is that good journalists read a lot, and learn to *borrow* techniques from fellow writers.

Betty Winston Bayé, a columnist for the *Louisville Courier-Journal,* recently told an audience of journalists:

> There's no substitute for a writer always being a willing student. I'm really hooked on books about writing, and books for writers only, about the passions of writing. Besides reading people who I really enjoy, I also tend to read a lot of books about the craft, because I am ever the student, and maybe there's something that I'm doing, that I'm wasting time, and that somebody else has found the solution to.[3]

Her statement could be used as a foundation for the whole of *The Journalist's Craft.* It explains why this book exists. The essayists here strive to help you by explaining the techniques that have worked for them over the years as they've reported and pondered and structured and written and revised stories.

—

Bayé was speaking at the Wilmington Writers' Workshop, an annual gathering sponsored by the *News Journal.* Editors at that Delaware newspaper had first conceived the idea of a large-scale writers' workshop in 1991. At the time, the Gannett Co. daily was experiencing budget restrictions. The paper's managing editor, John Walston, lacked funds to mount a quality in-house training program, or to bring in outside speakers who could generate excitement about good writing. Facing such limitations, he and other editors came up with the idea of staging an ambitious writers' workshop where renowned writers would agree to come to town and speak for no fee, and journalists from all over the East Coast would pay a modest registration fee that could be used to cover speakers' expenses and rent a hotel ballroom for two days.

---

3. Betty Bayé, "Putting Passion in Your Writing," Wilmington Writers' Workshop, April 2, 1995.

Newsroom veterans voiced doubts that such a no-frills workshop could ever attract enough registrants to pay for itself. How many writers and editors, they wondered, would be willing to sacrifice an April weekend to listen to people talk about what they do at work?

The skeptics were in for a shock.

More than 350 journalists from fifteen states registered for the workshop. Twelve veteran journalists, including syndicated columnists Molly Ivins and Chuck Stone, sportswriter Dave Kindred, and editorialist Richard Aregood agreed to come speak (without pay).

Organizers were further blessed with the fortuitous visit of best-selling novelist James Michener, who had come to Delaware to pick up an award. When someone casually passed along to him the brochure for the Wilmington Writers' Workshop, he asked if he might drop by and say "a few words."

So the Wilmington Writers' Workshop began on a Saturday morning in April 1992 with a frail, eighty-five-year-old Michener leaning into a microphone saying, "Hello, Fellow Writers."

His greeting delighted the crowd. His "few words" swelled into forty minutes. He talked about his writing life, his poor spelling, his devotion to an old manual typewriter that had served him through thirty-nine books, and about the immeasurable joys and lifelong agonies he had experienced as a writer.

It wasn't a bad start, for a low-rent writers' workshop.

Word got around. The next year, the Wilmington Writers' Workshop drew six hundred journalists.

———

By April 1994, the Poynter Institute for Media Studies had noticed the popularity of the Wilmington gatherings and had joined forces with the *News Journal* and other newspapers to jointly sponsor workshops in cities across the nation. The six Writers' Workshops that spring (all staged on the same weekend) drew 3,125 participants. The National Writers' Workshop—as it was henceforth called—has drawn more than 5,000 journalists every year since.[4]

---

4. For a longer history of the National Writers' Worskshop, see Winnie Hu, "The Training Track," *American Journalism Review* 21 (Oct. 1999): 56-65. The two-day workshops now take place at more than a dozen sites annually, in cities such as Atlanta, Hartford, Fort Lauderdale, Minneapolis, Oklahoma City, Indianapolis, and Seattle, as well as Wilmington.

No genre of journalism goes unrepresented on the programs for these events. Recent workshops have featured newswriters David Halberstam, James B. Steele, and Richard Ben Cramer; feature writers Ron Suskind, Madeleine Blais, Tom Hallman, and Rick Bragg; sportswriters Frank DeFord and Mitch Albom; columnists William Raspberry, E. R. Shipp, and Ellen Goodman; magazine writers Susan Orlean and Jeffrey Toobin; literary journalists Helen Benedict and William Least Heat-Moon; and humorists Art Buchwald, Roy Blount, and Dave Barry.

The workshops have also typically invited creative writers as speakers. Winston Groom, Philip Caputo, Soledad Santiago, Jack Butler, Robert B. Parker, and Rita Mae Brown are among the many novelists who've led sessions.

Wilmington Writers' Workshops have heard a "few words" more about writing from luminaries such as Nobel Prize laureate Derek Walcott (a poet and playwright), filmmaker Ken Burns, novelist-newsman Jim Lehrer, and playwright August Wilson.

Nearly every workshop at all the sites each year has featured at least one celebrated speaker who brought special electricity to the conference hall. In Hartford one year it was Pete Hamill (newspaper editor-reporter-novelist-memoirist) who sparked the audience. And in workshops further west, it was Pete Dexter (columnist-novelist-screenwriter), John Schulian (sports columnist and creator of *Zena, Warrior Princess*), and Jules Feiffer (cartoonist-journalist-novelist-playwright-screenwriter) who stimulated listeners by describing techniques they had used while writing in various genres.

Organizers have maintained the bare-bones status of the workshops. Registrants continue to pay only modest fees to cover the conferences' costs. The 170 or so speakers who visited the April 2001 workshops were all still donating their time.

Writing—as well as the attendant acts of reporting, interviewing, and editing—has remained the sole focus of these yearly gatherings.

These Workshops reflect the intense hunger that many working journalists have, a hunger to learn more about their craft. Such enthusiasm was fueled during the 1980s by the spread of the so-called writing coach movement in American newsrooms.[5] Newspapers then were facing their severest chal-

---

5. See Ray Laakaniemi, *Newswriting in Transition* (Chicago: Nelson-Hall, 1995), p. 49.

lenges ever, notably from around-the-clock TV cable news programming and the emerging capabilities of instant news delivery through the World Wide Web. Reporters and editors consequently began searching for fresh ways of telling stories that would grab and hold the attention of readers and possibly stir their hearts. This quest for new, more evocative storytelling techniques was led in many newsrooms by writing coaches.

Writing coaches differ from editors in the way they approach a reporter's work. An editor tends to concentrate most on the reporter's final draft and on "fixing" the story for publication. But a coach focuses more on the process of writing and revising and on ways the reporter might improve individual stages of that process to compose more interesting stories.[6] The presence and persistence of writing coaches, many believe, have led to a more nurturing environment for writers in some U.S. newsrooms.

The most influential of all the writing coaches—and the progenitor of that species—is Donald M. Murray. After collecting a 1954 Pulitzer for his *Boston Herald* editorials, Murray wrote for magazines and in 1963 began teaching at the University of New Hampshire. He has since published a score of books, many of them on writing and the teaching of writing. His latest, *Writing to Deadline: The Journalist at Work* (2000), demonstrates the methods he has used over the years as a writing coach for the *Boston Globe* and other papers. Murray acknowledges the primacy of writing "done away from the writing desk, when your unconscious and subconscious are playing with the subject."[7] But he ultimately seeks to demystify the journalist's task by breaking reporting and writing down to a sequence of steps *(Explore, Focus, Rehearse, Draft, Develop, Clarify)* that can each be consciously examined. If a reporter encounters trouble while preparing a story, he may turn to view his work in terms of this *process* and consequently see precisely where to concentrate on improving. Murray labors to "make the craft accessible"—and perhaps by so doing, ease some of that anxiety which, Jim Naughton believes, afflicts all writers.

Murray and the hundreds of other newsroom writing coaches of the past two decades have especially influenced the way newspaper stories can be organized. These coaches have opened up the structures of

---

6. Carole Rich, *Writing and Reporting News: A Coaching Method* (Belmont, Calif: Wadsworth, 2000), p. xiii. Rich writes: "Like a basketball coach who trains players how to improve their techniques on the court, a writing coach trains writers how to perfect their techniques in the craft."

7. All quotes from Donald M. Murray are taken from *Writing to Deadline: The Journalist at Work* (Portsmouth, N.H.: Heinemann, 2000), pp. 16–22.

newswriting to new modes of storytelling and have convinced many editors that such innovation must be encouraged if newspapers are to hold their audience.

Jack Hart, the Portland *Oregonian*'s writing coach, rightly underscores how "lexicon impoverished" journalists have been when it comes to naming the various story structures they use. He tells writers, "If you walk through the woods, and you know the names of all the plants, you'll see more."[8] His point is that journalists have needed a much sharper vocabulary of literary devices and strategies. Until recently, journalists have typically lacked the words to say much about a story beyond "this piece sings" or "it's not quite there, yet," or to point out lapses in the logic and order of its parts. Now—as you will see in *The Journalist's Craft*—journalists talk often about such things as *foreshadowing, focus, voice, rhythm, emphasis points, cadence, scene, metaphor,* and the significance of left- and right-branching sentences in stories.

These terms are not new—they are just new to the lexicon of most newsrooms. And their introduction there has been largely the result of the writing coach movement and the attendant new interest in writing that has been engendered in the exchanges of "Fellow Writers" at workshops and newsroom gatherings.

All writers represented in *The Journalist's Craft* have, at one time or another, spoken at the Wilmington Writers' Workshop. Most have served as writing coaches for newspapers. We've divided their essays into five sections: "The Writing Life," "Finding Good *Stories*," "Writing Nonfiction Narrative," "Developing Your Craft," and "Working With Words." The collection moves generally from the broader aspects of newswriting to more specific techniques that will interest all nonfiction writers.

Section I: The Writing Life

When you read Hugh Mulligan's witty, anecdotal essay, you will understand why we isolated it in a separate section. His recollections of his own long writing life provide a colorful overview of our entire collection. His essay offers a treasure house of memorable tips that Mulligan has picked

---

8. Quoted in Rich, *Writing and Reporting News,* p. 199.

up during his tour of duty. He talks about reporting (the need for accuracy, interviewing techniques, etc.), and he talks about writing (the creation of leads and kickers; the need to love words and avoid jargon and clichés; the vitality generated by anecdotes, wit, and humor). And all the while, he provides a tapestry of engaging examples drawn from his own stories, illustrating the traits of good writing he's describing.

The title for Mulligan's essay—"Breaking Out from the Herd"—presses home his insistence that journalists get out of the office and away from the pack of other reporters while pursuing stories. His essay establishes an argument that undergirds every essay in this book: Outstanding newswriting inevitably derives from accurate, sensitive reporting. Ken Fuson in a later essay puts it directly: "Good writing depends on good reporting the way human life depends on oxygen."

Section II: Finding Good *Stories*

Our second section features essays by three newsroom veterans addressing ways to recognize story ideas that, in Fuson's words, will "enchant readers from the opening note."

Amanda Bennett enumerates checks you can use to assess a story idea before you pitch it to an editor. She shows you how to test an idea to see if it possesses potential surprise, tension or conflict, movement (some new direction taken by something or someone), action, and anecdotes sufficient to compel readers. She reminds us that the strongest story ideas come not from the top of our head but from the legwork of reporting.

Ken Fuson maintains that reporters need to search for the "emotional facts" behind the drab numbers and abstractions that fill most news stories recounting the actions of public entities. He argues that newspapers' salvation from dullness lies in what he calls "real stories" that make readers laugh or cry, think or feel, stories that "mine the daily dramas of life" and explain how we live. He offers numerous suggestions about how you can find, report, and write stories that feature "interesting, sympathetic characters who face a dramatic conflict and resolve it."

John Sweeney suggests that such storytelling will force many reporters to unlearn bad habits developed through years of leaning on press releases, press conferences, police blotters, the calendar, and all predictable event-driven news sources. The journalist's job, he says, "is to uncover the emotions and make the connections that normally lie just below the surface in routine news accounts . . . to find and to tell the invisible stories that are all around us."

Section III: Writing Nonfiction Narrative

Fuson refutes the assumption of many 1990s newspapers that readers possess tiny attention spans and crave short stories. Fuson contends that readers *will* read long articles if the stories captivate, if they're written in such a way that "the 'story' element is strong and compelling." He demonstrated that convincingly in 1998 when he wrote a 16,000-word series, "A Stage in Their Lives," in the *Baltimore Sun.* The six-part series covered seventeen broadsheet pages, but the paper received indications that the stories were enormously popular with readers. For months Fuson had followed the backstage lives and fortunes of students seeking to play roles in their high school's musical, *West Side Story.* One media critic later wrote in the *Columbia Journalism Review:* "On one level, [Fuson's] series is a tale about the production of a high school musical. On a deeper level it is a masterful story about teenagers coming of age in the complicated 1990s."[9]

Fuson's brand of in-depth narrative storytelling has been dubbed "immersion journalism."[10] More newspapers today seem tentatively willing to devote space to such long-form stories. Donald Drake told a 1993 Wilmington Writers' Workshop that "narrative writing is the gold ring of journalism so far as readership is concerned."[11] He noted that his own *Philadelphia Inquirer* narrative stories typically range for an average of 150 column inches, with some series going on for well over 1,000 inches. Drake and two of the other master storytellers in contemporary newsrooms, Jon Franklin and Mark Bowden, contribute to our third section engaging commentaries on long-form storytelling.

Franklin was among the pioneers of immersion journalism. His gripping 1978 narrative account of a woman undergoing brain surgery—"Mrs. Kelly's Monster"—is now an often-anthologized classic of American journalism. It won for Franklin the first-ever Pulitzer given for feature writing. (He would score a rare second Pulitzer six years later in another new category, explanatory journalism.) In his brief essay here, he insists that nonfiction narrative is "chronology *with meaning,*" that it offers, like literature of any sort, a "kernel of insight, of vision." That vision, he says, is the "literary counterpart to a news peg." He predicts an emergence of narrative journalism in coming years because the genre flourishes in periods of

9. Steve Weinberg, "Tell It Long, Take Your Time, Go in Depth." *Columbia Journalism Review* 36 (Jan./Feb. 1998): 56–61.

10. See Weinberg's article.

11. Donald Drake, "Narrative Writing: Making News Stories Live," Wilmington Writers' Workshop, April 18, 1993.

momentous change, due to the way it *orients* readers to a shifting world of new issues, new values.

Mark Bowden stresses that such journalism means "approaching reporting with a storyteller's mind, looking for anecdote and setting, finding characters, scenes, and dialogue, and identifying a beginning, middle, and end." Using his own award-winning stories as examples, Bowden walks us from start-to-finish through the process he follows while developing stories. He leads us from his initial research, reporting, and interviewing, to his organizing and outlining of raw material, and on to his search for the most effective lead, structure, and voice for a story.

Drake, a long-time medical writer for the *Philadelphia Inquirer,* recalls how his early interest in playwriting and the theater led him to develop his own narrative storytelling strategies based on immersion reporting. (He once spent five years chronicling the progress of a class of University of Pennsylvania students through medical school, reporting their stories through scores of newspaper articles.) Like Fuson, Drake believes newspapers are often boring—causing readers to turn to films, TV, and sports events seeking the drama and suspense that reporters frequently fail to build into stories. He encourages journalists to start thinking like playwrights, and shows us how a reporter can use playwriting devices such as foreshadowing, scene development, and "cliffhanger curtain lines" to create anticipation and entice readers deeper into a story.

Section IV: Developing Your Craft

Bowden and Drake both discuss how they revise stories, but John Sweeney in the next gathering of essays offers a more fully developed "strategy for revision." He asserts that you need "discipline and a plan" for sculpting a story into final form. His strategy for revisions is flexible enough to guide you in polishing both breaking news stories and long-term projects.

Most other essayists in this section pick up threads stitched into earlier essays and develop them further. Richard Aregood, for instance, amplifies what Bowden writes about how reporters should (in Aregood's words) "let the tale find its own life." Aregood urges reporters to recognize that there are no one-size-fits-all story templates, that writers should avoid allowing facts to fall into familiar shapes that sometimes reflect clichéd ways of *thinking* as well as of structuring stories.

Lucille deView and Lynn Franklin expand suggestions made by others in *The Journalist's Craft*—that news and feature reporters should look to *borrow* techniques from other writers and other genres. DeView's whole essay is about looking at the work of other artists—novelists, nonfiction writers, songwriters, poets, screenwriters, radio and TV writers, playwrights, authors of children's books, essayists, even the performances of stand-up comics—to "see what we may borrow from them for our own selfish purposes." She makes it clear that a new sort of cross-pollination is going on in newsrooms (thanks to writing coaches such as herself) as journalists feel a new freedom to reach out to authors in other genres for structural strategies or literary techniques that may improve their newswriting.

That idea informs Lynn Franklin's essay on "stealing" techniques from classic fiction writers. Citing examples chosen from novelists Harper Lee, John Steinbeck, Mark Twain, and William Faulkner, she shows how journalists can make strong use of such classic literary tools as symbol, foreshadowing, rhythm, and dialogue as they produce newspaper stories. Her comments on foreshadowing—a technique seldom mentioned or mastered in newsrooms—are especially instructive. Franklin smartly demonstrates how foreshadowing is done, explaining that it's often the result of "backwriting," where a writer goes back into a draft of a near-finished story to add foreshadowing elements that may heighten tension and create resonance and power. She also shows how nonfiction writers can employ other fictional techniques to develop characters, describe places, create mood, and add extra layers of meaning beneath a story's surface level.

Tom Silvestri's essay encompasses the whole process of reporting, writing, and revising business stories, and you will find that his insights apply as well to all other newspaper genres. For example, he stresses the need all reporters have of working harder on story structure. It's what "keeps the writer on track and pulls the reader aboard," he says. He describes several innovative ways for structuring stories, all of them focused on a writer *visualizing* a story's structure before hitting the first keystroke.

Carl Sessions Stepp concentrates exclusively on structure as he complains that too many reporters labor over a lead and then just recklessly dump their notebooks into what Stepp calls the story's "murky middle." He urges that more thought be given to the second and subsequent paragraphs and describes two techniques that might clear up the muddle in the middle of stories: (1) the preparation of an "interior outline" that organizes the story's innards; and (2) the formulation of what he calls a "kickoff paragraph," which links the story's opening to its body. He also presents a toolbox of techniques (*previews, wrap-ups, signposts, connective tissues,* etc.) that may help a reporter maintain an orderly, accessible flow through a story's middle.

Section V: Working With Words

The three writers in our final group of essays highlight ways you can make individual words work more powerfully and evocatively.

Taylor Buckley's list of "Very Predictable Expressions" used by reporters reminds us of the need to keep the language of our stories fresh.

Jeanne Murray Walker follows with a discerning essay that illustrates one way reporters might do that, through the use of original metaphors. Walker is an accomplished poet. Some newsroom cynics might scoff at the idea of having a poet tell journalists how to write news. But Natalie Goldberg in *Thunder and Lightning: Cracking Open the Writer's Craft* (2000) wisely admonishes writers: "Don't be so rigid. If you learn a good move in one genre, use it in another. . . . Grab the reader's mind whatever it takes."[12]

Lots of good moves proposed by Walker in "Speaking of Metaphor" can be translated into immediate use by journalists. She argues that in a shrinking world where cultures are so rapidly being brought closer by science and technology, journalists *must* learn how to manipulate metaphor in the effort "to translate cultures to one another." Just as crucially, she declares, reporters will increasingly need metaphors as they strive to translate the "new reality" of a dazzling scientific revolution (in space exploration, computer intelligence, gene research, to name a few areas) into a reality that can be comprehended by readers still struggling to program their VCR. As Walker makes clear, metaphors are a great language tool, because they help us explain unknown things in terms of the known, to make a complex world seem a bit more understandable.

Dennis Jackson draws analogies between the work of writers and musicians as he shows how you can write with stronger rhythms and cadences. As he notes, *cadence* is another little-known word in newsrooms, and one often mistakenly used as a synonym for rhythm. Cadence is more important than rhythm, he proposes, because it helps more forcefully to create the voice readers hear as they read our words. That voice determines the extent to which readers experience our story's full intellectual and emotional impact. Jackson describes five techniques that may help you better convey a story's meaning and drama through your creation of more resonant cadences. He also discusses the value of using what he calls *right-branching sentences.* Renowned writing coach Roy Peter Clark has declared that the right-branching sentence "is the staple of effective journalism in the modern era."[13] Jackson's essay

---

12. Natalie Goldberg, *Thunder and Lightning: Cracking Open the Writer's Craft* (New York: Bantam, 2000), p. 93.

13. Roy Peter Clark, *The American Conversation and the Language of Journalism* (St. Petersburg, Fla.: Poynter Institute for Media Studies, 1994), pp. 10–11.

illustrates why that is so. He demonstrates how you can, by using such sentence constructions, infuse your writing with more energy and clarity.

—

One special feature of *The Journalist's Craft* is the frequent exercises the various writers offer—to help you analyze your writing habits in past stories, and perhaps prepare you to write better stories:

- Jackson's essay "Rhythm's Cousin, Cadence," is followed by "A 'StyleCheck' for Your Writing" that helps you determine if you're getting enough cadence, rhythm, and clarity into stories to make them distinctive. His exercise has the potential to: (1) tell if you've fallen into stylistic ruts that need attention; and (2) provide clues as to how you tend to build sentences, use emphasis spots and cadences, and place sentence modifications. His StyleCheck, he claims, can produce "a telling X-ray of your writing."
- Sweeney's essay "SpellCheck and Beyond: A Strategy for Revision" includes additional tests you can run on sentences, to see, for example, whether you have developed a tendency to overload them with prepositions or "to be" verbs.
- DeView concludes her essay, "The Zen of Newswriting," with a list of time-writing exercises and other workshop activities designed to refine your writing and stretch your imagination.
- Walker's essay, "Speaking of Metaphor," ends with "The Metaphor Kit: Tips for Writing Metaphor," a series of playful brainstorming practices that can help you learn to invent fresh metaphors.

We've also appended an annotated bibliography of our favorite books about writing, books that we believe can help you approach the task of writing with more skill and less of that gnawing insecurity Naughton describes.

—

Hugh Mulligan opens this collection of essays with a lament that traditional newspaper byline writer-reporters might be a vanishing breed, a species doomed by the challenges of cyberspace technology and instant electronic news delivery. He wonders if newspapers aren't destined to become as prehistoric as cave drawings. But the recent work of another reporter represented in *The Journalist's Craft* provides mighty evidence that Mulligan's fears may be unwarranted.

In 1997 *Philadelphia Inquirer* reporter Mark Bowden spent months researching and reporting on the 1993 Battle of Mogadishu, in Somalia. There, due to blundering commanders, U.S. Special Forces (sent to capture henchmen of a Somali warlord) became trapped in the city and had to fight their way out with the assistance of other U.S. troops. Bowden interviewed scores of American soldiers and Somalis who had been involved in the firefight that left eighteen Americans and more than five hundred Somalis dead. He gathered memories upon which he could base specific scenes and dialogue, and he gleaned information from transcripts of military radio transmissions and a classified combat videotape. He then reconstructed the battle in a minute-by-minute narrative that ran as "Blackhawk Down," a month-long twenty-nine-part series in the *Inquirer* in late 1997. It was the longest such nonfiction serial ever published in an American newspaper.

Bowden's stories won the Overseas Press Club's 1998 Boyle Award for Best Foreign Reporting.

He went on to expand the narrative substantially as a book, which was published in hardback by Grove/Atlantic in 1999 as *Black Hawk Down: A Story of Modern War.* (The *Inquirer* used "Blackhawk" and the book used "Black Hawk.") In 2000 Penguin Books issued *Black Hawk Down* in paperback, and by January 2002 the book sat atop the *New York Times* best-seller list. Simon & Schuster produced a four-cassette audiobook version. Meanwhile, KR Video (a division of Knight-Ridder, the company that owns the *Inquirer*) produced "Somalia: Good Intentions, Deadly Results," an hour-long Official Companion Documentary to Bowden's *Inquirer* stories. That film aired on the Cable News Network and received an Emmy. (The video now sells in bookstores.) Bowden and other writers helped Ken Nolan prepare a screenplay version of *Black Hawk Down.* That $90 million Sony Pictures reenactment of the Mogadishu battle—directed by Ridley Scott (*Gladiator*), produced by Jerry Bruckheimer, and starring Josh Hartnett—opened nationwide in January 2002 to immediate critical acclaim.

After running the twenty-nine-part "Blackhawk Down" series, the *Inquirer* established a Web site, *blackhawkdown.philly.com,* where those who logged on could click various links to get to: the *Full Text* of the newspaper series; *Maps* of the Somalia conflict; *Graphics* delineating battle highlights; *Photos* taken after the Mogadishu incident, including one shot through a bullet hole in a hotel wall; short *Videos* related to the story; *Audio* outtakes (clips from Bowden's interviews with soldiers, even clips of radio transmissions made by soldiers during the battle); gatherings of letters dispatched by soldiers involved in the conflict, and one mailgram informing parents of their son's death in battle; a *Who's Who* listing of participants; a *Glossary* of military terms ("Flash-bang," ".50 cal.," "Humvee," etc.); an interactive twenty-one-part *Question-and-Answer* session, where Bowden responds to queries about how he researched and wrote the story and about military details he may have overlooked, among others; a *Forum* or chat room where those who've read the book or served in the military can exchange views with others; a much-needed *Index* of the busy site; and a keyword search engine.

It was quite a site.

It's still accessible in 2002. Internet visitors can learn from the Web site how to purchase the book or audio versions of *Black Hawk Down.* They can order The Collectors' Edition of *Black Hawk Down* on a CD-ROM that includes Bowden's twenty-nine *Inquirer* stories, the KR Video documentary, and all the breathtaking multimedia offerings from the Web site. (The *Inquirer* has no financial interest in the *Black Hawk* movie.) While at the Web site, cyber-tourists can also subscribe to the *Inquirer* or access its free weekly internet archives or its older archives (at $1.95 per story downloaded).

Bowden's "Blackhawk Down" newspaper series obviously forms an extreme example—few reporters can expect ever to have their newspaper stories "versioned" in anything like the ways his work was. But this remarkable history of what happened to his stories does reflect some of the changes taking place in the newspaper profession at the beginning of the twenty-first century. It represents the new synergism being created between print and electronic media, and the ways enterprising publishers are finding to market the products of talented writers.

The signs are here: that newspapers will adapt somehow to all the latest electronic challenges; that there will continue to be a strong need for writer-reporters who can go out and find what Ken Fuson calls "real stories," and who can then create with them what Mulligan calls "the music of fine prose." The writers in *The Journalist's Craft* may not be able to help you accomplish such fine music in all your stories. But they can surely help you better tune your instrument before you sit down again at the keyboard.

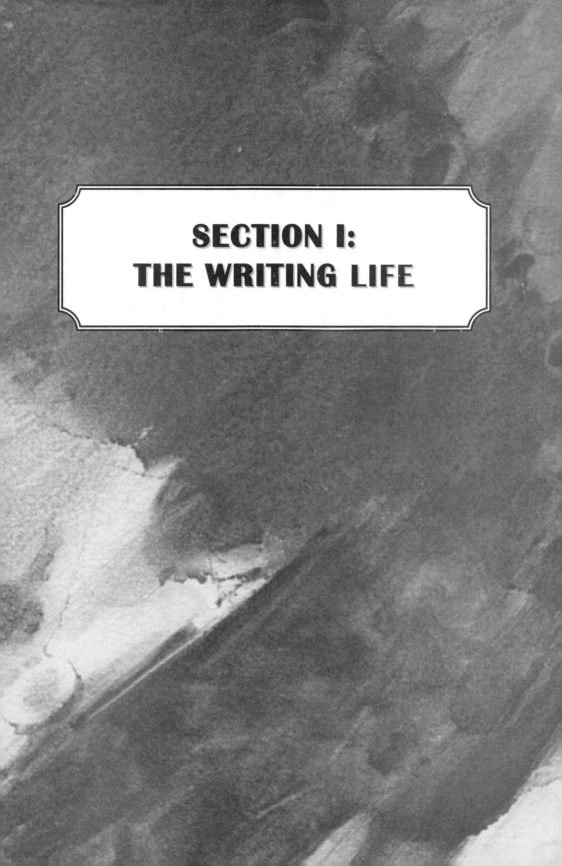

SECTION I:
THE WRITING LIFE

Breaking Out from the Herd

By Hugh A. Mulligan

[Mulligan worked as a Special Correspondent for the Associated Press for five decades before retiring in 2001. His assignments have carried him to 142 countries, various wars (including Vietnam), space shots, presidential campaigns, and on every major trip taken by Pope John Paul II. In 1972 and 1978 he received the AP Managing Editors award for outstanding reporting.]

Perhaps at the dawn of the millennium in cyberspace, it is already too late to consider the writer as a reporter on the scene, not just at the screen of a breaking story or a heartbreaking feature. Certainly, writers in the purest sense of the word seem to be a dying breed, an endangered species, really. These frail birds of paradise flutter their plumage in an obscure corner of the electronic newsroom, ready to be stuffed and mounted and, alas, put on display in Al Neuharth's Newseum. Graphic artists with their maps and charts and clever visual depictions already are gobbling up news holes once reserved for the byline writer-reporter. It won't be long before tomorrow's newspaper will seem like part of some prehistoric yesterday, when a communications breakthrough consisted of stick drawings of reindeer on the wall of a cave.

But take heart. A few Grub Street hacks are still required to fill in the blanks between that color-coded weather map and the diagram of the bomb that blew up the Federal Building in Oklahoma City.

So now, after my five decades in this business—adventurous decades of bouncing about the globe covering wars, disasters, popes, presidents, even a world nudist convention—the time has come to speak of many things that, unlike the walrus and the carpenter, are not yet available on disk or CD-ROM.

I have no profound theories that will make you a better writer or a more observant reporter in six easy lessons, but perhaps those years of experience, the winning and sometimes the losing of play on a story, can provide some hints, a few techniques and insider tips on how to handle a difficult interview, a reluctant source, a sensitive situation, even a challenging expense account. These ploys from the past may not always work, but, then, they often failed me, too.

Even the unclad conventioneers at Port Nature on the southern coast of France were shy about confronting the press. You would think nudists would be the last people in the world with something to hide. Yet the newly crowned "Miss Health Glow" declined to be interviewed for fear her mother would learn how she minimized her clothing budget.

I never have worked for a newspaper. I joined the Associated Press in Baton Rouge, Louisiana, straight out of Harvard Graduate School, where I had taken a master's in English Literature, concentrating on Joyce, Beckett, and Yeats. My Ivy League education and relatively easy entry into journalism always perplexed my first boss, Jim McLean, a crusty old hard news hawk right out of *The Front Page.* Jim's proudest boast was that he had never used a semicolon in his life. "A semicolon," he would say, rewriting Professor H. W. Fowler, "is a festering hemorrhoid hanging between two half-assed clauses." But Big Jim, may his tribe increase, gave me the best piece of advice anyone ever tendered me in this business. "No AP man has ever been sued for libel," he assured me, then added with a truculent grin, "but several former ones have." That, for me, is still journalism's only golden rule. No matter how you write it, you'd better write it right.

I can't recall the exact story—something about Governor Earl Long calling an opponent "a pernicious pismire"—but I still painfully remember the stage fright that attended my first byline. It looms firmly in memory because it is still there, quivering, leaking stomach acids, whenever I sit down to write. The condition is chronic, as verified by the Maalox bottle on my desk beside the AP *Stylebook.*

Perhaps running scared isn't a bad thing for a writer. Georges Simenon, the Belgian genius behind Inspector Maigret, wrote nearly four hundred novels in an amazingly prolific career. In his autobiography *Mémoires intimes,* he confessed to suffering stage fright every time he committed the words "Chapter One" to a blank sheet.

But fun, not fear and trembling, brightens my recollections of those halcyon days trolling for bylines in the bayous. It seems to me, in the rosy haze of hindsight, that the media didn't take itself quite so seriously back then. Editors seem to have been more daring, more imaginative, more tolerant—even encouraging—of individual writing styles.

I recall when, toward the end of his dazzling career, Rudolf Nureyev came to dance "Swan Lake" at the old New Orleans Opera House in the French Quarter. The lively afternoon tabloid, the *Item,* sent a sportswriter instead of its staff culture vulture to cover the event. His name eludes me, but I vividly remember his piece, which is glory enough for a writer. He incisively caught the quintessence of the balletic art when he wrote, "If my jockey shorts were that tight, I could jump that high and stay up longer." And he described a rather aging prima ballerina who danced the lead swan and packed a lot of lard into her leotard as "poultry in motion." Unlike many of today's slash-and-burn media critics, some of his remarks were constructive. "If the corps de ballet," he suggested, "recruited taller girls, they wouldn't have to spend so much time on their toes." The editor put the story on page one. And why not? Newspapers then entertained the delusion that one of their key functions was to amuse as well as inform their readers.

—

This is a nuts-and-bolts book about writing, but before I attempt to get down to the basic hardware, I should note that history is rife with confusion on this subject. *New Yorker* humorist Peter DeVries once observed that "all writing is formula writing: there is the beginning, the muddle, and the end." And as Somerset Maugham, that elegant master of the Queen's English, told a BBC interviewer: "There are three basic rules to good writing. Unfortunately, no one knows what they are."

I mentioned this to John Steinbeck one night in Saigon during the Vietnam War. He had the room next to mine in the Caravelle Hotel and occasionally dropped by to share the comforts of my PX liquor ration. The Nobel laureate took a stab at filling in the blanks for Maugham: "Never make excuses. Never let them see you bleed. Never get separated from your luggage." He then added a fourth: "Find out when the bar opens and when the laundry comes back."

A year or so later, James Jones came by my room in the same hotel for a can of PX grapefruit juice. The hard-boiled G.I. novelist of *From Here to Eternity* was on the wagon and on assignment for the *New York Times Magazine.* Cigar stub firmly clenched in his jaw, he growled out a more serious approach to Maugham's three unknown rules in the blunt lingo of the infantry grunt he still was at heart: "Fill your notebook with more impressions than quotes. Talk *with* people, not *to* them. Writers aren't trial lawyers doing a cross-examination. Sometimes, if you keep your ears open and your trap shut, you might learn something you never dreamed of asking. Lastly, tell it like you would to a buddy in a bar."

I love meeting authors. Over the years it's been my privilege to interview dozens: Tennessee Williams, Gore Vidal, William Kennedy, Walker Percy, Muriel Spark, Brendan Behan, Vladimir Nabokov, James Michener, John D. MacDonald, and a rare chat (not long before he died) with Patrick O'Brian, that delightful nautical novelist who in his eighties was still producing a book a year. The wonderful thing about talking to writers is that most of them don't have a clue about what triggers the creative process beyond sitting there and letting it happen.

Truman Capote told me that Gore Vidal advised him that one way to break writer's block was to put down any word at all just to get started. So he wrote the word "the," stared at it for forty minutes, then added, "Hell with it," and decamped to his favorite Brooklyn Heights bistro for a conscience-soothing double-dry martini. Later I learned Capote had lifted the anecdote from Robert Benchley with no input from Vidal.

—

Back in the thirteenth century the philosopher Thomas Aquinas posed six one-word questions that to me sum up the fundamentals of chronicling events or what we now call newswriting: Quando? Quomodo? Who? What? Where? Why? When? And How? Rudyard Kipling wove these into a delightful quatrain worth memorizing when you are trying to marshal the contents of your notebook into words that convey to the reader what happened:

> I keep six honest serving-men;
> (They taught me all I knew)
> Their names are What and Where and When
> And How and Where and Who.
>
> —"The Elephant's Child," in *Just So Stories*

Rene J. Cappon, the AP's writing guru and resident curmudgeon, not long ago asked me for some words of advice, based on personal experience, on writing leads. Alas, he did not choose an expert in the field. I am never comfortable writing a lead and seldom satisfied with what I eventually produce. In fact, I have always consoled myself at being better at finding a kicker line to end a story than an opening line that will enslave the reader.

My mentor for a strong finale was Barney Krebs, a savvy professional with great political contacts who covered the Louisiana legislature for the *New Orleans Times-Picayune.* His editors allowed him to write reams of copy, full of lively quotes and vivid descriptions of floor fights. His stories began on page one, then inexorably jumped from page to page, all the way back to the want ads. "But," Barney told me, "I always save one juicy quote or a droll anecdote for the last paragraph to reward the faithful few who have come so far."

In the AP, of course, brevity has always been regarded as the soul of wit, or at least self-preservation against the fiery-eyed Hannibal Lectors sharpening their scalpels on the editorial desk. Early on in our careers, we are reminded that one of the AP's most admired leads contained only two words. The story was under a San Juan Capistrano, California, dateline and concerned the annual return of the swallows on March 19. The lead said it all: "They're back."

I envy that lead writer but cannot bring myself to commit such wit so soon. I find that a lead that is too coy, too clever can often lead you astray, lead you down paths where the story isn't heading, and cost you paragraphs to get back on track. If you ever do. As fight manager Angelo Dundee always counseled his aspiring cauliflower champions, "Don't be a sucker for an easy lead."

Hurrying back from an assignment, in a taxi, a helicopter, or on foot, I begin thinking about the lead to my story by asking myself what pictures did the photographers take? What struck *them* the most about what we just covered? Another technique I've found helpful, especially when I'm struggling with a lead, is to guess what headline a newspaper might put over my story? Better still, what headline would a tabloid like the *New York Post* or *New York Daily News,* or even one of those supermarket scandal sheets, blare in boldface to summarize and dramatize the story lurking in my notebook and tape recorder? Down the years, some of journalism's most famous headlines have brilliantly suggested what happened and have coaxed the reader to find out more:

> WALL STREET LAYS AN EGG
> FORD TO NEW YORK: DROP DEAD
> HEADLESS TORSO FOUND IN TOPLESS BAR
> HICKS NIX PIX IN STICKS

(The latter was *Variety*'s lament for the way a flick with a multimillion-dollar budget had bombed at box offices outside urban areas.)

Alan Gould, the AP's longtime executive editor, recalled that as a rookie sportswriter, he was at ringside when Gene Tunney won the heavyweight championship from Jack Dempsey after the famous "long count." Gould froze over his typewriter beneath the ring apron in creative paralysis, unable to think of words worthy of such a controversial ending to the fight. Bob Considine, the versatile Hearst star, took pity on him. "Just tell them what happened," he counseled. The keys began to clack again.

Ernie Gobright, the AP's first Washington bureau chief, just told them what happened on the night of April 14, 1865, when Abraham Lincoln went to Ford's Theater: "The President was shot in a theater tonight and perhaps mortally wounded." Unconsciously, the AP's Bob Johnson filed an almost identical bulletin from Dallas on November 22, 1963: "President Kennedy was shot today just as his motorcade left downtown Dallas. Mrs. Kennedy jumped up and grabbed Mr. Kennedy. She cried, 'Oh, no.' The motorcade sped on." Neither of these AP leads told more than what the reporter knew from the then-available facts. Lincoln didn't die until the next morning. Kennedy was pronounced dead an hour after being shot.

Novelists seem to be telling us by example to begin at the beginning and keep it simple:

> "Last night I dreamt I went to Manderley again."—*Rebecca*
>
> "Scarlett O'Hara was not beautiful, but men seldom realized it when caught by her charm. . . ."—*Gone With the Wind*
>
> "Marley was dead, to begin with."—*A Christmas Carol*
>
> "You don't know about me without you have read a book by the name of *The Adventures of Tom Sawyer;* but that ain't no matter."—*The Adventures of Huckleberry Finn*
>
> "Call me Ishmael."—*Moby Dick*

Or, as Woody Allen rewrote Herman Melville, "Call me Ishmael, and we'll do lunch."

Thank heavens the venerable "inverted pyramid" lead of the wire service has at last followed the Prince Albert tobacco can into well-deserved retirement. Old-time telegraphers, like Gene Autry before he made his living with the guitar, used a tobacco can to resonate the dahs and dits on their primitive modems. The inverted pyramid lead was designed to fit a news hole of any size. The idea was to pack the most important facts into the first sentence, follow with essential quotes and pertinent color in successive sentences, and then wind down with lesser details so that an editor, like a tailor shortening a pair of trousers, could cut off from the bottom to make a perfect fit on the page. The result teetered, top-heavy and ungraceful, as would the Great Pyramid of Cheops if upended and balanced on its tip.

These days, when it comes to composing leads, many writing coaches seem to favor the narrative approach, using a storytelling technique to get into a subject. A dramatic, people-focused opening is certainly an effective way to grab the reader by the lapels. Here is one such opening that I wrote in 1969:

> Belfast (AP)—Just after dark on the wildest of wild nights the doorbell tinkled in a Roman Catholic greengrocer's shop in the Crumlin Road.
>
> "Tommy, come in," said the woman behind the counter, recognizing her Protestant neighbor and good customer of long standing. The man ignored the greeting. "I lost my home on Agnes Street tonight," he announced bitterly. "You have 15 minutes to get out before you're burned out."
>
> "Sure, I had nothing to do with that," cried the woman, bursting into tears. "I can't help that," the man said. "None of us can help anything any more." And he disappeared in the crimson glow of the crossroads where already a doubledeck municipal bus, symbol of government power, was a burned-out skeleton and just behind it a public house, stereotype symbol of Roman Catholic riotousness and rebellion, leaped into flames.

For nearly ten years I covered the "Troubles" in Northern Ireland. The tragedy was so sickeningly repetitive that the story I wrote in 1969, when the centuries-old violence re-erupted on Black Sunday, could've happened almost any year thereafter.

I should warn, however, that when such narrative leads are overblown or done too often, the result at best is second-rate melodrama and at worst numbing boredom.

Rather than being led astray by a lead that's too cute, too glitzy, or too burdened with narrative bathos, I often put off writing the lead on a story until the very last. Once you get by the muddle in the middle and see the light at the end of your tunneled prose, the start might suggest itself.

The nicest thing about that modern miracle, the word processor, is that it enables you, like Mary Queen of Scots, to proclaim bravely that "my end is my beginning" before facing the editorial ax. And, most consoling of all, the floor around you is not littered with printed evidence of your fits and starts, as in the dear dead days of Remington and L.C. Smith.

Also gone forever, I suppose, are the legendary leads of journalism's yellowest days. Like this one, from the old *New York Journal,* on a Chinatown gangland shooting: "They wanted Willie Wing, but they winged Willie Wong; another slip of the tong in Chinatown's vicious gang wars."

They don't write 'em like that anymore, which is probably just as well, but they sure had fun back then.

—

I think I had the final interview—in English, anyway—with novelist Vladimir Nabokov. I admire him most among modern writers for his dazzling use of imagery and language. Like Joseph Conrad, Nabokov did not speak English until well into manhood. Born into an aristocratic Russian family, he first learned French from his governess. He was schooled in Russian and wrote a half dozen novels in the language he adored above all others for its rich vocabulary. Then, in almost mid-career, after the violence of the Bolshevik revolution drove him into exile, he switched to writing in English. As his brilliant poetic imagery reflects, the variety and vivacity of English words and expressions fascinated him. He loved puns, palindromes, lavish alliterations, crossword puzzles, and double acrostics—any bizarre form of wordplay.

When Nabokov was lecturing on the English novel at Cornell, a nun approached him after class. "Professor," she complained, "I have trouble concentrating because the boy and girl in front of me are spooning all the time." Nabokov had never heard the word *spooning* used in the context of romance. "My dear sister," he replied, "you should be grateful they aren't forking all the time."

The right words, to Nabokov, were as lovely and as rare as the butterflies he collected. "Don't tell readers," he advised his students. "Show them. Give them an example." This word-wizard never needed to tell us Lolita was a sexy nymphet. Early on we had the example of her climbing into Humbert Humbert's lap to seduce him. "Examples," Nabokov preached, "are the stained glass windows of the mind."

Words are the only raw material available in our profession. And, oh, what you can do with them when the muse cooperates. And what they can do to you when the brain is out of gear. How you use words can even betray who you are. A Vassar professor feeding words into a computer nailed

Newsweek's Joe Klein as the anonymous author of the presidential satire *Primary Colors.* Words can glitter like diamonds in your prose or explode like booby traps planted in a placid paragraph. In my early days with Associated Press, we had a staffer on rewrite who tried to jazz up a rare murder in Boston's Chinatown. "Ho Fan Wing," he wrote, "was found shot to death today behind the counter of his Chinese laundry where for so many years he had happily fingered his abacus." Only a few seasons back, a CBS-TV sports roundup assured us that "George Brett's hemorrhoid problems are largely behind him now." Last summer I was driving to a golf course on Cape Cod when I heard a radio newscaster announce "that beached whale off Chatham isn't out of the woods yet."

None of us is immune to this sort of prose pratfall. Certainly not I, who have made a living weaving words for over five decades. In the final days of the Yom Kippur War, the Egyptian Third Army was trapped on the Israeli side of the Suez Canal at the same time as an Israeli parachute battalion was surrounded on the Egyptian or African side of the canal. Under an Ismailia dateline, I wrote: "The Chief Rabbi of Jerusalem arrived on the banks of the Suez Canal today to offer special prayers for all Jewish soldiers cut off at the front." Where were all those carping, gimlet-eyed, phrase-slashing desk folk when you needed them most? (Fortunately, they were there to cut me off at the wire.)

Webster's unabridged English dictionary defines more than 650,000 words. Almost any of them can lead to glory or grief. "Words," wrote the philosopher Gerald Brennan, "are as recalcitrant as circus animals, and the unskilled can crack the whip at them in vain."

There indeed are those performers who dazzle and delight us with their whip-cracking wizardry. Red Smith was always center ring, which is why I seldom lend out *Out of the Red* and my other treasured collections of his erudite and witty sports columns. They rarely come back. When heavyweight Tami Mauriello dispatched British contender Bruce Woodcock in the fifth round, in 1946, Red reported that Woodcock "[slipped] off into the deep, dreamless slumber that comes only to small children, the pure of heart, and all British heavyweights." Evoking Shakespeare in a nifty if naughty reference to the great American gelding Kelso, Smith wrote off some sports misadventure as "the unkindest cut since Kelso." Far be it from me to suggest that good writing is whatever you can get away with, but at times it seems to pay to be daring. When Lorena Bobbitt took the stand in her own defense against meaningfully maiming her erring, abusive husband, Amy Pagnozzi of the *New York Daily News* wrote: "Lorena cut through the prosecution's baloney as deftly as she did through his." Former

Boston Globe columnist Mike Barnicle compared TV evangelist Tammy Faye Baker's complexion to "a Vermont ski report: two inches of powder on a hard-packed base." And I bow deeply to the anonymous *Time* magazine writer who, in the days when Henry Luce granted no bylines, covered the return of Fritz Reiner and the Chicago Symphony Orchestra from a triumphant world tour. Some six thousand music lovers turned up at O'Hare airport in a blizzard to welcome them home. "But then," the writer rejoiced, "the Windy City's great big heart always has gone out to the spectacle of a dozen men arriving in town with violin cases that actually contain violins." Super Bowls usually generate mountains of slushy hyperbole, but sometimes a gem glistens among the muck. When six blimps hovered over the San Diego Super Bowl a few seasons back, a local columnist dubbed it "a day that will live in blimphany." For clarity and simplicity you can't beat the Back Bay dowager who was asked by the *Boston Post* reporter and later famous novelist John P. Marquand if it were true that she came to America on the maiden voyage of the Titanic. "Well," she replied, "part way."

Like a riveting film or play, good writing has pace and verve and builds to a climax in a setting illuminated by carefully observed details. Listen to what Somerset Maugham said about master storyteller Rudyard Kipling: "Kipling's vocabulary was rich. He chose words, often very unexpected words, for their color, their precision, their cadence. He knew what he wanted to say and said it incisively. His prose had pace and vigor."

Pace. Vigor. Cadence. One would think Maugham was discussing Mozart or Verdi, but there is music in fine prose. "The best sentences," said the poet Robert Frost, "have their own sound—with the stresses shifting with the sense." Anthony Burgess, the author of *A Clockwork Orange,* is in firm agreement: "The better writers write with their ears, listening to the inner music of sentences."

The AP colleagues I admired the most—Hal Boyle, Don Whitehead, Saul Pett, Pulitzer Prize–winners all—went around talking to themselves, orchestrating their prose. That's at least what I tell people *I'm* doing, when they catch me mumbling in the macaroni aisles at Safeway and walking about in a Walter Mitty–like reverie of creativity.

We can't all be Vladimir Nabokovs or Red Smiths or Maureen Dowds, but we can avoid the trendy, tediously au courant jargon that so quickly jells into a cliché. Words and expressions like: "send a message," "gave it his best shot," "hard ball," "the bottom line," "running on empty." And, oh, yes, is peace possible anymore, anywhere, without a "peace process"?

Let us then become jargon-nauts and launch into limbo this sort of media mumbling that without the saving grace of a swift sound bite lumbers onto the printed page full of pretense and flatulence. In reading so-called think pieces I find that first sentences containing the word *symbiosis* or any reference to Alexis de Tocqueville invariably become my last sentence. Actually, I have nothing against that peripatetic voyeur of American democracy, but to cite him ad infinitum, as the Beltway pundits do, diminishes the grandeur of Edmund Burke, my own favorite reference when a pretentious riposte is required.

Then there is the other danger of *under*writing as opposed to *over*writing, making as little as possible of something just to be rid of it. In these days of high-priced newsprint and tight news holes, it behooves us to try and make something of almost nothing. If a story is worth doing at all, it is worth doing well. Toward the end of his career, John Barrymore was asked why the greatest Hamlet of his era would stoop to playing the small part of King Duncan in a production of *Macbeth*. "There are no small parts," the Great Profile replied, "only small actors."

When it comes to routine stories (and devoutly do I wish there were no such category), newspapers and broadcasters seem to be almost surgically linked to some clichés, even unto death. Obituaries provide the deadly evidence. Have you noticed that whenever a prominent Catholic dies, he or she was always "a devout Catholic"? A prominent Jew was invariably "a pious Jew." Alas for the Reformation, the best they can say of an Episcopalian is that he or she was "a lifelong Episcopalian." But as the *New York Times* demonstrated when the humor columnist Erma Bombeck died, it is possible to inject some life into an obit. The obit told how she was motivated to write about odd happenings in her neighborhood, such as the time a garbage truck ran over the dog that the little boy next door got for Christmas. "Don't cry, Jimmy," his mother tried to console him. "Rover's in heaven with the Baby Jesus." To which the kid wailed, "What would the Baby Jesus want with a dead dog?"

An insightful anecdote, a dash of wit can make the most ordinary story stand out on a page. Ed Tunstall, who wrote sports for the AP when I was stationed in New Orleans, dropped by Curley's gym one afternoon on the way to the office. He bought a cup of coffee for a broken-down club fighter and came away with a delightful feature that began: "Lightweight Ray 'Jitterbug' Smith, who never has been anywhere, is planning a comeback."

Ed Tunstall was a reporter, and reporters, like cops and firefighters, are never off duty. Where I live in Ridgefield, Connecticut, the best-selling author of *The Longest Day* is buried beneath a stone that bears the simple legend, "Cornelius Ryan, Reporter."

The late Mike Royko considered it the highest praise when a wise editor on the *Chicago Tribune* called him "a great street reporter." Like Murray Kempton, another great sidewalk journalist, Royko, when stuck for an idea, used to wander into criminal court just to apply his reporter's stethoscope to the Windy City's troubled heart. Trials can be boring, but he often lucked out and came away with a story. But as Peter Arnett, my AP colleague of twenty years before he became a broadcast reporter, once told a journalism class, "There are lucky reporters and there are lazy reporters. But there are no lucky lazy reporters. Luck is getting off your butt and out of the office."

How well do you function out of the office, out in the real world away from your desk, the telephone, the Internet? Do you as a reporter use all the natural gifts available to you on every assignment, gifts more valuable than a tape recorder and a laptop? Have you learned to look as well as to listen? In this world of thirty-second sound bites and third takes, too many journalists have developed the notion that news is what happens when you stick a tape recorder or a microphone into a politician's face, and out pours tomorrow's headlines or the nightly news.

Georges Simenon armed his police inspector with all the basic tools of investigative reporting: "It was Maigret's way when he was working on a case to soak up everything like a sponge, absorbing people and things, even of the most trivial sort, as well as impressions of which he was barely conscious." Sometimes, impressions of which you are barely conscious can dictate the mood of a story when you sit down to write.

——

An alert reporter must be a loner, apart from the herd.

This is especially important on a big story, when the media herd gathers to brag and joke while the jury is still out or a fire is being hosed down or the presidential motorcade is still blocks away. As a reporter, you need to break out from the pack, do your own thing. Work the crowd or drop into a gas station or diner to tune in on how the community is reacting to whatever the herd is awaiting. To me there is nothing so dismal and unproductive in this business as a bunch of reporters and camera crews standing around swapping stories. I remember when President John F. Kennedy's coffin was being taken from the White House to lie in state under the capitol dome. Hundreds of us wearing press credentials lined Pennsylvania

Avenue to cover a story that already was being relayed live on TV around the world. The *New York Herald Tribune*'s Jimmy Breslin broke ranks and deserted us. He flagged a taxi to Arlington cemetery for a memorable interview with the gravediggers who were preparing the slain president's final resting place.

I learned a lesson there and then. People make better copy than events, most notably TV events. Breslin's example paid off for me when Pope John Paul II presided at a youth rally at the Galway racecourse in the west of Ireland. The pope at a racetrack? It seemed a bizarre setting for a pontifical Mass, so I passed up the press bus and went out to the track several hours ahead of the herd. Instead of attending a briefing on the liturgy by the local bishops, I was shown around the premises by a delightful track steward with a Barry Fitzgerald brogue who was as astonished as I was at the Vatican's choice of an outdoor chapel. He told me the flower-decked helicopter pad where His Holiness would alight was actually the winner's circle on race days. The altar, he noted, had been erected in front of the betting totalizer board, now concealed behind gold-and-white Vatican banners. The pope would be putting on his vestments for Mass in the jockeys' weighing-in room, but the cardinals and bishops would be suiting up in the paddocks—the stables—fragrant now with incense instead of the usual horsey aromas. Here was a rich opportunity for a reporter to use eyes and ears, and even the sense of smell, to dramatize the unlikely appearance of a pope at a racetrack. "Dramatize! Dramatize!" novelist Henry James implored writers. The tabloid *New York Daily News* had four reporters chasing the pope around Ireland. They bannered my story under the headline: "POPE WINS, PLACES AND SHOWS AT GALWAY TRACK."

—

On any assignment, if there is time, read up as much as you can on the topic you're to cover. This is so much easier now that computerized news libraries make back issues of major dailies and magazines instantly available. If you can avoid it, never set out cold on an interview. A little preparation unburdens you and your subject of time-consuming background questions, but more often spares you from asking ridiculous howlers. Researching your subject might enable you to ask an offbeat question that might soften the reserve of a cautious, uncooperative interviewee or at least win his or her respect. I can give you a good example. New York's John Cardinal O'Connor was a former Navy chaplain who rarely talked about his Vietnam experiences. While I was engaged in a one-on-one with the cardinal, en route to visit a women's prison, we passed a golf course. I asked if he still had the golf clubs he bought at the Navy Exchange and if he ever played that little nine-holer near Saigon's Tan San Nhut airport. This unleashed a flood of reminiscences. In no time at all, he was recounting a trip he had made in a helicopter that had come under groundfire and made a rough jungle landing. He recalled being crouched in a ditch, saying his rosary, while AP photographer Eddie Adams was dashing about photographing a firefight. My bit of homework about the golf clubs put him in a relaxed mood for me to ask the tough questions I had prepared.

Avoid, if you can, interviews by telephone or in hotel lobbies. Try to meet your subjects on their own turf: backstage, in the sacristy, down on the factory floor, on the stump, at home, but not in a bar—unless that's the subject's normal habitat. Mort Rosenblum, the AP's globe-trotting correspondent, makes a point of asking to use the bathroom in the home of an interview subject. It gives him a chance to peek in the den, at the pictures on the piano or in the hallway, at the bookshelf, the playroom, maybe the master bedroom.

As James Jones suggested, leave enough time between questions to let people ramble a bit. Sometimes you may hear a seemingly irrelevant anecdote that, when you get around to writing, is more revealing than dozens of expository and descriptive paragraphs. The best human interest stories often tell themselves.

Toward the end of his second term, New York Mayor Ed Koch had a visit from Mother Teresa at Gracie Mansion. She declined his offer of tea and cookies, explaining that since her order worked among the poorest of the poor, they never ate outside the convent.

"These cookies are awfully good," His Honor tempted. "My chef makes them without any butter fat."

"If you insist," Mother Teresa conceded. "Wrap them up, and we'll share them back at the convent."

Delighted, Koch ran to kitchen and whispered to his chef, "stick in a cheese cake too, I'll bet those nuns never had a genuine kosher cheese cake."

The anecdote gave a deft example of Mother Teresa's practicality and Mayor Koch at his best—playing the Jewish mother.

———

In this cyberspace age, with so much information available at the tickle of a keyboard, writers need to be extra wary of statistics, the numbing numbers that bury the reader under a slag heap of forgettable figures.

The *Wall Street Journal,* devoted almost exclusively to finance and the dismal science of economics, manages year after year to produce one of the best-written papers in the country by relegating the awesome procession of cardinal numbers to its stock tables. No publication is better at explaining and dramatizing a leveraged buyout or a hostile takeover without torturing the reader on a mathematical rack that would test the endurance of IBM's chess-playing Big Blue.

Sportswriters seem obsessed with the numbers game. We all recognize the formula: "Pint-sized quarterback Charlie Klutzmeyer passed for 195 yards, scrambled for 38 more, and connected on two touchdowns as 12th-ranked Old Siwash upset top-ranked Mensa State Teachers before 65,000 homecoming fans in the 58th renewal of this Little Seven rivalry."

Although I am not a sportswriter, I once won a Louisiana Press Association trophy for spot sports reporting by avoiding a statistical lead in reporting a basketball game from the LSU field house. "Bob Pettit kept the scoreboard singing like a supermarket cash register on a Saturday night in leading the Tigers to an upset over nationally ranked Kentucky." Against all AP rules, the score and his total of 60 points were in the second paragraph. When Pettit was named to the All-American team, he told me he still relished that comparison to a supermarket cash register.

My lifelong aversion to statistics was challenged while covering the funeral of Princess Diana. How else, except by the numbers, could readers fathom the blizzard of flowers that carpeted Kensington Gardens, Hyde Park, and the Mall leading to Buckingham Palace? On TV and in front-page color photos, the Queen and the Duke of Edinburgh were seen almost knee-deep in floral offerings as they approached St. James's Palace to pay their respects. The British Florists Association reported that 15 million tons of flowers were sold the week of Diana's wake and funeral. But who can comprehend even a million tons? How many funeral cars would they fill? Returning in a taxi to the AP office, I chanced to see the marquee of a West End theater offering a revival of George Bernard Shaw's *Pygmalion.* I had the cabbie take me immediately to old St. Paul's church in Covent Garden where, before the rain-swept portico, Eliza Doolittle, in the film *My Fair Lady,* had flogged her flowers. Sure enough, there was a flower dealer hustling bouquets from a little green barrow just like Eliza's. To strike up a conversation, I bought a bouquet for £10 (about $15). All week long, the florist said, he had been selling more than a hundred an hour, twice as many as at Christmas and St. Valentine's Day, the peak seasons. In fluent Cockney that would have pained Professor Higgins, he insisted that it was not "us blokes jacking up the prices, out of respect for the Princess"—the blame was to be laid entirely on "the bleedin' 'olesalers in 'Olland." Well, I had to settle for that statistic, a hundred bouquets an hour, but I think it conveyed more to the reader than 15 million tons.

And it paid off to have read Shaw's *Pygmalion* in an otherwise dreary postgraduate literature course. To write well, you really should read well. ("Reading," said the British essayist Richard Steele, "is to the mind what exercise is to the body.") For one evening a week, give up TV news and your favorite sitcom and lubricate your mind with literature. You might start with Dickens, Kipling, Hemingway, Willa Cather, Graham Greene, George Orwell, Doris Lessing—all of them former journalists. Or try Evelyn Waugh's *Scoop.* It is still the best and funniest novel ever written about foreign correspondents, and not a bit dated in its satire.

—

We hear a lot lately about media credibility. Some polls rank the press just ahead of used-car dealers and a tad behind telephone hucksters when it comes to public trust. If readers are to have any confidence in our major investigative projects, it behooves us to be right in reporting the most fundamental truths, like spelling a person's name correctly and getting the score right in a Class D high school lacrosse match. Letters to the editor that begin: "Not only was I misquoted, but that turkey couldn't even spell my name right" are the most painful to answer. Correction boxes on the front page may proclaim our integrity, but they also broadcast our incompetence. Here I definitely would include spelling, while freely confessing to being one of our craft's more imaginative spellers. Like Oscar Wilde, I can't stand those narrow-minded people who can only spell a word one way. Alas, the computer's SpellCheck has sunk from sight even that jolly rejoinder to a livid editor.

—

Look beyond the handout. Read between the lines of the government news release. One day in the AP's Saigon bureau, George Esper was going through a stack of handouts from the U.S. Military Command. A one-sentence item intrigued him. B-52 pilot Michael Heck, the report noted matter-of-factly, was being "disciplined" for refusing to fly missions over the North. Using the complex military phone codes, George patiently dialed bases in Guam, Thailand, and the Philippines where B-52s were assigned. Three hours later, he tracked down Capt. Heck at the bar in the officers club at U Tapao in Thailand. The pilot blurted out that his tormented conscience no longer allowed him to drop tons of bombs from 30,000 feet without knowing who or what was beneath the cloud cover: a SAM-site or a hospital? a school, an orphanage, or a supply convoy destined for the Ho Chi Minh trail? George's persistence resulted in a searing human interest story that led the TV evening news, made banner headlines everywhere, and earned him a rare page-one byline in the *New York Times*.

How long should a story be? On street assignments, when I first came to the AP's New York bureau, I sometimes ran into *Herald Tribune* feature writer Tom Wolfe, now the legendary author of such best-sellers as *The Right Stuff* and *The Bonfire of the Vanities*. I envied his long, vividly detailed, elegantly written articles, wishing my editors would allow me half that length. Over coffee in a diner, he confided that he once asked city editor Dan Blum how long he could let a piece he was working on run. Blum advised him, "Till it gets boring."

Sometimes long is good; other times, short is better. In Saigon I wrote a one-paragraph story that perhaps told as much about that seemingly bottomless quagmire as all the hundreds of thousands of words I wrote in Vietnam over a period of four years. Here is the entire story:

> SAIGON (AP)—Rama Dama Rau, Premier Ky's personal astrologer who predicted five years ago that the war would be over in six months, was drafted today.

People stories often get to the heart of a matter more surely than statistics or political pronouncements. In my to-ing and fro-ing about the globe in search of local color, I frequently find that real estate agents, automobile dealers, missionaries, local pastors, even undertakers are better sources of information than political big shots. They invariably are in better touch with the everyday people of the community.

And writers are people who need people. If people don't really fascinate you, amuse you, and, more often, irk you, then you may be in the wrong profession.

I was in Berlin when the Wall came down. Christmas time, 1989. All the big-name anchors were there in fur hats and stylish belted overcoats.

Peter Jennings, Dan Rather, Tom Brokaw, Pierre Salinger for French TV. Night after night, they took turns doing stand-ups in front of the historic backdrop of the Brandenburg Gate. Yet nothing was happening there. The gate wasn't opened until weeks later for East-West traffic. It loomed under the TV lights as a symbol of political power, but now that power belonged to the people, ordinary people.

Just a few blocks away all sorts of human comedies and tragedies were being acted out live. Happy Berliners were chipping away at the wall with pickaxes and crowbars, making holes big enough for Trabants—those one-lunged Czechoslovakian cars—to pass though. A Trabbie broke down right in the middle of what had been the death strip. A half dozen laughing young men ran out to carry it the rest of the way. Weeping old women and men were placing flowers along the wall where dozens had died trying to cross to freedom. The machine gun towers were still occupied by vigilant guards waiting for the word to open fire. The revelers waved and whistled at them and kept chipping away. French paratroopers arrived in a jeep pulling a trailer and began passing out bottles of champagne to refugees now pouring through the gaping holes. They kissed all the young girls and the old grandmothers, too.

It was a cold day, with a sharp wind blowing down the Spree River. I didn't pay much attention, but about noon an elderly man in a long over-coat unfolded a camp chair near Checkpoint Charlie, which now bore the graffiti message, "Charlie's out to lunch." Seated with his back to the wall, he removed a cello from its case, tuned the strings, and commenced play-ing. He played beautifully, a happy, lilting air. I was ready to move on when a young girl, probably a music student, cried "Maestro!" and fell to her knees. She was the first to recognize Mstislav Rostropovich, the world-class cellist, who had vowed he never would perform a concert in Berlin until the Wall came down.

I was in luck again, the luck I had made for myself by getting out of our warm office and deciding against listening, through an interpreter, to a live telecast of an emergency meeting of the East German parliament. The cello solo grabbed more front pages than the swan song of the commissars.

Lady Luck even gave me a bonus. Only once did the VOPOs, the feared East German militia, employ force to save the wall from further damage. They brought in a huge water cannon, the kind the British army used in Ulster riots, and began power-blasting the pickaxe-wielding cele-brants off the Wall. One very drunk Berliner, fat and jovial as a Bavarian braumeister, stood defiantly astride the ramparts, unzipped his lederhosen and fired back.

There was no need for punditry or political analysis, no reason to search out any officials for official comment. History was being written by ordinary citizens whose actions spoke louder than press conferences. Don't be so overwhelmed by important personages at any news event that you forget that ordinary people reacting to extraordinary events add up to a more meaningful story. People who had lived in the shadow of that Wall made the story, not the East German parliament in its unmourned dying moments.

The best reporting is sometimes just letting it all happen without benefit of Q-and-A. The pope manages to make news without ever holding press conferences or granting interviews. I've covered John Paul II on trips to more than fifty countries on every continent except Antarctica. Along the way, I've interviewed any number of cardinals, bishops, and monsignori, including several members of the Curia. Yet my most memorable encounter along the papal trail took place at Trinity College in Washington, D.C., during the pope's first American visit in 1979. Rows and rows of sick and handicapped pilgrims were out on the lawn in wheelchairs and on stretchers hours before his arrival. They eagerly awaited his blessing, some hoping and praying that they might be healed by a touch of his hand or just by looking into that compassionate face. I talked with Michael Burns, an angelic-looking seven-year-old with the enormous blue eyes of a Raphael cherub. He was stretched out on a gurney in his First Communion suit, his polio-twisted legs tucked into useless shiny black patent leather shoes. Michael was back in the fourth row, tended by a nurse who kept fanning his blond curly head with a newspaper. The boy told me he was so excited about meeting the pope he had hardly slept a wink.

I caught up with him later, after the pope had passed, just as he was being loaded into a hospital van.

"Michael," I asked, "did you get to see the pope?"

Those lovely eyes brimmed with tears. "Yes," he answered, "but he didn't see me."

So I wrote: "It must be a sad job being a pope—not being able to perform instant miracles for people reaching out to you, to go on praying for peace everywhere and often finding only violence and misery."

The point here is that observant, sensitive reporting is the raw material of good writing.

Do you always make full use of your eyes, your ears, your nose—even your emotions? Do you dare put your heart into a story? Or have you become so hard-boiled, so cynical, so "been-there, seen-it-all," as never to wonder how people feel down deep, below the surface of your questions, in the privacy of their misery? Do we as reporters mostly concern ourselves with public wrongs and political rights and rarely, if ever, with the private desolations of the heart that for most people are the unwritten headlines of their everyday lives? As Ring Lardner asked, "How can you write, if you can't cry?" They say that when Gustave Flaubert described Madame Bovary's suicide, he vomited as if he had taken the arsenic himself.

Well, sometimes I've tossed my cookies as well as copy into the wastebasket, more often in disgust than in empathy. Nonetheless, after years in this business, I agree wholeheartedly with Flaubert that "writing is a dog's life, but it's the only life worth living." And I enjoin you to live it to the full by using all the tools, all the senses, at your command.

SECTION II:
FINDING GOOD *STORIES*

Testing Your Ideas:
Ten Pre-Proposal Checks

By Amanda Bennett

[Bennett was part of a *Wall Street Journal* team that won a 1997 Pulitzer Prize for reporting. After working for two years at the Portland *Oregonian* as managing editor in charge of investigative and long-range projects, she joined the *Lexington Herald-Leader* in Kentucky as editor and senior vice president.]

Here are ten ways to assess a story idea before you try selling it to an editor:

1. *Where did your idea come from?*
   If it came off reporting, it's probably a stronger idea than one you just got out of your head. Did your reporting suggest a trend? Did it turn up a fascinating person? Did something just not seem right? Did something about your reporting puzzle you, or intrigue you, or surprise you?

2. *Is the idea original?*
   Have you done your library research to see what else has been written on the topic? You don't want to spend weeks or months reinventing the wheel. If something has been written about your idea already, look for opportunities to take an intensely local perspective or a particular new angle on the subject.

3. *Does the idea surprise you?*
   If it doesn't surprise you, will it surprise your readers? Will they invest the time to read fifty inches of a story if it is so predictable that they already know pretty much everything about the story's main idea by reading the headline?

4. *Does the idea have movement to it?*
What's *movement?* It's change, direction, motion—it's
something that's new, something that's more than it used
to be or less than it used to be, something that people
are suddenly developing interest in or losing interest in,
something they're starting to talk about, or think about,
or plan for.

5. *Is there a* story *there?*
For some stories—profiles, social stories, stories of towns,
regions, people—you want a story that has a beginning, a
middle, and an end. Can you show how someone or
someplace grows, changes, develops? Will you know
more about this person or place at the end of the story
than at the beginning? Is there a *tale* in your idea that will
draw the reader along?

6. *Is there tension?*
Tension comes with conflict, the unknown, a problem to
be overcome, a mystery to be solved. Tension is reading
the first paragraph of a story and not knowing what the
last paragraph is going to say—or knowing, but not knowing how you'll get there.

7. *Is the story true?*
There are an awful lot of compelling ideas—about inven-
tions, and social movements, and diseases, and vitamins,
and truisms, and philosophies—that just turn out *not* to be
true. Before you propose a story, do enough work to make
sure you know what you are talking about. But remember:
If something that everyone thinks is true turns out to be not
true in some way you can prove, you've got a great story.

8. *When you talk about the story to your editor and friends,
do you find yourself using a lot of verbs and talking about
specific incidents?*
If you find that you just can't help using *action verbs* in
talking about your story—how doctors are pushing for

some change, how a particular group is annoying its opponents, how someone is defending something she believes in, or agitating to change something he hates—you are likely onto something good. Are you just dying to tell someone the amazing *anecdote* of how this guy got the developers to back off his land? Or how she kept the secret for years that she was actually a famous opera star? Do you laugh inside when you think of some of the anecdotes you are going to use? Do you feel moved?

9. *Or do you find that you just can't help falling back on weasel words?*
When you try to sell the story to your editor, do you find that you just can't help using the word "interesting"? Or "fascinating"? Or "important"? Do you find that you just can't avoid saying: "I want to take a look at . . ."? These are all telltale signs that you have a *topic,* but not yet a *story.* Remember that the need to show, not tell, applies to proposals as well as to stories. If something is indeed interesting, your reporting should make that clear without your having to say so. If something is important, it should be the details that make it important that you present to your editors—don't make the editors take you on faith.

10. *Do* you *like the story?*
You're going to be spending an awful lot of time working on this piece. Shouldn't it be something you really love doing? And that means assignments, too. If you find yourself, as many of us do all the time, doing something that has to be done, shouldn't you find a way to make it as fun and meaningful for yourself as possible? How can you expect your editors and readers to enjoy a story if you haven't?

Tammy Gaudette Wants Real Stories

⌒

By Ken Fuson

[Fuson, a reporter for the *Des Moines Register,* received the 1998 American Society of Newspaper Editors Distinguished Writing Award for non-deadline writing. He has won numerous other honors for his reporting and writing.]

As a feature writer, I'm often accused by the real reporters—those folks who write about bauxite and leading economic indicators and such—of not getting to the point fast enough in my stories. They say that my forte is spot fluff, that I'm on the broken-wing beat, writing about the disease of the week and other misfortunes. And they fully expect to pick up the paper someday and read a story of mine that begins like this:

> Tramp was Johnny's favorite pet. They laughed together, ran together, and slept together. And now they're in heaven together. Tramp was with Johnny yesterday when a nuclear bomb struck the state of Iowa and killed 3 million people.

Well, those reporters may have a point. But my own point is this: *I don't think we write enough stories.*

I know what you're thinking—"What the hell are you talking about? I'm out here at my newspaper writing two stories a day and three for Sundays. I'm writing so many stories I can't keep them straight. Let's see, was Mr. Jones the check-kiter or the philanthropist? Are you about to offer another one of those 'let's boost productivity' pep talks?"

No. What I mean is, we don't write enough *STORIES.* Stories that enchant readers from the opening note . . . stories that have a beginning, middle, and end . . . stories that make readers look for the byline when they're finished and cause them to make a mental note to look for that reporter's work another day . . . stories that leave readers calling out to a roommate or spouse, saying "You have GOT to read this" . . . stories that take readers places they've never been . . . stories that make them laugh or cry, think or feel. A friend of mine compares reading a great story to seeing a great movie. There comes that moment right after the initial credits when you lean back in your seat and say, *Here we go,* and then get lost in the tale. I'm talking about stories like this:

> In the cold hours of a winter morning Dr. Thomas Barbee Ducker, chief brain surgeon at the University of Maryland Hospital, rises before dawn. His wife serves him waffles but no coffee. Coffee makes his hands shake.
>
> In downtown Baltimore, on the 12th floor of University Hospital, Edna Kelly's husband tells her goodbye. For 57 years Mrs. Kelly shared her skull with the monster: No more. Today she is frightened but determined.
>
> It is 6:30 A.M.
>
> "I'm not afraid to die," she said as this day approached. "I've lost part of my eyesight. I've gone through all the hemorrhages. A couple of years ago I lost my sense of smell, my taste. I started having seizures. I smell a strange odor and then I start strangling. It started affecting my legs, and I'm partially paralyzed.
>
> "Three years ago a doctor told me all I had to look forward to was blindness, paralysis and a remote chance of death. Now I have aneurysms; this monster is causing that. I'm scared to death . . . but there isn't a day that goes by that I'm not in pain, and I'm tired of it. I can't bear the pain. I wouldn't want to live like this much longer."
>
> As Dr. Ducker leaves for work, Mrs. Ducker hands him a paper bag containing a peanut butter sandwich, a banana and two fig newtons.
>
> Downtown, in Mrs. Kelly's brain, a sedative takes effect.[1]

---

1. Jon Franklin, "Mrs. Kelly's Monster," *Writing for Story: Craft Secrets of Dramatic Nonfiction by a Two-Time Pulitzer Prize Winner* (New York: Plume/Penguin, 1994), pp. 28-29. [Originally published in the *Baltimore Evening Sun,* Dec. 12-13, 1978.]

You may recognize that as the start of Jon Franklin's story "Mrs. Kelly's Monster," which first appeared in the *Baltimore Evening Sun*. It won the first Pulitzer Prize given for feature writing, in 1979. Franklin followed that up in 1985 by winning the first Pulitzer Prize given in explanatory journalism. He has written a valuable book, *Writing for Story,* that talks in exacting detail about writing nonfiction stories—how to find them, how to write them, why we should do them.

I share Franklin's obvious love for newspapers. I've loved them since I was a kid in Granger, Iowa, where every morning I'd go to the milk box—we had milk boxes then—to get the *Des Moines Register.* I never knew what to expect. Maybe the *Register* would tell me a story about the woman who gave birth in her car during a blizzard, or maybe it would be the morning that a reporter took readers into an operating room, or maybe it would tell me about the teenage girl from Union-Whiten High School who scored a hundred points in a basketball game. I didn't know what I'd find, but I knew it would be thrilling, or exciting, or sad, or thought-provoking.

People talk all the time in the newspaper business about connecting with readers, and newspaper executives hire consultants who charge thousands of dollars to organize focus groups to tell us that Joe Six-Pack doesn't have time to read the paper because he has to mow the lawn. Richard Ben Cramer—another Pulitzer-winning storyteller who learned his craft writing for the *Baltimore Sun*—asks a simple question: Why don't those corporate types ever ask themselves why Joe Six-Pack would rather mow his lawn than read the paper? Why don't those executives see to it that their newspaper includes some *stories* that would give Mr. Six-Pack an excuse *not* to mow his lawn?

People buy newspapers for a variety of reasons. Maybe they're seeking a coupon for soap. Maybe they want to know if the local high school won its game. Maybe they just want to know what time *Rocky VIII* starts at the movie house.

Or maybe they're seeking *stories* that will engage their interest.

Newspapers are filled with stories, aren't they? Isn't that what we call those things between the ads? No. Newspapers are filled with crap. Dull, boring crap. Reporters will list all the bills filed in the legislature for the week; or they will tell you that the school board is interested in something called "competency testing," whatever that is; or they will tell you that the City Council is applying for revenue-sharing money so a private-public foundation will give the seed money to the downtown sector. No wonder Joe Six-Pack is reaching for his lawn mower. Worse, reporters themselves often don't read their own newspaper. They're bored by their own stories.

But Tammy Gaudette isn't reading this stuff. I first met her several years ago, when the *Register* invited a panel of readers to tell us what they thought of the paper. Tammy Gaudette, a housewife and mother of two, said she read the paper every day. Somebody at the gathering asked what she read. "Well, I don't read the news," she replied. "I like the interesting stories."

I wrote that down and pasted it to my computer: *I don't read the news. I like the interesting stories.* Stories that put her on the street with the cop who is wearing a bullet-proof vest for the first time because his buddy got shot the night before. Stories that put her in a classroom as a first-grader struggles to read. Stories that take her behind the scenes at a City Council meeting to describe the shouting match that precedes the vote to raise her taxes.

Walt Harrington's wonderful book about such story-writing, titled *Intimate Journalism,* starts this way:

> As journalists for the tribe, we remember many things well. Yesterday's weather, always. Michael Jordan's amazing 69-point tear against Cleveland. Instability in Istanbul. Insurgency in Peru. Politician caught in love nest. Celebrity gets married, celebrity gets divorced. The Dow. The death of an old man in Omaha, Nebraska. The birth of a baby girl on the same day in Taos, New Mexico. Hurricanes in Jamaica. Massacres in Rwanda. Revolution in Russia. The speeches—oh, the speeches. And elections far and wide.
>
> The tribe is grateful.
>
> But other things we remember for the tribe almost not at all. The *feeling* a child has when she takes the power of the Holy Spirit into her heart at first communion. The feeling an old farmer has when he latches his barn door for the last time on the night before his homestead is sold. The feeling a teacher has when a bad student becomes a good one. The feeling a mother has when her daughter pitches the winning game in the Little League championship. The feeling a father has as he buries his firstborn son. The feeling a man has when he learns that he has beaten the cancer. The feeling a woman has when she learns that she has not.
>
> . . . But to most journalists honored with the job of remembering the stories of the tribe, these momentous events of everyday life are virtually invisible.[2]

2. Walt Harrington, *Intimate Journalism: The Art and Craft of Reporting Everyday Life* (Thousand Oaks, Calif.: Sage Publications, 1997), p. xi.

As Harrington reminds us, journalists should mine the daily dramas of life. We should look for stories that explain how we live. Every day, someone is born, someone is buried, someone gets married, someone gets divorced, someone heads to the operating room, and someone goes to jail.

There are real *stories* out there, even for beat reporters. There are stories for the writer who covers City Hall. Maybe next week, the city will shut off someone's electricity for failure to pay. A story likely lies inside that action. Every single vote the City Council takes affects someone, for good or ill. Real stories are there, subsequent to that official action. Courthouse reporters have a rich store of stories to mine. Right now, today, someone is in small claims court for the first time, accusing a neighbor of owing money. There's a story. Right now, today, someone is on trial for murdering her boyfriend's old flame. There's a story. Right now, today, a young couple is filing for bankruptcy because a downturn in the Dow Jones average has wrecked their dream of running a florist's shop. That's another of the many stories that fill a courthouse daily. Likewise, if you're the school beat reporter, you'll find intriguing stories down every hallway. Spend a day with a new teacher fresh out of college. Spend the day with a kid who dropped out of high school, or with one who is graduating despite overwhelming odds. Spend the night with a senior who works all the time to pay for his car, then sleeps during first-period English. Spend time at a junior-high dance with a nervous seventh-grader. Spend a few hours in the auditorium with student actors, as they await the drama teacher's posting of the cast list for the upcoming musical. All these stories could manifest intense drama, if they're reported and told well.

I believe stories—real *stories*—are powerful enough to save our newspapers as they compete against so many other media thriving today. It's taken for granted in newsrooms that readers won't read long stories. But it's not so. In Des Moines, reporter John Carlson wrote a five-hundred-inch series about an Iowa family that lost several members—all hemophiliacs or their loved ones—to AIDS. It was a gripping saga. The biggest complaint the paper received was that editors had divided the story into three parts instead of publishing all five hundred inches at once. Before this story, the record for reprint requests at the *Register* had been eight hundred. This series received seven thousand requests.

Readers will read long articles—if the stories captivate, if they put readers on the scene of some unfolding situation. They will read stories about interesting, sympathetic characters who face a dramatic conflict and resolve it. It's up to the reporter to write the material in such a way that the "story" element is strong and compelling.

Here are a few suggestions, focusing first on the story *idea,* then on the *reporting,* and finally on the *writing.*

Finding Story Ideas

As you look for story ideas, look for drama. Remember what you learned in seventh grade: The best stories have a conflict (or complication), a plot (or action), and resolution. Jon Franklin describes and illustrates this conflict-resolution form extensively in *Writing for Story.* The more basic the conflict—those involving love, hate, triumph, travail—the better. Franklin says the best stories can be organized using three-word descriptions, such as: "Ken dreads speech"—"Ken gives speech." Now, obviously, there are different levels of conflict. The dread I feel before giving a speech is not on a par with the fear someone feels before undergoing open-heart surgery. Franklin points out that it's a conflict if a fly lands on my nose, but the resolution is simple: I shoo it away. It's not so simple if I'm paralyzed. He also observes that most newspaper stories tend to present resolutions without bothering to set up any conflicts that are involved. In other words, someone wins an award, a vote is taken, a game is won. Franklin suggests we go back and find out what the conflict was that has since been overcome. That, he proposes, is where the reporter will find real stories.

Let's look at a story that has it all—a universal conflict, surprising plot twists, a dramatic climax, and satisfying resolution. It's *Are You My Mother?* by P. D. Eastman. In it, a baby bird is born, but its mother has flown off in search of food. That is a pretty basic conflict or complication: *Baby loses mother.* We follow the baby bird in its search. It talks to the cat, the chicken, the dog. No luck. It finds a car and a boat. No luck. Finally, the bird is picked up by a giant crane—the Snort—and deposited safely into its nest, where its mother waits. So, we have this resolution: *Baby finds mother.* I actually outlined this simple book, to see what I could discover about P. D. Eastman's storytelling techniques. You can do this with anything—a book, a movie, a television show. In outlining, you try to recognize in its most elemental form the conflict, the plot twist, and the resolution. Such outlining can become habit-forming, because by doing it, you can learn so much that can assist you in your own storytelling.

The key to doing real stories on deadline, I believe, is to think *small.* You're writing one slice, not the whole loaf. If your city lays off ten firefighters for budget reasons, follow one firefighter who now has to find somewhere else to work, or locate someone whose house has burned down. Real stories do not need to be five hundred inches long. Spend the day with a garbage crew on the day after Christmas. Spend the day after Thanksgiving with the manager of a department store. Go with someone who is applying for a job. One of my colleagues, Lisa Pollak, not long ago wrote that perennial, the "teacher of the year" story, by locating students who had studied under the teacher years ago. It was beautifully done, and it was a real *story*.

We simply have to change our mindset about stories. A real story is not the mayor talking about the need for a tax increase. That's important, of course, and must be written, but for a story, go to a widow's home as she struggles to balance her budget and find the story of how the increase will affect her. A story is not how some business fared in the third quarter. It's important, and must be written, but for a story, find the store owner who is going out of business after twenty-five years because time has passed him by. A story is not a report on the increasing number of divorces in your community. It's important, and must be written, but a story is how two local high school sweethearts simply grew apart and separated.

Granted, these stories are not always easy to get. The reason we write so many stories about politicians and meetings and court papers and other "official" stories is that they're readily available. These are often the sorts of stories you're handed by an editor who spends his or her workdays sitting in the office. And if, in seeking story ideas, you wait for an editor's assignment, you're lost. The best stories, typically, are the ones you find on your own. If you're trolling for stories, real stories, you're probably going to have to get out of the office often to talk to real people. You'll find it's not as hard as you think. To find good stories, follow Jon Franklin's advice: Look for conflicts and resolutions.

Reporting the Story

Good writing depends on good reporting the way human life depends on oxygen. And that's no less true of feature writing than it is of hard news reporting. There are a few simple things about good reporting that we tend to forget, as we slog from story to story meeting deadlines:

- Most reporters deal with numerical facts. Real stories often deal with emotional facts—what did something look like, sound like, feel like to you, or to the person you've interviewed? Can you make the reader feel the experience?
- Weave facts into a story the way a baker weaves chocolate chips into cookie dough. If something is boring to you, it'll be boring to readers. Find another way to tell it.

- Honesty works. I once interviewed an eighty-year-old grandfather accused of robbing a bank. I went to his home. His wife answered. I told her who I was and that I wanted to write about her husband. Why? Instead of coming up with some story about crime and the elderly, I told her it wasn't every day that an eighty-year-old grandfather was accused of robbing a bank. "Let him in," the grandfather said. (While he admitted nothing, he did say he had seen a movie called *Going in Style* about three old men who rob a bank.)
- Dare to be dumb. This has served me well. Gene Roberts, the former editor of the *Philadelphia Inquirer* and former managing editor of the *New York Times,* says his hero was Homer Bigart. Bigart, he recalls, could do anything, as he reported stories for the *New York Times,* but he was best at bumbling: "Homer would show up on a story, mumbling, `Wha-wha-what's going on?' And everyone would be helping poor old Homer. They helped him to win two Pulitzer Prizes."

Writing the Story

The best tale I ever heard about writing also comes courtesy of Roberts. He says he once had an editor named Henry Belk, who was blind. Belk would call reporters over and tell them, "Make me see. You aren't making me see."

How can we make our readers see? Here are ten suggestions:

1. *Organize your stories into scenes.* The best stories have a you-are-there quality to them. Be there when the drama happens, so you can describe it. In the long history of journalism there's never been a memorable story written based on a telephone interview. Get out of the office. What did the experience you're reporting look like, sound like, smell like, taste like? Search for the most telling details, and cast them into descriptions of *action.* One of the best examples I've seen was in the *Wall Street Journal,* in a story by Charles McCoy that began with this scene:

   VALDEZ, Alaska—It is 9:32 last Thursday morning, and Otter 76 is fighting for her life. She is pinned to a makeshift operating table in a clammy elementary school gym, lungs scored by petroleum poisons. She rattles and gasps, slow spasms rolling up in waves from her hind flippers to her bewhiskered snout. She foams at the mouth and she excretes crude oil. It takes four men to hold her down.

"Come on babes, hang on," exhorts Jeanie Clarke, a volunteer otter attendant from England. Veterinarian Riley Wilson, also a volunteer, frantically pumps drugs into the animal. "Live, damn it," he mutters, and implausibly, Otter 76 does live. The seizure subsides. At 9:43, Otter 76 goes back into her pen, and Mr. Wilson shakes his head and tells a colleague: "I didn't think she'd win that battle."[3]

2. *Be sensitive to the pace, or rhythm, of your prose.* The following paragraph—from a Susan Orlean story in the *New Yorker* about a gospel singing group—combines a reporter's keen eye with a sense of rhythm. The result is lyrical.

I heard people at gospel concerts call eyeglasses "helpers" and a gravel road "a dirty road," and I heard an infant called "a lap baby," and a gun called "a persuader," and dying called "making it over," and an embarrassed person described as "wanting to swallow his own teeth," and a dead person described as someone who was "having his mail delivered to him by groundhogs." Everybody talked about Jesus all the time. He was called a doctor, a lawyer, a lily of the valley, a lamb, a shepherd, joy in the morning, a rock, a road, peace in the evening, a builder, a captain, a rose of Sharon, a friend, a father, and someone who is always on time. I met a man named Porkchop and a man named Midget and a little boy named Royriquez Clarencezellus Wooten. I heard other gospel groups perform: the Christian Harmonizers and the Sensational Harmonizers and the Harmonettes and the Religiousettes and the Gloryettes and the Gospel True Lights and the True Gospel Singers and the Brotherhood Gospel Singers and the Five Singing Sons and the Mighty Sons of Glory and the Fantastic Disciples and the Fantastic Soulernaires and the Fantastic Violinaires and the Sunset Jubilaires and the Pilgrim Jubilees and the Brown Boys and the Five Blind Boys and Wonder Boy and the Spiritual Voices. The concerts were like big public conversations. The exhortations that people called out to the singers most often were "Take your time!" and "Let Him *use* you!" The exhortations that Huey and Roger called out most often were "Do you believe in Jesus?" and "Can I get just one witness?" and "Are you with me, church?" and "You know, God is *able*."[4]

---

3. Charles McCoy, "Heartbreaking Fight Unfolds in Hospital for Valdez Otters," *Wall Street Journal,* April 20, 1989, p. A-1.

4. Susan Orlean, "Devotion Road," *New Yorker,* April 17, 1995, p. 69.

3. *Strive to pick up good dialogue.* Nothing moves a story faster than dialogue. This goes for beat reporting, too. Meetings and trials are great places to pick up dialogue for use in stories.
4. *Approach stories with the passion of a columnist.* That doesn't mean you should tell me your opinion, but strive for an intimate tone. Readers can tell if you care about your work.
5. *Appreciate the sound of words.* Read stories aloud. Bill Keller of the *New York Times* was listening to the sound of words when he composed this lead:

> With the commanding dignity that has carried him through more than a half century of defiance, captivity and conciliation, Nelson Rolihlahla Mandela became the first black President of South Africa today.[5]

6. *Use the most evocative, striking details you have to tell your story in a fresh way.* I once indicated just how remote a small town was by locating it fifteen miles from the nearest McDonalds. A *Washington Post* reporter covered the birth of a baby on an airline flight and described how an internist on board had used a man's shoelaces to tie the umbilical cord. When two boys shot four of their classmates to death in Jonesboro, Arkansas, Rick Bragg of the *New York Times* described the town this way:

> It was a place where only one store carries *Playboy* magazine and you have to ask for it "under the counter." There are no blinking beer signs or hotel happy hours because there is no booze—Craighead County is dry as old bones—and faith in God is a given. In a town dominated by the Church of Christ and Baptists, the Methodists are about the most liberal people in town.[6]

7. *Find a tone and stick to it.* Each story has a personality. Do you want the tone to be sad, or thoughtful, or funny? Once your tone is established, don't veer from it. When David Finkel was with the *St. Petersburg Times,* he wrote an entertaining story about the fat man at the circus, using the tone of a carnival barker.

---

5. Bill Keller, "South Africa's New Era: The Overview; South Africans Hail President Mandela; First Black Leader Pledges Racial Unity," *New York Times,* May 11, 1994, p. A-1.

6. Rick Bragg, "Bloodshed in a Schoolyard: The Impact; Determined to Find Healing in a Good and Decent Place," *New York Times,* March 27, 1998, p. A-1.

8. *Try anything.* I once wrote a one-sentence weather story that ranged for 290 words—but it nonetheless managed to earn its way onto page one of the daily paper. A reporter for *USA Today* wrote his obituary of Dr. Seuss in verse. The idea is to do whatever it takes to get read.

9. *Sprinkle in similes and metaphors, but make them yours.* Rick Reilly of *Sports Illustrated* says he tries never to repeat a sentence or description that he has seen before.

10. *Search for the humor inherent in a story.* Humor is one of the most underappreciated and least-used tools in our kit. A few years ago, I wrote a narrative series about a small town in Iowa. One of the big controversies was a town council edict to clean up old cars from yards. This is how I described the resulting council meeting:

> The meeting draws 60 residents. Two Marshall County deputies stand guard. Duwane "Cooter" Miller, a bar regular, talks first. This is his 54th birthday, but he has promised to remain sober for the meeting.
>
> "You're moving too fast for these people," he tells the council. "This isn't Ames. This is a small town. . . ."
>
> *BANG!*
>
> Rich Goodman accidentally knocks over a folding chair. Everybody in the room jumps, then laughs, like after a scary moment in a horror movie.
>
> Bohnsack also defuses the tension. All the council wants to do, he says, is enforce ordinances that have been long ignored, to bring in people and businesses, to save the high school. But he agrees that using a policeman to spread the word was a mistake.
>
> "If that's part of the reason you're all here tonight, I guess I apologize for that, and I think the council should, too," Bohnsack says.
>
> From the back of the room: "It'll never happen."
>
> Bohnsack: "What will never happen?"
>
> "An apology," bellows Bruce Sautter, 32, a city employee.
>
> The economic development group, Bohnsack continues, should mediate complaints. His face red, he calls for compromise.
>
> "All we're doing is pissing everybody off," he says. "You've pissed me off. I've pissed you off. The council has pissed you guys off, and you've pissed the council off. . . .
>
> "I think basically we need to put our heads together and quit being so damn bullheaded and stubborn."
>
> But it's not going to be easy. As soon as the mayor finishes, Terry Collier lambastes Councilman Wise for smiling while Miller was talking.

"If you were sitting there smarting at me outside, you wouldn't be smarting for long," Collier yells.

And halfway through the meeting, after Bohnsack asks him to quit interrupting, Sautter saunters to the council table, slams his hand on the table and says:

"Mayor Bohnsack, you remember this. I'm done. I quit. I've got a better job somewhere else. Up your nose. Good night, Irene."

Sautter returns to work the next day. He says he may have drunk too much before the meeting.[7]

A final word of advice: Don't turn in a story you wouldn't read. Do the Tammy Gaudettes of the world a favor. Write an interesting story for them.

---

7. Ken Fuson, "Lack of Teamwork Hinders State Center's Fight to Survive," *Des Moines Register,* Oct. 16, 1988, pp. A-1, 4-5.

Are Plumbers News?—
What Makes a Story a *Story*?

By John Sweeney

[John Sweeney is public editor and newsroom writing coach for the *News Journal* in Wilmington, Delaware. He has worked with the Wilmington Writers' Workshop since 1992 and currently directs that annual program.]

I f we are to be storytellers, we must have stories to tell.
    We can learn sentence structure, develop an engaging style, and master complicated narrative forms, but, in the end, if we have nothing to say, we will not be read.

The best writers always seem to come up with the best stories. Is it luck? Or is it art?

Jon Franklin, a two-time Pulitzer Prize–winner, says it is all in knowing how to look:

> Chance, as the historians of science sum it up, favors the prepared mind. The odds are overwhelmingly against the prepared scientist making any particular discovery . . . but it's a foregone conclusion that he'll discover *something*.[1]

Writers are no different.

---

1. Jon Franklin, *Writing for Story: Craft Secrets of Dramatic Nonfiction by a Two-Time Pulitzer Prize Winner* (New York: Plume/Penguin, 1994), p. 71.

The prepared writer may not find a particular story, but the chances are excellent he will come back with a solid story—one that readers will want to read.

For reporters—as opposed to fiction writers—that solid story we are talking about cannot be made up. The best reporters come back with dramatic, engaging, and informative stories that are based on genuine interviews, thorough reporting, and first-hand observation. None of it is fudged, piped, or imagined.

That stipulation, though, only makes us wonder all the more how these writers do it.

For one thing, the best writers know what a story is. They know what will amuse, horrify, and fascinate their readers. The best writers know what will affect their readers' lives. They can recognize a good yarn. And, most importantly, they are not afraid to tell it to their readers.

Compelling and dramatic yarns do not come along every day. So the second skill the best writers share is a method of finding good stories. Most of them search systematically. They are eternally curious, constantly asking themselves, "Is there a story here?" Most of the time, the answer is no. But every now and then—far more often than mediocre reporters—they are able to dig below the surface of an event and find the dramatic story lying beneath.

My intent here is to examine briefly what it is that makes a story a "story." What are the essentials that will entice readers into paying the writer the ultimate compliment—reading all the way to the end and, even better, remembering it? Subsequently, I will suggest some strategies for finding those essentials. How can a writer rise above the routine of the modern newsroom and consistently find stories that readers want to read?

What to Look For

A few years ago I attended a "family fun night" at my son's elementary school. Moms and dads and grandmoms and granddads happily played bingo with their kids and grandkids in the school's cafeteria. Then the bingo caller announced that the prize for the next game would be a Beanie Baby. Squeals filled the room. I was baffled. "What's a Beanie Baby?" I asked my fourth-grader. He dismissed it with a wave of his hand. "It's just something third-graders like." As it turned out, neither of us held the winning bingo card, so I forgot about the squeals.

That is, until I read about the latest kid mania on the front page of another newspaper. Soon after that, McDonald's offered Beanie Babies with its "Happy Meals." These same moms and dads and grandmoms and granddads lined up at fast-food counters to get all the Happy Meal prizes they could. Only then—when the fad held no more surprises—did my newspaper report on the craze.

By that time, it was old news. We lost an opportunity to surprise and delight our readers with early reports of a developing trend. Instead, we merely confirmed something many of them already knew.

Unfortunately, that's not so unusual.

We fill most of our newspapers with predictable, event-driven accounts that rehash what every other news outlet is reporting. Today's newsrooms do a good job of covering the obvious. Elections, crashes, murders, tax increases, official meetings, and pronouncements. They hold drama, but it is obvious drama.

Yet reporters deal with drama every day. They report and write stories about winners and losers, conflicts and resolutions, institutions that work and institutions that fail, people who overcome the odds and people who succumb to temptation.

It is life.

Behind every government action is a power struggle. One group wins; another loses. Sometimes justice is served; sometimes it is battered. And the best writers know this. They know too that behind every trophy handed out at the annual sports banquet is a tale of someone who overcame adversity, someone who set a goal, struggled, and then won. The best writers know that is a story.

How many times have we come across a reporter who put together all of the little things we had noticed in our own lives, like the Beanie Babies squeals, and made a story out of it? How many times have we picked up another newspaper and found that a writer discovered drama—edge-of-the-seat drama—in everyday life?

Ken Fuson did just that. He followed a group of high school students through their production of the musical *West Side Story*. His six-part series in the *Baltimore Sun* kept readers coming back day after day to find out which student won the part of Maria, and what happened to the boy who fell in love with his co-star.[2] That's not earthshaking stuff, but the readers loved it.

---

2. Ken Fuson, "A Stage in their Lives," *Baltimore Sun*, June 1–6, 1997. Reprinted in *1998 Best Newspaper Writing: Winners: The American Society of Newspaper Editors Competition*, ed. Christopher Scanlan (St. Petersburg, Fla.: Poynter Institute and Bonus Books, 1998), pp. 1–65.

None of this is magic. It takes time, and it takes imagination and practice. But it does not take magic.

We are in the business of providing our readers with the Five Ws—who, what, when, where, and why. They are the fundamentals. Everything else is built on them. But in this age of instant communication, live TV, and Internet coverage, simply telling readers what happened and whom it happened to may be too little. Readers are looking for answers to questions about what *really* happened and, more important, why.

Even if we could answer these questions every time, it may not be enough. Few topics interest everybody. James B. Stewart, a Pulitzer Prize–winning journalist who now writes for the *New Yorker,* suggests something he calls the 90 percent rule:

> When thinking about potential stories, I began to focus on what I estimated to be the 90 percent of readers who were *not* interested in the proposed subject. Indeed, I consciously tried to ignore my own particular interests, finding that I was far more effective if I could act as a surrogate for readers who weren't interested. After all, I wasn't worried about losing the readers who were interested in a given subject, but in attracting those who weren't.[3]

So how do we interest that 90 percent?

Just look at the great storytellers. Homer succeeded because he wrote about an interesting character trying to get home over the objections of a few gods and goddesses. Homer's listeners, at the least, stuck around to find out if the guy made it.

In the not-so-ancient past, 1948, Curtis MacDougall in his classic text *Interpretative Reporting* suggested eight elements of reader interest: personal appeal, sympathy, unusualness, progress, combat, suspense, sex and age, and animals.[4]

Every practicing journalist can vouch for the validity of the last item. Animals, especially baby animals, will draw more reader interest than anything else in the newspaper. Write about a human in trouble, and you will touch a few hearts. Find a calico kitten stuck in a sewer line, and the world stands ready to open its heart and its pocketbook.

---

3. James B. Stewart, *Follow the Story: How to Write Successful Nonfiction* (New York: Touchstone, 1998), p. 18.
4. Curtis D. MacDougall, *Interpretative Reporting,* 6th Ed. (New York: Macmillan, 1972), pp. 63–65.

No matter how tempting it is, we cannot fill our pages with cats in jeopardy. So we must go beyond the cute and cuddly and find the reader's basic interests.

Consider what four successful practitioners of the art have to say. James B. Stewart, William E. Blundell, Donald Murray, and Jon Franklin are all highly successful journalists and top-notch storytellers. Each has written a book on the art. Each also offers what he thinks to be essential elements of reader interest.[5]

- They believe readers are looking for stories that have significance. Readers want a story that means something to them.
- Good stories also should provide information as well as news. News is something the reader didn't know. Information goes beyond news because it connects the new with the old. It helps readers understand by providing a context.
- Good stories are universal. The situation should appeal to readers as human beings, not just as members of an interest group. It has to make them care. This is Stewart's 90 percent rule.
- All four authors also stress how keenly readers are interested in *people.* Murray says readers are looking for faces. Franklin believes good stories focus on a character who is caught in a complication. Blundell asserts that readers are much more compelled by watching people move as actors in a story or as recipients of some action, than they are in hearing talk from people who serve as experts or witnesses providing explanations and background for that action.
- This leads Blundell to insist: Reporters should have a bias for *action* and should look for stories with movement, where something happens. Franklin holds that the best stories consist of a sympathetic character caught in a universal complication who through his own action somehow resolves that complication.
- Finally, both Franklin and Stewart hit on one of Curtis MacDougall's important elements: suspense. Franklin says that a character trying to resolve a complication creates suspense, the need in the reader to find out what happens next. Stewart, talking about the same thing, calls it *the question:*

---

5. William E. Blundell, *The Art and Craft of Feature Writing* (New York: Plume/New American Library, 1988); Donald M. Murray, *Writing to Deadline: The Journalist at Work* (Portsmouth, N.H.: Heinemann, 2000). Franklin and Stewart are cited above.

> Curiosity sends writers on their quests, and curiosity is what
> makes readers read the stories that result. These days, when
> there is increasing competition for people's time, writers cannot
> count on anyone to read their work out of a sense of obligation,
> moral duty, or abstract dedication to "being informed." They
> will not read because someone else deems a subject to be
> important. They will read because they want to, and they will
> want to because they are curious.[6]

To do this, the obvious must go. The easy-to-find is out. We cannot be satisfied with just the visible news. Our job is to uncover the emotions and
make the connections that normally lie just below the surface in routine
news accounts. Our job is to find and to tell the invisible stories that are all
around us.

That is not an easy task in a business that often mistakes the news conference for the news. We must unlearn bad habits.

"A good way to measure the vigor of a newspaper," Don Murray writes,
"is to count the number of good stories that were not produced by journalism routine: the calendar; the police radio; the competitor's newspaper;
the publisher's second cousin; or the PR release."[7]

We can begin by looking at the news in front of our nose.

News coverage historically has been event-driven. We wait—to take a
cue from the nineteenth-century editor Charles Dana—for Providence to
provide us with a public event that we can photograph and report.[8]

Much of this news is scheduled, often at our own convenience. But a
lot of news oozes its way onto the public agenda with no one noticing.
The spray-painted message of the 1960s was: The revolution will not be
televised.

The radicals of the left were supposed to deliver the revolution, and the
people would rise up and put down their oppressors.

The revolution did come. And parts of it were televised. In fact, television was the revolution. The revolutionaries were in the laboratories and
the marketing departments.

Gene Roberts, former editor of the *Philadelphia Inquirer,* has pointed
out that no newspaper covered the single-most important development of

---

6. Stewart, *Follow the Story,* p. 17.
7. Murray, *Writing to Deadline,* p. 40.
8. Charles Dana, quoted in Stephen Bates, *If No News, Send Rumors: Media Anecdotes* (New York: St. Martin's Press, 1989), p. 76.

the 1950s: the flight of middle-class whites from the cities to the suburbs.[9] No one called a press conference. No one issued a report. If a reporter or editor had suggested it as a story, he or she would have been laughed at. That's soft news. That's for sociologists. Get back to City Hall and cover the council meeting.

But look at the consequences. America is a different place because of that shift. And how much did we learn? Not much, I'm afraid.

Few people noted the switch to Japanese cars until it posed a serious problem for American automotive workers. No one considered the implication of the Walkman tape player, but it allowed young people to listen to any manner of lyrics without reproach from parents. The microwave oven was first marketed as a new way of cooking roasts and other meats, but wound up changing our cooking habits and altering the way families dine, forever.[10]

Imagine if you had found these stories when they were beginning to break.

We cannot catch all of them, but, like Jon Franklin's prepared scientist, we can find a lot more if we know how and where to look.

Change Your Point of View

Ask yourself this question: Are plumbers news?

Say you are the editor of a newspaper, and a staff reporter proposes two story ideas, the first concerning a discovery in microbiology and the second dealing with an improvement in plumbing. Which would you likely urge her to pursue first?

Chances are, you would pick the one about the microbiologist. Why? Perhaps it's because journalists accord microbiologists greater prestige than plumbers. Or maybe the sponsoring institution, a well-known hospital or university, has a greater cachet than a plumbing parts manufacturer. The decision is perhaps made before the real questions are asked: Which is more important? Which will affect readers more?

We have an idea of what is news and what isn't. We know who makes it and who doesn't.

9. Gene Roberts, "Covering the Big Story, Welfare Reform," Keynote Speech, Freedom Forum Pacific Coast Center, San Francisco, April 28, 1997.

10. George Kennedy , Daryl R. Moen, et. al., *Beyond the Inverted Pyramid: Effective Writing for Newspapers, Magazines, and Specialized Publications* (New York: St. Martin's Press, 1993), p. 24.

That's our first mistake. As the sociologist Herbert Gans and other critics point out, mainstream journalists follow mental models that determine
how we view the news. There is nothing wrong with this. It is how the
human mind works.[11]

Peter Senge of M.I.T. writes:

> None of us can carry an organization in our minds—or a family
> or a community. What we carry in our heads are images,
> assumptions, and stories. Philosophers have discussed mental
> models for centuries, going back to Plato's parable of the cave.
> "The Emperor's New Clothes" is a classic story, not about fatu-
> ous people, but about people bound by mental models. Their
> image of the monarch's dignity kept them from seeing his naked
> figure as it was.[12]

Think back to the Watergate scandal. Who broke the stories? It wasn't the
heavyweight political reporters of the day.

Switching viewpoints can produce good stories. You can talk with the
experts who never get their hands dirty, or with the people digging the
ditches.

Don Murray says, "You may want to imagine your beat being covered
by a screenwriter, a historian, a mystery writer, a *New Yorker* profile writer.
Write a few pages in this new genre using the approach and the language to
help you see the familiar anew." Blundell says we can either be on the
mountaintop or in the valley.[13]

Hugh Mulligan, in his essay that appears earlier in this volume, mentions a variation of this: the "Gravedigger" theory of journalism, so named
after Jimmy Breslin's famous column on the assassination of John F.
Kennedy. The president's body lay in the Capitol Rotunda. Celebrities
lined up to be seen by the television cameras and the hundreds of print
journalists on hand. Breslin, alone, went to Arlington National Cemetery,
where he found an old man digging the president's grave. Breslin described
the man's actions and talked with him about his feelings for Kennedy. No

---

11. Herbert Gans, *Deciding What's News* (New York: Vintage, 1979), pp. 26–27.

12. Peter M. Senge, *The Fifth Discipline: The Art and Practice of the Learning
Organization* (New York: Doubleday, 1990), p. 174.

13. Murray, *Writing to Deadline*, p. 45; Blundell, *The Art and Craft of Feature Writing*,
p. 19.

one reads the other accounts today. Breslin's column has been reprinted and is still capable of moving the reader to tears.[14]

Breslin, in essence, asked himself how big the story was that he was covering. Was it confined to the personages assembled in the Rotunda? Breslin realized it was more than that. He realized there were other players in the drama, some who would forever remain hidden in the shadows. The other journalists played it safe. They stuck with the pack.

That type of thinking has become an embarrassment to journalists. Now, with live television broadcasts from every press conference, journalists are seen and heard asking inane or insulting questions of beleaguered public officials. Now cameras pursue crime victims or scandal celebrities down courthouse steps to waiting cars, poking microphones in their faces, shouting rude questions, pushing and shoving against family and friends. No wonder credibility is so low.

In addition to being rude, the "pack" mentality makes whimpering conformists of the people supposedly protecting democracy from itself. One answer to the follow-the-pack mentality is occasionally to employ contrarian thinking. If the world is going up, try going down. If businesses are going gaga over a downtown developer's plan for the waterfront, find the local dockhand who will lose his job.

This can be overdone and easily slip into cynicism. Yet a healthy skepticism can be a tonic for mindless conformity. The *Wall Street Journal* did just that by taking seriously a story that most of America mocked. Most of the nation laughed when an elderly woman won a large court award because McDonald's coffee was too hot. Having been scalded when the coffee spilled on her lap, she contended that the coffee was hotter than it should have been. People scoffed: The legal system has gone insane, they said, lawyers are running amuck, and so on. But the *Journal* took her contention seriously, instead of moaning about the seeming ridiculousness of the situation. It found the lawyer who tested the temperature of coffee from other fast-food restaurants and found McDonald's coffee was several degrees hotter.[15]

Think about it. Even the *Journal* didn't need the lawyer. Many of us were laughing about the court award at the same time we were wondering about the coffee. It was the talker of the week. Why didn't hometown

---

14. Jimmy Breslin, "It's an Honor," reprinted in *The Art of Fact: A Historical Anthology of Literary Journalism*, ed. Kevin Kerrane and Ben Yagoda (New York: Scribner, 1997), pp. 466–68.

15. Andrea Gerlin, "A Matter of Degree," *Wall Street Journal*, Sept. 1, 1994, p. A-1.

reporters dip a thermometer into cups of coffee from Burger King and McDonald's? A writer with a light touch could have had some fun with it. Then readers would have been talking about the hometown newspaper.

Question, Question, Question

Amanda Bennett of the *Lexington Herald-Leader* teaches reporters an important lesson: *personify, personalize,* or *puncture.*

- Can we personalize the information, telling exactly what the development means to the reader? People don't care about education. They want to know about their children.
- Can the story best be told by finding someone who personifies the problem? Find real people to represent issues.
- Or should we puncture an assumption? Bennett says all political and business decisions are based on assumptions. For example, school reform is based on an assumption. Environmental regulations, likewise, are based on assumptions. The writer should ask: What are those assumptions, and are they really true?

Bennett did that when she was a reporter with the *Wall Street Journal.* Her efforts helped win the *Journal* a Pulitzer Prize for its coverage of AIDS. She started with the assumption that had been laid down by a massive U.S. Government public relations campaign, that the entire U.S. population should be taught that *anyone* could get AIDS. Most Americans accepted the conventional wisdom, since federal officials were saying this over and over in lectures and advertisements. But was that assumption true? Were large numbers of heterosexual non-drug users in America truly at risk?

Bennett and fellow *Journal* reporter Anita Sharpe detailed the story. They told how the decision had been made, how health officials had purposely misled Americans and, in the end, possibly misspent millions of dollars and hurt their own cause. The money and the advertising had been aimed at AIDS prevention among low-risk groups, while high-risk groups (gays and drug users) were virtually ignored.[16]

---

16. Amanda Bennett and Anita Sharpe, "Health Hazard," *Wall Street Journal,* May 1, 1966, p. A-1.

Go Below the Surface

I once sat on a panel with a public relations consultant who told the audience that one of the greatest problems facing people and organizations today was reputation management. It is your reputation, he said, and you have the right to manage it, the right to control what people print and broadcast about you. Naturally, the audience applauded. Everyone wants protection from the evil news media. And, of course, who better to provide the best protection than a public relations expert.

The press certainly is guilty of ruining some reputations. Innocent people have been badgered. Reporters have been known to get things out of context. But a greater failure of the press is its willingness to accept some people at their word. Reporters often fail to go below the surface.

Public officials are thus free to claim problems have been solved or crises averted through their intervention. Too many newspaper stories consist of: (1) self-serving comments from a public figure denouncing a problem; and (2) fawning reaction from a beneficiary of that intervention praising the official's foresight and courage. Sometimes, the situation is turned upside down. Victims of a problem demand action, and the public officials are forced to come up with a solution. Sometimes, the story rolls out just the way it should. More often, some big questions are left unasked.

The solution is not cynicism. It is skepticism. A little healthy digging below the surface is called for.

- *Keep asking yourself: "What is the real story?"* The story is not the press conference; it is the backroom brawl. The story is not the hero's medal; it is the hero's actions, the choices he was forced to make. The mayor honors a neighborhood woman for public service. The story isn't the mayor's proclamation. The story is finding the men and women who were influenced by the woman when they were kids. The preacher eulogizes a music teacher, and a chorus of adults joins in the praise. The story isn't the praise, but the people who were affected by the teacher's methods, his character, his determination, his inspiration.
- *Find the emotional center of the story.* Find the flare point, the anger, the aggravation. Find the joy, the relief. The *Washington Post* did this in an article about "DWB" or "Driving While Black," an examination of what it's like to be hassled by police for no other reason than being a black male.[17]

17. Michael A. Fletcher, "Driven to Extremes: Black Men Take Steps to Avoid Police Stops," *Washington Post*, March 29, 1966, p. A-1.

- *Find the tension, the underlying conflict.* Rick Raber, a reporter at the *News Journal* in Wilmington, Delaware, looked at a dispute between a large chemical company and a youth baseball team. Raber rightly recognized that the story (headlined, "Little folk take on mighty Hercules") was not the legal entanglements over a field, but a public relations battle between two groups who each knew well how to manipulate public images.
- *Find the faces behind the news.* People make decisions, people suffer the consequences for those decisions. Who are the human beings making the decisions? What is the effect on real people? Another *News Journal* reporter, Dale Dallabrida, took a humorous look at everyday office life. In every office, someone, without title or reward, has become the in-house expert on whatever new technology that lands. What is it like to be the unofficial expert on the photocopying machine or the latest word processing program?
- *Find your way below the surface of a story by using "mapping" techniques.* Most of us are familiar with this concept by now. Mapping (or "clustering") has been advocated by a variety of authors as a way of unleashing the inner writer. You're not likely to hear much talk in newsrooms about "unleashing the inner writer," but mapping has its uses. For one, it can help a writer get his thinking, conscious or otherwise, down on paper. Don Murray is an advocate. He suggests journalists use it when they want to get past more formal outlines.[18]

In mapping, the reporter writes the central concept in the middle of a page, and then begins associating that word or phrase with whatever comes to his mind. The associated words are jotted down. They in turn lead to more associated words. As the exercise develops, the writer can make connections between words and start to shape ideas. For example, a reporter starting with the concept "burglary" could find himself associating it with: police, statistics, patterns, neighborhoods, insurance claims, costs, fears, security systems. The list could lead to a story about which neighborhoods spend the most for security systems. Or the concept "burglary" could go along these lines: police, criminals, unsolved, fences, loot, market. This list could lead to a story about what items are targeted by burglars and what happens to them after they're stolen. Both ideas could make interesting stories.

Another advocate of mapping is William Blundell. In *The Art and Craft of Feature Writing,* Blundell suggests submitting a story concept to

---

18. Murray, *Writing to Deadline*, pp. 41–42.

cause-and-effect reasoning by mapping the moves and countermoves surrounding an event or development. Blundell uses the example of a shortage of physicians. Using cause-and-effect mapping, the shortage can be treated both as an event and as the possible cause of other events, such as the greater use of paramedics.

Blundell says the approach has two effects: (1) it helps identify in advance potential action elements in the story; and (2) it helps visually stake out the story's boundaries. He cautions that no one will use all of the possible angles a map would uncover. Stories must be limited to one idea.[19]

Peter Senge adds another caution. In *The Fifth Discipline,* a book about systems thinking and organizational management, Senge warns that all human actions take place in a complex network of actions and reactions. Most of the time,

> "cause" and "effect" are not close in time and space. By "effects," I mean the obvious symptoms that indicate there are problems—drug abuse, unemployment, starving children, falling orders, and sagging profits. By "cause" I mean the interaction of the underlying system that is most responsible for generating the symptoms, and which, if recognized, could lead to changes producing lasting improvements. Why is this a problem? Because most of us assume they are—most of us assume, most of the time, that cause and effect are close in time and space.[20]

This is a common human tendency.

Gutenberg, for example, could not have realized his printing press would lead to the Reformation. Likewise, Henry Ford had no idea affordable automobiles would lead to a sexual revolution among teenagers. But historians were able to make that connection, and journalists can, too.

The Story Wave

Journalists use the word "story" to describe everything. A two-hundred-inch investigation is a story. A plane crash is a story. Even a brief about the chess club is a story.

For the moment, let us consider a "story" as something longer. The news event is when the action bubbles to the surface. Then there is the follower. Or the backgrounder that explains where all of this came from. The story of the event includes all of this.

---

19. Blundell, *The Art and Craft of Feature Writing,* p. 26.
20. Senge, *The Fifth Discipline,* p. 63.

Consider the "story" the unfolding of an event in its many parts. The "story" of a murder is more than just the discovery of the body. It includes the search for the killer, the trial of the accused, and the punishment if convicted. We tend to put endings on an event just for the sake of storytelling. The "story" never ends for the parent of a murdered child. But there comes a point when we should get out of their lives. Most "stories" are not tragic, and dramatic endings are harder to find. Society's spotlight has to move on at some point.[21]

Therefore, we can break the "story" into segments:

- The building wave is the coming story, when few people are familiar with the event or trend.
- The breaking wave is the effect the story has on readers. Is the event good or bad for people? Who is winning and who is losing?
- The retreating wave is the reaction, the countermove. Who is trying to stop the development, to counteract it, to slow it down?

Our approach will depend on whether the "story" is building, breaking, or retreating.

Thus, if we come to a story late, we can still break new ground. Blundell says, "While [a reporter's] competition is clustered around the main development, he can move on to some of the impacts they haven't had time or vision to cover, or he can jump all the way to countermoves."[22]

Minds Fossilize

The world is more interesting than our newspapers portray it. There are stories waiting to be told, but they have to be found first. What can we do about it?

Don't let our minds fossilize. Come alive. Talk to people we don't know, people who aren't like us. Listen to what they really say, not what we expect them to. Read. Read everything. Read against type.

Systematically look beyond the convenient patterns, the usual suspect, and journalism as usual. Break out of the patterns. Expand the small ring of official experts.

Act as if plumbers really can make news.

---

21. James W. Carey, "The Dark Continent of American Journalism," in *James Carey: A Critical Reader,* ed. Eve Stryker Munson and Catherine A. Warren (Minneapolis: University of Minnesota Press, 1997), pp. 144-88.

22. See Blundell, *The Art and Craft of Feature Writing,* pp. 11-12.

SECTION III:
WRITING NONFICTION
NARRATIVE

The Narrative Tool

By Jon Franklin

[Jon Franklin won the first Pulitzer Prizes ever awarded in the categories of feature writing (1979) and explanatory journalism (1985). He holds the Merrill Chair in Journalism at the University of Maryland.]

Narrative is a simple thing, at bottom: chronology with meaning. Soap operas have it, and so do daily newspapers. What are our pages for, if not the episodic revelation of our public (and sometimes private) lives? When an editor moves a story, the word "story" refers to a particular piece of copy. But when we talk about "the Watergate story," we mean the whole nineteen acts. When a good reporter sits down to write, the first task is to place the daily story in the context of the overarching social narrative. Presumably, the reader is aware of that narrative, and the hard news story can therefore plug directly into it.

But our standard techniques fail us when the overarching narrative isn't there, or when it's wrong, or when it's too shallow. Then there is nothing to plug our daily episode into, and the hard news form fails us. We need to orient the reader to the history, issues, and values that lie behind the facts.

Narrative is important because it is the penultimate orientation technique. We learn best by experience, but experience has a cost. Narrative is the next best thing because it allows us to live, vicariously, the experience of others. So it's not surprising that narrative journalism thrives in moments of great change. The last golden age of news narrative was the late 1960s and the early 1970s, when we were reorienting ourselves to a world undergoing revolution in every aspect, from civil rights to the environment to sexual behavior. The sagas of the civil rights marchers reset our social values, as did tales from Vietnam, Chicago, and the City of Love.

The intervening years have marked a period of consolidation, during which narrative journalism fell out of favor. Now the world seems on the brink of yet another period of change, and it's not surprising that narrative is coming back.

As it does, my strongest advice is that we should remember that narrative is chronology *with meaning.* It is all too easy to forget that last qualifier, to focus our narratives on messages that are no more than conventional wisdom. Narrative journalism, like literature of any sort, must contain a kernel of insight, of *vision*—this is the literary counterpart to a news peg. The narrative that lacks vision will suffer from exactly the same weakness as an inverted pyramid story that lacks a piece of hard news. It will seem pointless. Worse, narrative, being by nature stronger, will seem not only pointless but also vacuous and self-indulgent.

Vision is no more magical than a news peg. Like the news peg, it results from reporting. In the case of narrative, that means depth reporting—talking to many people, doing library work and searching the Internet, and, most importantly, doing the heavy lifting that is contemplation and consideration. In this way we can see beyond what we expect to see and what we are supposed to see, and lift our stories to the level that merits narrative. Then, when we have something to say, the complex of rhythms, styles, and devices we identify with literature can serve journalism as well.

Nonfiction Storytelling

By Mark Bowden

[A reporter for the *Philadelphia Inquirer,* Bowden has written four books, including *Killing Pablo* (2001). His earlier book *Black Hawk Down* became an international best-seller and provided the basis for the recent Sony Pictures film by that title. *Black Hawk Down* began as a twenty-nine-part *Inquirer* series that received the Overseas Press Club's 1998 Boyle Award for Best Foreign Reporting.]

My first full-time reporting job for a newspaper was to cover Anne Arundel County, Maryland, for the now-deceased *Baltimore News-American.* Anne Arundel extends south from Baltimore down the western shore of the Chesapeake Bay. It encompasses Annapolis, the state (and county) seat, and rural points south.

Every morning on my forty-five-minute drive to Annapolis, I would stop by county police headquarters in Millersville. It broke up the drive and gave me a chance to review all the police reports from the night before. Only on rare occasions did the reports reveal anything notable. Major crimes were picked up by the paper's police reporters in their normal daily phone checks, but by stopping in every morning, I became friendly with Captain Bill Lindsay, who, among other duties, served as the department's media spokesman. The Captain was amused and a little impressed with my dogged regularity, and I enjoyed his laconic insights into larger goings-on in the county. In time, he would have a hot cup of coffee waiting for me each morning next to the neat pile of reports, and he would put on top those I might find interesting or amusing.

One day he offered me an exclusive. County detectives planned to stage a late-night drug raid on what Lindsay called "some of the major suspected dealers in Annapolis." There would be a press conference the following morning, but if I wanted, I could actually ride along and witness the raids. He introduced me to the detectives responsible, and I drove out to head-quarters late that night.

To my great surprise, the pre-raid assembly point resembled a fraternity party. There was beer, loud talk and laughter, and a steady parade of officers wobbling out to a street lamp off the parking lot to urinate. The raid itself was conducted with gusto, lots of door banging, shouting, and bullying followed by the emergence of half-dressed, handcuffed, sleepy-eyed "perpetrators." But the site of the raid turned out to be Annapolis's public housing project, which struck me as somewhat low-rent for "major dealers." And, sure enough, early the following morning when the raid's take was spread out for the press conference, there were dime bags of marijuana, crumbs of hashish, multicolored pills, paraphernalia, and other minor contraband. To the older reporters present—this was 1974—it no doubt looked impressive. The event was good business for all concerned—great publicity for the cops and something sensational enough to kick off that day's local news reports. To me it was a joke. As the youngest person in the room, and therefore the one closest to the then-booming recreational drug culture, what I saw gleaming under klieg lights and the detectives' smiling poses were the collected paltry stashes of about a dozen drug users, hardly the inventory of even a minor dealer.

Which left me in a difficult spot. How could I reward my friend Captain Lindsay's generosity by exposing this charade? Indeed, could I expose it? I had been a reporter for less than a year, and I was unsure of my own observations and insights. I felt strong pressure just to write the same straight story everyone else did and fill in my account with some drama from the nighttime raids. I could leave out anything controversial. Maybe beer drinking by cops about to conduct an anti-drug raid wasn't that outrageous. How was I to prove that the officially quoted "street value" of the drugs seized was ridiculously inflated? At a bigger or better newspaper, an editor would have helped me answer these questions, but my work at the *News-American* was basically unsupervised. With so little experience of my own, it was daunting to write an account so much at odds with the official version.

Writing a traditional news lead—

> Anne Arundel County police yesterday raided the homes of a
> dozen suspected drug dealers just outside Annapolis, seizing an
> estimated $10,000 worth of narcotics.

—would mean accepting the fiction of the event. A brutally honest alternative—

> Beer-drinking Anne Arundel County police detectives broke
> down the doors of a dozen sleeping suspected drug users in the
> Annapolis projects last night and seized a few hundred dollars
> worth of their personal stashes.

—placed an equal and even more sensational emphasis on my own inter-
pretation. In both cases there would be room later in the story to spell out
nuances and present opposing points of view, but with either lead, the tone
of the story would be heavily cast at the outset.

Instead, I decided that the best way to proceed was simply to tell the
story. Here's the lead I wrote:

> Sergeant Bob Brown of Anne Arundel County police's vice and
> narcotics squad set one denim-clad leg over a corner of his desk
> and cleaned his fingernails with a six-inch switchblade. Two shot-
> guns lay alongside his leg.
>
> "I haven't slept in two days worrying about this thing," Brown
> said.

The story took off from there. I offer this not as an example of a great lead,
which it is not, but to identify a turning point in my newspaper writing career.
I had grown up reading, or trying to read, the *Morning Sun,* Baltimore's
sage old newspaper of record. I say "trying to read" because much of the
time I couldn't understand it. Few events the *Sun* reported ever happened
outside the halls of government—local, state, or national—and always seemed
to take place on some abstract plane disconnected from the real world, in
places like "The House Appropriations Committee" or "The State
Insurance Commission." As best I could tell, readers of news reports were
usually expected to know a lot about the subject matter. They were assumed
to be following the twists and turns of these reports from day to day as carefully as the newspaper's editors evidently were. The articles in the *Sun* may
have been important, but they weren't very easy or fun to read.[1]

---

1. Today, the *Sun* has vastly changed. Under the editorships of John Carroll and Bill
Marimow, it has become one of the best-written daily newspapers in America.

What excited me enough to try my own hand at writing nonfiction was the terrific New Journalism of Tom Wolfe, Gay Talese, Truman Capote, John Hersey, Norman Mailer, and others who wrote stories about things that happened to real people, in real places. Until I wrote the drug raid story, I had not seen how to apply the techniques of this storytelling journalism to my own newspaper writing. Suddenly it afforded not just an alternative, but an answer. Instead of choosing beforehand how to interpret the material, as the more conventional leads required, why not just tell the story? Why not start at the beginning and just let it all unfold? The account would include all that the detectives wanted to get across, but also things that they probably assumed I'd edit out—or that they couldn't imagine would fit in a conventional newspaper article. Just telling the story was more truthful than either of the other two approaches would have been. It didn't reach conclusions about what happened or offer my interpretations or place more emphasis on my observations than the department's. When it got to the part about the seized drugs on display, I was able simply to describe the displayed items in all their evident insignificance, and then let the detectives hang themselves with their boastful rhetoric.

Captain Lindsay wasn't happy with the way it turned out, but he had no complaint. He knew I hadn't made any of it up. Best of all, the story was fun to write and fun to read. I recently rooted out the yellowed clipping, and unlike my response to most of my work from those early years, I got so caught up in the story I was disappointed when I couldn't find the jump to read it through to the end.

There is plenty of good writing in the traditional forms. Straightforward (often inverted pyramid style) coverage can be elegant, clear, and richly informative. In many instances, it remains the best way to write a newspaper article. In fact, nowadays, newspapers can go overboard, gussying up reports that ought to be unembellished with distracting anecdotal leads and other literary rococo. When covering a continuing story, for instance, or late-breaking news, traditional newswriting is often the only way to go. But whatever larger success I've enjoyed as a writer—for newspapers, magazines, books, and film—I owe to this determination to tell stories.[2]

It means more than just shaping the material differently. Telling stories means approaching reporting with a storyteller's mind, looking for anec-

---

2. For the purposes of this essay, I am writing about those stories that you have time to develop and write fully. At a newspaper, alas, I know this is not often (and for most reporters rarely) the case. Just today, for instance, a Wednesday, an editor assigned me a rather ambitious story for Sunday's paper. He wants me to profile a major public figure whom I have virtually no chance of interviewing. The time constraints rule out traveling to, say, the subject's old hometown or, frankly, doing any ambitious primary source reporting beyond making scores of telephone calls. So, the story will end up primarily being a "clip job," drawn mostly from secondary sources, something I hate, but sometimes there is no alternative.

dote and setting, finding characters, scenes and dialogue, and identifying a beginning, middle, and end. Even before beginning work on a story, I ask myself, Who and What is it about? Where does it take place? Whose life has been changed? How? What emotion does this story tap? Is it funny? Inspiring? Infuriating? Sad? How can I best tell this story? In chronological order? Backwards? Episodically? Thematically? Should it have a strong narrative voice or an invisible one? Should it be told through one character's point of view or shifting perspectives? In my own words or through the words of those involved—or both?

In the course of reporting and writing, answers to the above questions change, sometimes often. As a young reporter, I was troubled by this. Each new piece of information or point of view cast my material in a new light. Sometimes the alteration was so dramatic, my first reaction was to feel the story was ruined. I can remember sitting at my desk with a daily deadline approaching, afraid to make a last-minute reporting phone call, for fear the story would get turned around so completely I wouldn't be able to write it in time. Yet, if I didn't make the call, then the story might lack something vital and remain that much more distant from the truth. Making the extra phone call was always worthwhile. Instead of "ruining" the story, the new perspective always gave it more accuracy, fairness, depth, and nuance. Thorough reporting is the absolute first principle of writing nonfiction. You may not use everything you learn; in fact, you usually shouldn't. But the more you know, the better story you will write, everything from finding better descriptive detail to achieving a deeper understanding of the material.

Any project, whether a daily newspaper story, magazine piece, or book, begins with a review of what has already been written: Old clippings from newspapers and magazines, Internet pages, books, and so on will provide history, context, and leads. The real reporting starts when you begin seeking out primary sources, visiting the places where the story took place, and finding those whose lives are or were caught up in it. If your story is going to break new ground and avoid repeating misinformation (one of the plagues of modern cribbed journalism), you must deal as much as possible with primary sources and restrict what you use from them to what they experienced firsthand.

Researching my 1997 newspaper series "Blackhawk Down"[3] meant interviewing scores of American soldiers who fought in Mogadishu, Somalia, on October 3, 1993, and then visiting Mogadishu to explore the

---

3. This series of twenty-nine stories first appeared in the *Philadelphia Inquirer* between Nov. 16 and Dec. 14, 1997. The *Inquirer* used "Blackhawk" and the subsequent book and movie titles used *Black Hawk*. The material was later published in revised and much-expanded form as *Black Hawk Down: A Story of Modern War* (New York: Atlantic Monthly Press, 1999). (The newspaper series amounted to roughly one-third of the book.)

battle sites and interview Somalis who fought against American troops. I tried in all these interviews to focus only on what each interviewee himself had experienced. Second-hand stories nearly always turned out to contain significant distortions or errors.

Information gathering can be addictive. Most good stories are potentially bottomless. In researching "Blackhawk Down," for instance, I found that in order to fully understand the battle, it was important to understand the weeks and months that had preceded it. The United Nations (and United States) intervention in Somalia had begun in December 1992 and had evolved over eleven months into something quite different from what it had been at the beginning. The battle of October 3 would not be understood without this recent historical background. But to understand the prior eleven months, wasn't it important to know something about the whole modern history of the country? How much of this back story did I need? My series of stories would focus primarily on the 140 or so men of Task Force Ranger, who roped from helicopters into central Mogadishu on a sunny Sunday afternoon and wound up trapped overnight, fighting for their lives against thousands of heavily-armed Somalis. But what about the five hundred soldiers, including Pakistani tank crews and Malaysian soldiers, who fought their way into the city to rescue the trapped task force? How much of their story should be told? There were significant events that happened in the days and weeks after the battle. For instance, Black Hawk pilot Mike Durant was captured during the fight and held captive eleven days. The story wouldn't be complete without an account of his ordeal. And what about the families of the men killed? How did they learn of their sons' and husbands' deaths? Surely it was important to ground the sacrifice of these young lives in the context of everyday American lives. And what about political fallout from the battle? Shouldn't the story explore its broader political and diplomatic consequences? The more you learn, the more you realize you need to know.

Unless you begin to make decisions early on about where your story begins and ends, you can become paralyzed by this need to report. I have known superb reporters, some of the best I have ever seen, who utterly lack the ability to assemble the information they collect into a coherent story. They are familiar newsroom characters, surrounded by boxes and file drawers crammed with documents, notes, faxes, reports, clippings, and other items, slowly burying themselves in facts. Reporting is more than just collecting information or investigating. It is an ongoing process of drawing, disassembling, and then redrawing the story in your mind, letting your vision of the story feed your reporting and letting the additional reporting, in turn, reshape the story. This process steers your reporting intelligently and tells you when you are ready to draw back from reporting to write.

I've probably made this sound more complicated than it really is, so here's an example.

I wrote a story some years ago called "Finders Keepers," which was about an unemployed Philadelphia longshoreman named Joey Coyle who found $1.2 million in cash lying in the gutter.[4] The money had fallen off the back of a poorly secured armored car. As it happens, it is a crime to keep something of significant value without making any effort to return it, and Coyle spent the next seven days doing a terrible job of trying to do just that. Reporters and detectives had little trouble discovering who found the money. Over the week of his clumsy flight, stories surfaced about Joey giving money away to friends, family, and strangers. With an evidently effusive nature that made it impossible for him to keep a secret, Joey was apparently telling everyone he encountered about his amazing find. He was finally captured at an airport in New York with a one-way ticket to Acapulco and thousands of dollars stuffed into panty hose he had donned under his pants.

The twists and turns of Coyle's odyssey were big news in Philadelphia for months. Coyle emerged from his fifteen minutes of fame with something of a charming image—and was, in fact, acquitted by a jury of all charges connected with his find. This was the story I had in mind when I started: a lighthearted modern-day Robin Hood tale with a hero every reader would love. I would reconstruct the week of his giddy flight, relying on police reports and interviews with Coyle and his friends.

Very quickly into my reporting, however, I learned that the true story was quite different. Coyle was a hopeless drug addict. The frenetic aspect of Joey's flight and his compulsive desire to tell everyone of his find were symptoms of being continually stoked on amphetamines. The legend of his giving money away stemmed not from feckless generosity, but from Joey's foolhardy effort to "launder" the cash (which was unmarked and unsequenced, so there was no need to launder it). The "strangers" to whom Joey had given money were South Philadelphia mobsters, and people he was afraid might turn him in. The real story of Joey Coyle was still very funny, but it was much darker than anyone imagined. I saw it as a parable of addiction: one troubled young man acting out the fantasy of effortless redemption, of having lifelong success and happiness just fall into his lap.

---

4. The story ran as a three-part magazine article in the *Philadelphia Inquirer* (Dec. 21 and 28, 1986, and Jan. 4, 1987) and was eventually substantially altered and made into the movie *Money for Nothing* (1993), starring John Cusack as Joey.

The money Joey found worked on him like a drug hit. It gave him an unbe-
lievable rush that lasted for about forty-eight hours, and then became a
nightmare.

To illustrate this nightmare meant approaching the reporting differently. Instead of just collecting anecdotes about his frantic wanderings over
seven days, I would have to get inside Joey's head. I needed to track the
process by which the money had gone from joy to torment. I had originally planned to do only one or two long interviews with him, but now I began
talking to him in person and on the phone several times a day for months,
raiding his memory over and over again. Joey's mind was somewhat drug-
addled, and he found it difficult to reconstruct where he was and what he
had done during those seven days, much less what he had thought and how
he had felt. He grew surly and impatient with my repeated questions about
the same things. By reviewing my notes of each conversation and compil-
ing them carefully, I was gradually able to piece the chronology together,
matching Joey's vaguer memories with events I could nail down from other
sources.

To show how possession of the money gradually drove Coyle crazy, I
redoubled my efforts to stir his memory about even the least significant
periods of time. Earlier on in my reporting, for instance, I would have just
accepted Joey's offhand account of a particular morning—"I just stayed
home and hung around"—as being uninteresting and unimportant. Now
the time he spent alone doing "nothing" could potentially hold vital clues
to his changing state of mind. I began pushing him for details about this
morning. The conversation went something like this:

"I told you, I just stayed home," he said.

"What did you do at home?"

"Nothing."

"Did you sleep?"

"Yeah, some of the time."

"What did you do when you weren't sleeping?"

"What difference does it make?" (Whereupon I would soothe Joey and
explain that writers are born dimwitted and ask all sorts of stupid questions;
it's just what we do.)

"I don't know what I did. I moved around the house, looking out the
windows. I was real paranoid. There were cop cars all over the neighborhood. I hid the money a few places."

"You hid the money in the house?"

"Yeah."

"A few places? Why not just one place?"

What emerged from Joey, after much protesting and sighing with impatience, was an account that became the centerpiece of "Finders Keepers" and a perfect illustration of its theme. Home alone, speeding and paranoid, Joey had tried hiding the cash in three different places. He had disassembled the water heater in his basement and stuffed the cash into the insulated lining around the heating tank. After reassembling the heater, he thought twice about it, afraid the money might somehow catch fire, so he took it apart again, retrieved the money, and reassembled the heater. Next, he took apart a toilet upstairs and hid the money in the empty space under the porcelain bowl. Unhappy with that, he took the toilet apart a second time, removed the money, and bolted the toilet again. Then he decided to hide the money in the narrow space between the outer brick wall of his row house and the inner plaster walls. To accomplish that, he had to crawl into the ceiling of his mother's bedroom, from where he slipped and fell, crashing through the tiles of the drop ceiling to the floor and hurting his back. Coyle's slapstick paranoia that morning explained better than I ever could how his blessing had become a curse.

The reporting feeds the story, and the story feeds the reporting.

To make this concept work means keeping an open mind, not just at the outset but all the way through the reporting and writing. There is a virtue in Zen practice called "Beginner's Mind." It expresses the idea that, in any pursuit, experience can be just as harmful as it is helpful, to the extent that it habituates us to certain forms and limits creativity. "Beginner's Mind" means approaching familiar problems or tasks as openly as you did the first time, when you were not weighted down with instruction and experience. It is easy, for instance, for a reporter to let preliminary facts fall into the shape of a "familiar story." This attitude is endemic at newspapers, especially some tabloids, where it is the guiding philosophy. Crusty old scribes grumble that there are no "new" stories. A dozen or so of the same old stories have been happening over and over again in updated settings since Eve offered Adam an apple. A clever variation of this insight is popular just now in New York and Hollywood. All stories, the experts say, fall into certain basic patterns. The writer's job is to discern which pattern fits the particulars of a "new" story and follow it faithfully. I don't believe it. After reporting and writing stories for more than a quarter-century, I still find they come in as many shapes and varieties as human experience.

This isn't just a matter of lazy writing and reporting. Letting a story fall into a familiar pattern nurtures stereotypes and misconceptions, and doing so defeats the larger purpose of good reporting. In 1997, I was asked to do a story about a supposed "racial attack" in a South Philadelphia neighborhood. The story, as reported to that point, concerned a black woman and her son who had allegedly been senselessly attacked by a mob of neighborhood whites. Grays Ferry was primarily a white, blue-collar neighborhood with a sad history of racist violence dating back two or three decades. So this poor black woman's story fell into a familiar pattern. Muslims and civil rights leaders began calling for marches and protests, the police expressed alarm, the mayor interceded. Grays Ferry was making national news. I managed to track down the primary sources of this story on both sides and learned that the truth was substantially different from "the same old story."

The supposedly racist, white, blue-collar neighborhood had, in fact, quietly and successfully integrated over the last decade. On the block where the "attack" occurred, nine other black families had lived peaceably with their white neighbors for years. It was not a case, as everyone assumed, of white racists trying to scare a black family off their block. The incident had started when the woman's son, a big nineteen-year-old recently released from prison for armed robbery, got in a fight with a white man out on the sidewalk. The white man's friends spilled out of a nearby social hall and came to his aid. Racist insults and threats were made during the scuffle, but no one was seriously hurt. It was an ugly episode, but certainly not enough of one to attract the kind of national attention Grays Ferry was getting. Residents there, black and white, were far more troubled with the way the press had presented their neighborhood than they were with the fight. Many feared that the hard-won gains of racial tolerance were being undone by reporters writing stories based on assumptions that were no longer true.

One of my tests for determining if I've done enough reporting is whether or not I am surprised. The truth nearly always has that effect. If the material doesn't surprise in some way, then more reporting is probably necessary—or the story isn't worth the effort. The story should emerge honestly from the reporting, crafted on its strengths and around its weaknesses. This approach, if you manage to pull it off, makes each story you tell unique. It is also slightly dangerous, because it often means standing alone in what you write, and it risks failure every time out.

Great stories are not once-in-a-lifetime opportunities, like the phone call to the *Washington Post* with news of a break-in at the Watergate Hotel. In my experience, most great stories are excitedly and incompletely covered by the press and then discarded.

Joey Coyle's story is an example. When I undertook "Finders Keepers," the overwhelming response of other reporters and editors at the *Philadelphia Inquirer* was, "Don't we already know that story?" Yet no one had ever talked to all the principal characters and pieced it together. There was widespread coverage of the Battle of Mogadishu before I started "Blackhawk Down" but no one had systematically interviewed the men who fought there in order to find out exactly what happened. The same is true of most nonfiction classics. When Tom Wolfe undertook *The Right Stuff,* which is about the original seven astronauts, the early U.S. space program was thought to have been one of the most overcovered stories of the 1960s—yet Wolfe showed us on page after fascinating page how much we didn't know. When John Hersey wrote *Hiroshima,* certainly the world had seen plenty of coverage of the first nuclear attack. He was the first to detail the blast from point zero, detailing the horrible human consequences of the blast. In both instances, Wolfe and Hersey went to the primary sources of events thought to have been fully covered and found a deeper story. Not every story is worth a long second look, but many of the big ones are. Every reporter has had the experience of working a story hard, and then being disappointed by having to tell it too early and too briefly. My advice is, save your notes. Go back after those stories once some time has passed and those closest to it feel freer to talk. Just because a story is old does not mean it has been told.

Start thinking about the form of your story as soon as you begin reporting. By the time you sit down at a keyboard, you will have at least a sketchy notion of how to write it. For me, this process has become mostly internal on shorter pieces, but years ago, even for daily newspaper articles, I found it very helpful to begin sketching outlines on paper. My old pads were filled not only with scribbled notes, but with hastily scrawled lists. I would begin by enumerating all of the main elements of the emerging story—scenes, dialogue, description, explication, quotes, and so on—writing them down in no particular order, just a way of surveying what building blocks I had. After reducing the story elements to these abstract components, I could begin arranging them in different ways, playing with the story's structure. That way, by the time the story was ready to be written—or deadlines forced the decision—I already had a well-formed idea of how to proceed. For me, this shorthand outlining is something that must be done by hand. It probably stems from my earliest days in newspapers when we wrote on typewriters, which meant that correcting mistakes and making revisions were far more laborious than they are on a computer screen. Before you began pounding away at the typewriter keys, it was best to have at least a summary notion of where you were going—otherwise, there would a lot of starting over (and retyping) or a great mess with scissors and paste. Even though the computer has made starting over and revising mechanically effortless, I find outlining the first draft of a story on paper beforehand remains a valuable exercise.

By far the hardest part of writing anything is getting started, and no matter how thoroughly I have reported or outlined my story beforehand, the first few lines are always a struggle. This is not simply a matter of getting something down on the page. We've all heard the advice: "Just start writing. Don't worry about how good it is, you are going to rewrite it anyway." It doesn't work for me. There is an element to writing that goes beyond preparation and organization. A story requires the right narrative voice, its own tone and style. I shop for this voice in my head and heart, and it's not always easy to find. Until I find it, usually most of the writing I do is wasted. For me, the right voice doesn't slowly emerge from the prose on screen. It has to pop into my head, and until it does, I can't get started. So I start trying to find it early on. My notepads usually contain pages of handwritten passages that may or may not eventually find their way into the story. These are usually efforts to find the right voice.

Often, I find that voice in something I'm reading or that I've read, and when that happens, the discovery is a very distinct moment, something I remember. The narrative voice for "Finders Keepers" came from a comical narrative line in the film version of John Steinbeck's *Cannery Row*—"Nobody knows how greatness comes to a man." I went back and read a few chapters from the book and found just the right mock epic narrative tone. The narrative tone of my second book, *Bringing the Heat,* was inspired by passages in a satirical essay by P. J. O'Rourke in *Rolling Stone,* which combined serious reporting with a voice that did not take itself or the subject matter too seriously—perfect for a story about pro sports. Often, the voice of the story is suggested by one of its principal characters. If I'm stuck on the first page of a story, I sometimes find it helpful to leaf through some of the favorite books in my library, reading passages, looking for a sentence or paragraph that strikes the right tone. It is hard to describe how this happens, but I know it when I feel it. Something I read or recall strikes precisely the right key for the story I'm trying to write. I have written stories without discovering the right voice, forcing myself to meet a deadline, and I'm rarely happy with them when I'm done. I know no sure-fire tricks for finding the most compelling voice for a story. Sometimes I have found it helpful, when stuck, to talk about the story—my wife bears the brunt of this, I'm afraid. All of us have certain storytelling instincts, and sometimes the best way to tap them is just to sit down, look someone in the eye, and let 'er rip.

Much is made of writing leads, the first lines of a story, and there's no doubt that an arresting sentence or image is vital to grabbing a reader's interest. But a great lead does not make a great story. Splicing a snazzy lead onto an otherwise conventional article strikes me as false advertising. If twenty years ago the anecdotal lead—as opposed to the old *who, what, when, where, how,* and *why* standby—was a daring innovation, today it has become formulaic. Better in most cases to start by telling the story in simple, declarative sentences, leaving out as much official verbiage as possible in order not to slow the reader down. In truth, a person's official title, or the name of an agency (things reporters love to recite right off the bat, as I did in that old drug raid story—"Sgt. Bob Brown of the blah, blah, blah"), is often the least interesting or descriptive thing to report. It can certainly wait for a line or two. The lead should establish the tone and voice of the story and make the reader want to keep reading. The standard anecdotal top on a story these days is akin to the hackneyed public speaker whose idea of good rhetoric is to begin his speech with a joke—any joke—just something to get the audience laughing. Best not to begin your story with a cheap trick. Sometimes the best anecdote in a story works better as a kicker. After all, the final lines (assuming a reader gets there) are the ones most likely to be remembered.

The most readable stories are driven by action, scenes, and dialogue. Popular fiction is often a caricature of this, offering poorly imagined, clichéd characters and trite dialogue, but reporters can learn from it. Michael Crichton writes stories on complex scientific topics but never lets the learning slow down his story. Elmore Leonard tells convoluted tales with many characters and multiple subplots, but the pace of his stories never slows from the first page to the last. The same storytelling principles drive filmmaking, where explication (unless the director opts for a voiceover) must take place within the action. There is plenty of great writing, even great journalism, that flaunts this rule.

Artists sometimes complicate a narrative for effect. Writers from Laurence Sterne to Thomas Pynchon and David Foster Wallace are masters of the sublimely ridiculous digression—Wallace in hilarious footnotes that often rival the main text. Anthony Lucas's acclaimed nonfiction book *Big Trouble* is an exercise in digression gone mad; the narrative of his turn-of-the-century murder yarn in North Dakota branches off in more directions than the Paris Metro. Much of Tom Wolfe's journalism is as notable for its dazzling explication as its story line. But the guiding principle for a newspaper writer should be to keep the story moving. And nothing reads faster than action and dialogue.

To write a story in this way demands much more detailed reporting than conventional journalism. I have already written about seeking out primary sources. You must also visit the scenes of the action, track down minor characters and seemingly insignificant details—what was on the TV in the hotel room when the payoff was handed over in the plain brown bag? Gabriel García Márquez, a formidable journalist as well as a Nobel Prize-winning novelist, has written about how often making a nonfiction scene come into clear focus demands the addition of a small, otherwise irrelevant detail. In many crime stories these days, actual dialogue can be gleaned from police surveillance tapes and court transcripts. Much of the dialogue in "Blackhawk Down" comes from tapes of the radio calls made during the battle. When there is no exact record, my practice is to reconstruct dialogue based on the best memory of those involved—noting the fact that I'm doing so. This is going further than some journalists are willing to go, but I think vivid storytelling demands it. In a scene where two sources remember the same conversation differently, I either avoid reconstructing the dialogue or offer both versions and let the reader share in the ambiguity of the situation. A writer doesn't need to be able to answer all questions in a story. Sometimes it's more compelling, and real, to show that in real life one faces conflicting accounts of events.

In "Finders Keepers" there is a dramatic scene in which a well-known Philadelphia mobster meets with Joey Coyle's friend Carl Masi to discuss "laundering" Joey's money. Coyle and two of his friends who were present identified the mobster, but Masi, for what I think were evident reasons, insisted that the others were mistaken. The mobster was not present, Masi said. I could have just gone with three sources over one, but Masi was the most likely to know the man, the late Sonny Riccobene. I struggled for weeks with this question, opting finally to tell both versions. In the story, Coyle and the others recount seeing Riccobene, while Masi denies it. The story doesn't conclude which version is correct. Not only did this approach preserve a certain dramatic ambiguity, it also underscored the nature of a man like Riccobene, whose very presence strikes fear and prompts some people—without saying whom—to lie.

Eliciting enough information to write scenes means demanding anecdotes from sources. For instance, if someone says he found a character "scary," you ask, "What did he do to make you feel that way?" In the case of the mobster, one of the young men with Coyle answered this question by remembering how the man had paused on his way out of the meeting, put one finger to his lips suggesting silence, pointed his index finger at the boys with his thumb upraised, and then ominously dropped the thumb. Keep after sources, re-interview them until they kick you out of their houses, until you get them to tell you the stories you need to write your own.

Description is essential to good storytelling, but it is also perhaps the most difficult thing to master. Bad writing drips with description that distracts the reader and that is too often hackneyed or clichéd.[5] Good writing keeps description to a minimum, or uses it so artfully that it moves the story forward. In *Of a Fire on the Moon,* Norman Mailer produces a page-long description of NASA's Vehicle Assembly Building, the largest building (by volume) in the world.[6] But there is nothing static about it. Mailer leads the reader through the front doors of the VAB, takes them up a long elevator ride to its top, and then metaphorically throws them off a scaf-

---

5. For one of the best discussions of how to avoid cliché, and one of the best essays ever written about writing, see George Orwell's "Politics and the English Language," in Orwell's *Shooting an Elephant and Other Essays* (New York: Harcourt, Brace & World, 1950), pp. 79–92.

6. Here is Mailer's description of NASA's Vehicle Assembly Building, from *Of a Fire on the Moon* (Boston: Little, Brown, 1969), pp. 55–56: "Once inside, however, it was conceivably one of the more beautiful buildings in the world. Large enough to assemble as many as four moon-going Apollo-Saturn vehicles at once, it was therefore open enough to offer interior space for four tall bays, each of these niches tall enough to house the full rocket, which was thirty-six stories high. Since the rocket in turn sat on a transporter, called a crawler, of some dimension itself, the doors to the four bays were each over forty stories and therefore high enough and wide enough to take in through their portals the UN Building or the Statue of Liberty. Yet for all its size, the VAB was without decoration inside, rather a veritable shipyard and rigging of steel girders which supported whole floors capable of being elevated and lowered, then rolled in and out like steel file drawers in order to encircle each rocket with adjustable working platforms from either side. Since some of these platforms had three complete stories contained within them, the VAB was a complexity of buildings within buildings which had been first maneuvered then suspended ten and twenty and thirty stories above the ground. Because the sides were usually open, one could look out from the platforms to other constellations of girders and buildings and could look down from whichever great height to the floor of the VAB, sometimes as much as forty stories below. Note however: one was still inside a closed space, and the light which filtered through translucent panels rising from floor to ceiling was dim, hardly brighter than the light in a church or an old railroad terminal. One lost in consequence any familiar sense of recognition—you could have been up in the rigging of a bridge built beneath the dome of some partially constructed and enormous subterranean city, or you could have been standing on the scaffolding of an unfinished but monumental cathedral, beautiful in this dim light, this smoky concatenation of structure upon structure, of breadths and vertigos and volumes of open space beneath the ceiling, tantalizing views of immense rockets hidden by their clusters of work platforms. One did not always know whether one was on a floor, a platform, a bridge, a fixed or impermanent part of this huge shifting ironwork of girders and suspended walkways. It was like being in the back of the stage at an opera house, the view as complex, yet the ceiling was visible from the floor and the ceiling was more than fifty stories up, since above the rockets were yet some massive traveling overhead cranes. To look down from the upper stages of the rocket, or from the highest level where the crew would sit, was to open oneself to a study of the dimensions of one's fear of heights. Down, down, a long throw of the soul down, down again, still falling was the floor of the building, forty floors below. The breath came back into the chest from an abyss. And in one corner of the floor like a stamp on the edge of a large envelope was a roped-in square of several hundred tourists gawking up at the yellow cranes and the battleship-gray first girders."

folding and plunges them down to the bottom. It is a classic example of a purely descriptive digression that leaves a vivid mental image without slowing down the narrative in the least. If it weren't so original and superb, this long paragraph could serve as an example of a writer's getting carried away with his descriptive powers. But faced with such a truly monumental structure, Mailer generates a description that in its very breadth helps convey the VAB's enormity. Too often, writers fall back on unhelpful and subjective descriptions, saying, for instance, that a woman was "pretty" or a man "handsome." To whom? Be mindful of all five senses when drawing a picture in words. Note not only how something looks, but where appropriate, how it sounds, smells, tastes, and feels. This last may be the most important of all—note Mailer's evocation of vertigo. Often it is the least tangible sensation about a person or place that conveys the most lasting impression. Telling me that an old woman made you feel angry relates far more than the mere fact that she had a big nose.

That said, as a general rule, description should be kept to an artful minimum. Action propels a reader forward. "Blackhawk Down" begins with U.S. Army Rangers stepping out of helicopters and roping down into battle with bullets cracking around them, and ends when the exhausted survivors stagger to safety the following day. When I first sat down to write, I mapped out a long opening section meant to introduce the main characters and set the context for the battle that would follow. This seemed the only way to proceed, given the complexity of the situation (why were elite U.S. troops in Somalia trying to capture a neighborhood warlord?), the difficulty of the story, and the great number of characters involved. In Sebastian Junger's popular book *The Perfect Storm,* the storm itself doesn't start to blow until about halfway through the 225-page story. In Cornelius Ryan's classic, *The Longest Day,* the invasion of Normandy doesn't begin until halfway through the book. In *Of a Fire on the Moon,* an account of the Apollo 11 moon mission, the rocket doesn't take off until page 210. But after writing this long first section of "Blackhawk Down," lovingly introducing all my main characters and setting the scene for the fight, I found it was simply not as compelling as the battle. The big narrative challenge became weaving all that background information into the battle story itself.

For me, once the tone and general shape of a story have been set, constructing the narrative becomes a very deliberate, almost mechanical process. In "Blackhawk Down," I drew up a detailed chronology of the battle, using official U.S. Army sources and my own more detailed information. The Rangers roped into Mogadishu at the start of the battle from four Black Hawk helicopters, so I created four folders, one for each chopper.

Into each went the interviews with the men who rode in on them. Culling the best anecdotes from this material, I drew up outlines that moved the story of the initial minutes of the battle from scene to scene. Later, when the soldiers found themselves either thrown together on a convoy of vehicles or at one of the three locations where they were pinned down overnight, I reshuffled the interviews into new folders, one for the convoy and one each for the other sites. Then I reviewed all the notes again, looking for details, anecdotes, dialogue, and scenes that would drive that phase of the story. I reshuffled the folders several more times before I was finished, gradually working my way through the interview notes each time.

Once a story has been fully plotted, I find it is hard to keep myself from trying to write too much too fast. I generally start writing first thing in the morning, at about 8:00, and I stop by noon or 1:00. I find my ability to write well falls off rapidly after four or five hours. When I try to write longer, I usually end up spending an hour the next day rewriting the sloppy prose I finished with the day before. The novelist John Barth gave me a tip long ago that I have found useful. When you stop writing, stop in mid-sentence, never at the end of a paragraph or chapter. That way, the next day you will find it much easier to pick right up where you left off.

When I write, I have source material in file drawers and scattered around on both sides of a large desk, a rack of reference books (dictionary, encyclopedia, atlas, thesaurus, and whatever reference material I have gathered for the story at hand), and a blank pad of paper and pen. I may stop three or four times a day to quickly resketch an outline to remind myself of what I have written and where I am going. Writing a long story or a book is like walking through a thick fog. You lose track of what you've written, and you aren't always sure what you're going to write next. Writing is a process of thinking something through, so you don't know where the journey will lead until you take it. In writing a first draft I do a certain amount of jumping back to revise or expand on what I have already written, but I try to keep this to a minimum, valuing forward progress above everything. The overall shape of the story I'm writing is never considered fixed until I've rewritten it several times. I have often come upon a passage well into writing a story that strikes me as the natural lead, which of course necessitates a fairly major, mid-project revision—and sometimes a break in the writing to do more reporting.

When I'm writing a book, the completion of a first draft is an occasion for some time off. Maybe a week or two. I try to force myself to stay away from the manuscript altogether. I'll sit around with a pen and pad sketching out the design—as best as I can remember it—and playing with different ideas, but I find the break is helpful for regaining a fresh perspective on the material. If I'm writing a magazine story, the break will last only a day or two, or for a long newspaper article (given the luxury of time) maybe just a few hours. I believe much creative thought is subconscious and can only take place when the conscious mind is occupied with something else—playing tennis, say, or sleeping. So stepping away from a project is not just good for your mental and physical health; it actually improves the product. Many, many times, I have gone to sleep at night perplexed by some seemingly insoluble narrative problem and awakened the next day with a clear answer.

The second draft is the time for major structural revision. This was where, in writing "Blackhawk Down," I decided to do away with the whole first fifty pages or so and incorporate as much of it as I could into the narrative of the battle. On the second pass through the manuscript I work on cleaning up the prose, by eliminating repetition, clichés, needlessly difficult syntax, and clumsy or meaningless expressions. It is also a time to scrutinize the reporting carefully. Am I sure I want to include this anecdote? Am I sure it's true? Is there somebody else I ought to check with? Should I re-interview the subject and get more detail? Is this number or date accurate? By now the final shape of the story is clear, and it is easier to notice the things that are missing, or that don't belong. Young writers tend to fall in love with their first drafts. The joy of actually completing a thing takes hold. But a first draft is usually just a beginning, a point of departure. It's when the serious work of writing begins.

One of the first long newspaper series I wrote was about the threatened extinction of the black rhino in Africa. The *Inquirer* dispatched me to Africa for months in 1981 to travel and study the problem, and I returned with my brain and notebooks crammed with stories and images and ideas. I labored over the series for months, and when I thought I was finished, my editor, Charles Layton, went to work on it. Charles began attacking my first draft the way good writers (or editors) do. His patient enthusiasm for the work drove me nuts. One day, as I paced and fumed, battling to keep things exactly the way I had them, Charles said,

"I thought you loved to write, Mark."

"I do!"

"Well, this is writing."

Charles was right, both about what writing is and about the absolute necessity of working with a good editor. No writer, no matter how advanced, can look at his or her own work with objectivity. A good editor is a skilled first reader. If you ignore a reader's input, you cannot claim to be genuinely interested in the final product of your labor. In my first decade as a writer, I avoided editors. I would actually file a story late to help it escape detailed scrutiny. Now I look for editors, supplementing the efforts of whoever formally plays that role with two or three volunteers.

When you are at the point of finishing the work, with or without the help of a good editor, it's time to stop worrying about larger issues of form and content and to start thinking small. On my final passes through the manuscript, I deliberately try to shorten every sentence, not because shorter is inherently better, but because it's a useful discipline. I use my word processor to enlarge the type so that only one sentence at a time appears on screen. It forces me to rethink every word, turn sentences inside out, or break them in two. As a young writer, I was amazed when a good editor sat down with me and performed this exercise on a story I thought was finely polished. She was able to excise at least a word or two from every sentence I wrote, improving each one. I have never finished a story since without doing it to myself. In the one year I spent as an editor at the *Inquirer,* one of my favorite tasks was magically to reduce a reporter's thirty-inch story by five inches or more without lopping anything of substance. It is in this fine editing that plain prose becomes exceptional and that experienced writers develop a personal style.

It is not always easy to do your best work, but if you take writing seriously, it is necessary. Writing for a newspaper, in particular, demands daily compromises. Young writers often complain they aren't given the time or space to tell stories the way they'd like. My advice is to make time and find space. When the *Baltimore News-American* wouldn't give me the opportunity to do longer, more ambitious stories, I took contracts with *Baltimore Magazine.* When a *News-American* editor noted that my best work was appearing in the city magazine, he began offering me more time and space in the newspaper. All serious writers are at work on something that stretches them, even if it means stealing time for it. And I've never met a good editor who didn't fall in love with a good story. Rules evaporate if the story is strong enough. I was told at one point that the *Philadelphia Inquirer Magazine* would never publish a story as a serial over several weekends. It would demand too much of readers, I was told. But when I got a story that was too good to shortchange, I wrote it at the length it needed and delivered it to my editor with a challenge: "If you honestly think you can make this a better story by leaving out two-thirds, I'll help you do it." He didn't.

The world is so rarely what we expect it to be that, for me, nonfiction writing long ago became more of a calling than an occupation. I believe that we understand our world and ourselves through the simple stories we hear and repeat. The vast majority of these stories are full of misunderstanding, fiction, and half-truth. Anyone who has ever tried to write truthfully about an event in his or her own life, or who has spent an hour on a psychoanalyst's couch, knows how much more there is to learn about even the simplest things. The same is true of the world at large. Good nonfiction storytelling reminds us how much richer and more interesting the truth is than what we thought we knew, and it teaches us always to be humble in the face of all we don't.

Narrative Writing

By Donald Drake

[Drake works on special projects and serves as narrative editor at the *Philadelphia Inquirer,* where he has been an award-winning reporter since 1966. He is the author of three books about medicine and was Newsday's first science and medicine writer.]

For many years now, there's been a malignant movement in American journalism calling for shorter, snappier, more superficial stories. The conventional wisdom is that the lives of Americans have become too busy for them to read newspapers. Following this thought to its logical conclusion, the greatest service publishers could provide would be to stop publishing stories altogether, and then readers wouldn't have to waste any of their valuable time reading.

The conventional wisdom is conventionally wrong. Americans have plenty of time to read newspapers. It's just that they have more enjoyable things to do like going to movies, watching television dramas, attending sports events. Newspapers are boring. That's why people don't read them. And making stories shorter isn't going to make them any more interesting.

What is it about movies, television, and sporting events that make them more interesting than newspapers? The common factor is that they are all essentially narrative stories.

Sporting events in particular meet the most important criteria for a good narrative. They have beginnings, middles, and ends, with building drama and anticipation leading to the inevitable climax of winning or losing. They have many interesting characters and a lot of dramatic scenes. Will he make the field goal? Will he get a hit or strike out? Will he make the basket? It's the unknown and anticipation that make a sporting event exciting. The only reason that a replay is less exciting than the real thing, which looks exactly the same, is that the outcome is known.

Conventional news stories lack suspense and anticipation. The inverted pyramid story, with all the "important" facts crammed into a few sentences at the top, robs the piece and gives the reader ample reason to stop reading at the jump and start watching television.

So, what's a journalist to do?

If the main pull of these competing events is their narrative quality, then wouldn't it make sense for writers to do what writers do best—write stories?

There are many reasons why journalists don't do this, the main one being that the people in control don't want it. It's not politically correct these days for editors to say they don't like narrative stories, but they really don't, because such stories create problems.

Assigning editors don't like them because they take a long time to report and write, and they require considerable skill to edit. Editors have "more important" things for their staff to do. Newsdesks don't like them because they are invariably long and displace a lot of the stories that news editors feel compelled to fill their pages with—along with a lot of color, graphics, and white space—even though readers often don't feel compelled to read these other, shorter kinds of stories.

And reporters are scared of narrative stories because they require a lot of work and are far more likely to fail than a conventional story if the reporting and writing aren't top notch. No matter how mediocre the reporter, a five-fatality automobile crash told conventionally is always an adequate story or close enough to adequate that an editor can fix it. But telling the story of ghetto children who don't have mothers to care for them takes a good eye, a good ear, and an awful lot of good writing.

So no one really likes narratives—except readers and the Pulitzer committee, which has distributed a disproportionate number of its prizes for narrative stories, considering how few are published. (Even then, crime, violence, and death still garnish the bulk of these Pulitzers.)

I'm not suggesting that all or even most stories in a newspaper be narratives. The inverted pyramid style remains clearly the most efficient way of transmitting information, which is the primary purpose of newspapers. What I am urging is that readers be given reason to expect that every issue of their newspaper will contain one or two narratives that will delight them.

Just what is a narrative story?

A lot of people think it's just a feature story or a yarn. Superficially, it might not look like much more than that. You might say that a narrative is an anecdotal lead that keeps on going until the end, unlike conventional stories with anecdotal leads, which are to storytelling what a stripteaser is to sex. An anecdote lead excites, but the story seldom delivers what it promises.

Narrative storytelling is far more than just another way of writing—it's a completely different way of looking at journalism, and it's a markedly different way of doing it. Practically everything a reporter does in preparing a traditional story is the exact opposite of what the narrative writer does.

Narrative writers don't think in terms of cleverly written sentences or paragraphs, or of startling leads that attract attention. They think of *scenes.* They think visually and sensorially, describing colors, sounds, and smells to put the reader into the scene. They don't cram all the information in the top of the story to seduce fickle readers before they run away, but hold back information and force the reader to anticipate. They don't use quotes from disembodied sources because this wrenches the reader out of the scene, but they do want dialogue between characters because it builds the scene.

The narrative writer uses many other playwriting devices, such as foreshadowing and cliffhanger curtain lines that create anticipation—which is by far the most important element of a narrative. Writers build anticipation by holding back facts, a tactic that drives typical editors to distraction but keeps the reader reading. This is why Romeo and Juliet die in the last scene, after the audience has gotten to know and care about the characters and feel emotionally involved in their fate. Consider how the play would have read if Shakespeare had been of the inverted pyramid school:

> Two teenagers were found dead in a crypt yesterday after what appears to have been a brutal double suicide. No motive was found for the deaths, but one source, who spoke on the condition of anonymity, said it may have been linked to a disagreement among families.

Once the audience gets to know Romeo and Juliet, they care deeply about what will happen to them. They anticipate the lovers getting together, once an all-important message is delivered. This anticipation is far more seductive than the jarring fact of two young people having killed themselves.

The importance of anticipation and the negative effect of the newswriter's tendency to lead with the most important facts cannot be overestimated. A well-known example used in playwriting courses on scene construction dramatizes this. The challenge before the young playwright is how to get the most drama out of a scene in which a burglar, hidden in the closet of the heroine's bedroom, jumps out and rapes her. The scene could be written this way:

The curtain goes up on an empty bedroom at night. A woman, who has just returned home from a party, comes into the room. She takes off her blouse and skirt, and, while sitting in her slip in front of a mirror, starts combing her hair. The burglar jumps out of her closet, drags her to the floor and rapes her.

The scene has all the unpleasant gore that heightens the journalistic value of a crime story, but it lacks the most important element of a good narrative—suspense. The only excitement is when the burglar jumps out of the closet.

But a simple adjustment will make the scene work: Put the man in the closet. Open the scene with the burglar coming in the window and starting to go through the jewelry box. He hears the downstairs door opening and hides in the closet. Now do everything exactly the way it was done in the first draft. The significant difference between the two versions is that this time the audience knows that the man is in the closet and worries that he might burst out and do something awful. Instead of being a boring representation of a woman preparing for bed, the scene builds tension as the woman becomes increasingly vulnerable by disrobing.

The narrative writer searches for the drama in every interaction, in every scene, in every story. This is the most important criterion in deciding whether to do a story as a narrative. Does the story have potential for drama? Often, stories with little conventional news value make great narratives and can be done successfully in no other way.

For example, consider what possibilities the following information might offer for a major story in the "A" section of your newspaper: The local hospital does heart transplants, an operation that your newspaper has frequently written about. On any given day, there may be a dozen people waiting in the hospital for the surgery. This particular medical center doesn't do the surgery any better or any worse than comparable centers. There are no medical breakthroughs to report. There is no incompetence to expose. The hospital has been doing these operations for years and will probably continue to do them for many years to come. Using traditional criteria, there appears to be little here that could justify a big story, right?

But my paper, the *Philadelphia Inquirer,* generated a six-part series on this subject. The story, written by Stacey Burling, a talented reporter with a good eye for dramatic moments, turned out to be a powerful and well-received piece because it met the most important criteria for a great narrative: drama, a lot of good characters, and, even more, anticipation. Think of it. A dozen or so desperately ill patients living together in the hospital. They're all waiting for heart donors to be found, knowing that this is the only way they can leave the hospital alive. They wait for months, seeing other patients, people who have become their friends, getting hearts and leaving. Their medical condition is slowly deteriorating. Can they hold out? Will they get their new hearts?

Burling did a prospective narrative. She started out on New Year's Eve with the dozen or so patients in the hospital at that time and followed them until every one had gotten a transplant.[1] Prospective narratives are the best kind because the writer can witness the events and pick up subtle details more casual observers would miss. The only disadvantage of a prospective narrative is that there is no guarantee that it will lead to something interesting, let alone newsworthy. And since it takes so much time to do a prospective—a prospective birth announcement would take almost nine months to report—you're taking a big gamble on an unknown.

Often, a reporter has no choice but to do a retrospective narrative, which is about something that has already happened. The advantage of a retrospective narrative, and it's a big one, is that you know what happened and how newsworthy it is. The disadvantage is that you have to reconstruct events on the basis of extensive interviews of many participants and other secondhand data.

I prefer to do prospective narratives. Not only are they more fun and exciting to report, because you're there sharing the experience, but they can be used to make a routine conventional story special.

Let's say you want to tell a story about women in the police department and how well they're doing. The first step is to do the traditional reporting. You find out what percentage of the force is female, how many arrests they make relative to male officers, whether they are as good, better, or worse than males, in all the measurable ways. You find out the unique problems confronting females.

Once this information is in hand, any other reporter would be ready to write and be done with it. But for a narrative writer, this is just the beginning. Now comes the matter of staging the narrative—that is, determining what human story, what narrative drama, will best illustrate the most vital

---

1. Stacey Burling's series on heart transplants ran on page A-1 each day, June 2 through June 7, 1996, in the *Philadelphia Inquirer.*

facts collected through research and interviews. Since human beings are invariably more interesting than concepts or statistics, it's best to tell your story in terms of people or characters, in this case through female police officers. It's usually better to focus on one person, using other people as supporting characters.

Once you have the character, then you have to cast her in a drama. If nothing better comes to mind, one fallback drama is a day, week, or month in the life of your character. I once did this with medical students, following them through four years of medical school and their first year of internship for a series called "The Making of a Doctor."[2] Maybe you could follow a policewoman on patrol from roll call to check out.

· The trouble with day-in-the-life narratives is that they tend to have weak narrative arch; there is not much of a build-up in dramatic action from the opening to the final scenes. She comes to work. She rides around, answers a few calls, makes a few arrests, and goes home. What you have to do is ride with that police officer until you figure out what the dramatic arch is. That means it's unlikely that you can complete the narrative in a single day.

So you ride a couple of more days, looking for the elements that most dramatically represent what it means to be a woman in the police department. As you ride with her, winning her confidence, you discover that fear is the most difficult thing these women have to deal with—not because they are more likely to be afraid than men, but because they can't show it to their male colleagues, whom they think are looking for things to justify their prejudice against women officers. Women officers have to deal with their fears silently.

A dramatic arch is beginning to build.

You talk some more to your main character and find out that she is a single mother who was abused by her son's father, long since gone. Since becoming a cop, she's seen a lot of men beating up women, and it's the call she most hates to get on the radio. More interviewing reveals that she is particularly distressed by calls to the projects because they so often involve domestic abuse.

Just as a conventional reporter keeps looking for material to support the lead, the narrative writer is looking for elements to provide an effective, dramatic arch. In this case the subtext of the dramatic arch will dramatize the constant fear women cops confront. It is now clear what must be done.

---

2. These stories were published in revised form in *Medical School: The Dramatic True Story of How Four Years Turned a Class of Raw Students into Qualified Physicians* (New York: Rawson, 1978).

You have to ride with her until she gets a call for a family disturbance in the projects, which shouldn't take long, since they get several calls to the projects every week.

After you ride with her for three days, she finally gets the call and goes racing to the projects. When she gets there she sees that there's no backup for her. She can't wait for another patrol car to arrive because she knows a woman is in trouble, very likely being beaten up just as she used to be. She has to go in.

Her concern was for naught. The man isn't very big. He goes away as soon as he sees her, not wanting trouble with the police. Our character comforts the woman and resumes patrol. Many reporters would think the story was a bust. No one was hurt, let alone killed. Told conventionally, it would look like this:

A woman police officer went into the projects yesterday and told a man to stop annoying his wife. He did, at least for the moment.

But being a narrative writer, you know it's a great story—the story of a woman cop dealing successfully with fears she can't even admit to.

Now comes the fun part of building the story: intertwining the narrative of the police woman on patrol with the basic material that would have constituted the conventional news story. It's not just a matter of thinking up a lead and "nut paragraph." Because narratives are so dependent on foreshadowing and anticipation, they have to be carefully constructed. I usually write out a plot line, segment by segment, working out the opening and closing of each scene. (By the time I write my first paragraph of such a story, I know what the very last one will be, too.) A narrative must have movement, and the movement runs from the first scene to the climactic last scene. By knowing both in advance, you know what direction the story will travel and the elements needed to make the journey.

You decide that the opening scene will show the policewoman giving her child breakfast as she herself prepares for work. The final climactic scene will be responding to the call in the projects. If this is your plot, you will have to interview the woman carefully to reconstruct exactly what she did before reporting for work the day she got the call to the projects, assuming you didn't have the foresight to start each day of reporting with her at home.

This opening will give the reader a chance to get to know the character as both a cop and a mother. But in writing the opening, it's essential to describe the fear that is a constant part of her professional life and to indicate that she fears most of all getting a call to the projects. Most crucially, you must somehow set it up that, before the day is over, she would get that dreaded call. It's the anticipation of that final scene that keeps the reader reading.

Once you've established the opening narrative scene, you can start telling the main story—the overall piece about women on the police force and how they are doing. For the sake of space and to change the pace, you write this segment expositionally. You tell the readers when the first woman cop was hired, years ago, and relate how many are now on the force. You explain that in many ways they perform just like their male counterparts, and they've done fairly well, but women have some particularly difficult concerns. One of them is fear. This first expositional segment should not be long—maybe seven or eight inches—or else the reader will lose sight of the narrative and think he's been sucked in by an anecdotal lead.

Now, you cut back to your chief character and resume the narrative. The next scene probably would be her arrival at the station house for roll call, with a lot of detail showing how the male and female cops interact. It's important to link the narrative scenes so the reader has a sense of forward movement. If you close a scene with the character walking out to go to work, the next narrative scene should be her arriving at work.

When you reported the roll call scenes, you were careful to watch the male-female interactions, looking for little dramas with important subtext. For instance, your expositional reporting determined that the women act particularly "macho" to offset the female stereotype, so you were very careful to note how many of the women cops hoist their pants up and tell off-color jokes and act particularly tough. This contrasts nicely with the gently maternal way your cop treated her child in preparing breakfast.

The second narrative scene might end with roll call and a warning from the sergeant that there have been some problems in the projects and patrols should make extra pass-bys. (Once you start working on a concept, it's surprising how often real life cooperates if only you're primed to be on the lookout for the right stuff.) Now, you have a chance to dip back into another expositional segment where you provide more information about women police officers in general.

And so it goes, alternating narrative scenes with expositional segments, keeping in mind that neither the narrative nor expositional segment will be so long that the reader loses sight of the other. I like to think of the expositional sections as a way of educating readers—in this case about women on the police force—so they can better understand the unfolding narrative drama.

Once you get to the climactic scene at the bottom of the story, you have to bear down and start doing some serious writing. Actually, you should have been doing this all along, but the climactic scene is particularly important in a narrative even though it is way at the bottom on the jump page. It's as significant in a narrative as the lead is in a conventional news story.

Because this particular climax is so subtle, it requires especially careful writing. You decide to focus on the few minutes between the time the police officer reaches the projects and discovers she's without backup and the time she sends the man on his way. Make use of her anticipation—her dread of a possibly dangerous situation. You describe how she gets on the radio and says she's going into the projects. You show her walking across the debris-strewn walkway in front of the enormous building looming in front of her. You take the reader into the building and describe the smell of urine and the elevator that is so small that you feel trapped inside. The elevator climbs slowly to the twenty-third floor. It stops at twelve, and two big guys get on. And all the time, she is wondering what she will find when she gets off and goes to Apartment 23D.

This might be a good time to recall what it was like for the cop being beaten up by her child's father, how he was so strong that there was nothing she could do but take the beating and hope that this time it wouldn't last long. Finally, the elevator gets to twenty-three, and she walks out into an ugly, dark hallway. As she moves slowly down the corridor, her hand feels for her gun and nightstick as she checks the numbers on the doors. She can feel her heart pounding and hear her heavy breathing. 23A. 23B. 23C. Finally, 23D. She can hear the yelling on the other side of the door.

She remembers her training in the police academy. Be tough. Don't let the assholes know you're afraid. Be alert. Always wait for backup, don't take chances—a rule she's already broken. Taking her nightstick, she raps it against the door several times.

"Police," she announces. "Open up." The door opens and you have a quick resolution.

Apparently nothing happened. But everything happened. You showed it by taking your time and using a lot of detail, by building the tension and giving the reader a chance to anticipate. That's why you want to slowly take the reader down the hall. 23A. 23B. 23C. Unfortunately, reporters are so well trained to move a story along quickly, they're afraid to do this. They don't give readers a chance to respond to things emotionally.

Once you've finished writing the first draft—yes, narratives usually require a lot of revisions—you edit the story, mercilessly. Almost invariably, the first draft of a narrative is long, fat, and lumpy. It's not aerodynamic. It's such a blob that you're afraid to let your most trusted friends see it, let alone your editor. But don't get discouraged at this point. You're a sculptor who's just plopped in the lumps of clay in place to resemble the figure she's doing. Now comes the sculpting.

A narrative is very unforgiving of rambling thoughts, unnecessary words, or redundancy of any kind. Once you have made your point, move on. Here are some things to be on the lookout for:

- If you've shown the same thing in two different paragraphs, then get rid of one of them, no matter how beautifully it's written or how much time went into getting the information.
- Avoid stating what you are about to show. For instance, you wouldn't want to write, "The police officer was very frightened as she walked into the projects," because you're damn well going to show this.
- Excise quotes that merely repeat what the reader is effectively *shown* elsewhere. For instance, if you describe a beautiful park so evocatively that readers feel like they're actually there, you don't want to quote people saying in a lot of different ways how lovely this park is. Let readers discover these things and come to their own conclusions.
- The most common mistake is subtext redundancy, which is the telling of several different incidents that illustrate the same thing. For instance, the subtext of the woman's trip up to Apartment 23D is her terror. You're showing the fear that this police officer must deal with. If during the patrol that day she has to deal with a huge unruly drunk, you wouldn't want to spend a lot of time showing her fear as she walks up to confront the guy. It would rob from the climactic scene.

Once you've finished editing the first draft, the story probably will have shrunk by as much as 30 percent if you've been as ruthless as you should have been. And the story will likely read 500 percent better. This is the "Well, I'll-be-damned" phase of doing a narrative, as in, "Well, I'll be damned, I think this story is going to work."

With the emphasis on small stories these days, many reporters think it's a waste of time perfecting a writing technique that requires a lot of time and space, because their papers only want quick hits. It's true that you're not likely to be successful if you go to your editor and say that you have a great idea for a narrative story, and it'll take only a month to do, and you will need just 120 inches. So, don't do that: Use subtler tactics.

Come up with a story idea that is timeless, so that you won't be under deadline pressure. For your first narrative, pick one that is easy to tell, with an obvious beginning, middle, and end, clearly defined dramatic elements, and an obvious climax. A good example of such a narrative is the story of a woman giving birth. How can you justify an everyday story like that, you ask?

Let's say that your hospital has opened a new birthing center. Instead of writing the typical "ain't-it-grand" piece, tell the story of the new center through the experience of one woman giving birth.

The story has a good narrative arch. You have the drama of a woman arriving at the center with her husband, anticipating the pain and joy of bringing a new life into the world. That's a good opening. And you have a great climax: the actual birth. In between is the building tension and drama as the contractions become more frequent and the moment of birth approaches. It's also a story where you have access: most people are eager to share this experience, and the doctors have nothing to hide. Finally, it takes place over a short period.

Once you have reported, plotted, and written the story, don't take it to your editor. The first attempt at a narrative invariably fails. The editor will be right in saying the story doesn't work, and she'll probably be wrong in the suggestions offered to fix it. (The usual advice is to cut the story in half, make the point in the lead, and put a lot of quotes up high.)

Instead of showing the first draft to the editor, take it to a trusted colleague, preferably someone who enjoys writing as much as reporting. Ask for an honest response. When the person says it's okay but not great, don't ask how to fix it but, rather, seek specific reactions.

"Did you get bored, halfway through?" "Were you sympathetic to the character?" "Was the story exciting?"

Go back to the computer and rewrite. Find a way to make the story interesting from beginning to end. Build the character so the reader will care. And make the excitement come out.

Show the revisions to another trusted colleague. Get her response. Rewrite some more. Show it again.

Only when someone finally tells you that it's one of the best stories he has ever read is it time to show it to your editor.

Be prepared for an unexpected reaction. She'll probably like it and go to bat for it at the news meeting. Even the most skeptical editor loves a narrative when it's done right. And it's a feather in the editor's cap when it happens on his or her watch.

As for you, journalism will never be the same. It's a lot of work doing narratives, but nothing is so sweet as writing the story everyone is talking about—not because of the importance of the event, but because of your artful storytelling and the beauty of the writing.

SECTION IV:
DEVELOPING YOUR CRAFT

In Search of the Magic Bullet . . .

By Richard Aregood

[Aregood's editorials have claimed two of journalism's major honors: the 1985 Pulitzer Prize for commentary and the American Society of Newspaper Editors Distinguished Writing Award. He has won the latter prize an unprecedented three times. He is editorial page editor for the *Newark Star-Ledger*.]

The secret of good journalistic writing is that there are no secrets, no one-size wonders that can accommodate any kind of story. Naturally, journalists believe differently. We are the original single-bullet theorists, and the people who employ us would like to have a template in which everything fits.

Many newsroom writers believe that just about any story can be poured into an anecdotal opening. Such leads remain popular because they have a kind of literary feel to them. And that is why they are overused to the point of bringing tears to the eyes of the average newspaper reader. Everybody wants to be an artist. So we end up with reporters beginning a story with how bad a day it was for Joe Doakes, then consuming fourteen inches of page-one type before divulging over on the jump page that the reason Joe was in the news is that he was driving the train that derailed and flattened downtown yesterday.

We must always bear in mind that our function is only partially literary.

Our primary mission is to explain what the hell happened in a reasonable, understandable manner. It may take the edge off some imagined slowly blossoming drama, but we owe it to our readers to tip the hand a little: "It was a lousy day for Joe Doakes yesterday. That was even before he drove a locomotive through the sporting goods section at the Wal-Mart." It ain't pure, but it will work.

In fact, exactly the right technique for most stories is to let the tale find its own life. I once interviewed a child star, by then in middle age, whose embittered rants were so entertaining and had such momentum that the eventual story was 95 percent his quotes. In that case, the smartest thing to do was to step back from the material and see how good it was without extra help. All it needed was a little midwifery.

Most stories are likely best told as simple narratives. Most of us go through life experiencing it in time sequence; it is comforting to read somebody else's life the same way. (It works so well that Harold Pinter successfully made one of his plays work in backward time sequence.) So if there is any excuse to employ it, narrative is the way to go, no matter what the current magical fad is.

An excellent corrective to believing in magic is the application of a little breakdown technique devised by Donald Murray, who invented the concept of "coaching" writers as he moved along in his own considerable career as a writer. (He won a Pulitzer Prize for commentary and later authored numerous books on writing.) Murray broke the writing process into these categories: *Explore, Focus, Rehearse, Draft, Develop, Clarify.*

The genius comes with the analysis of the process. The problem is never in the part of the process with which you are struggling. It comes from the one before. For instance, if you are having unrelieved misery trying to report a story, it is likely that the problem is in the earlier stage—the block-head who made the assignment. Similarly, if the first write-through is not going well, the problem is probably in the reporting or organizing.

That is not meant to say that any of this is easy. Decent writing is brutally hard, lonesome work that is virtually impossible to do according to format. Most of the truly bad stuff you see in daily newspapers is the result of denying these basic facts.

A "nut paragraph" that is as dense as a dwarf star and as hard to cough up as a hairball is the result of going beyond the reason for a nut paragraph (i.e., to tell the reader why he or she should waste his or her time reading this) and lazily attempting to cram everything remotely resembling a fact into one indigestible mass.

A story that seems rushed is often the product of a writer struggling endlessly for a perfect lead. It does not come when summoned. Sometimes, it makes more sense to use an old rewrite man's trick and write the rest of the thing while your subconscious churns away at a lead. Sometimes, it doesn't come; but frequently, it does, because writing the entire story reminds you what the lead is.

That is not a bad idea, generally—to take some subconscious time to let things sort out. Even in a newspaper with the general attitude of a word factory, you can steal time to think by choosing to do mindless tasks first. Walking your beat is a great way to organize your thoughts, as well as something you should be doing anyway. Taking the time to think your story through may bother an unthinking editor—who may believe that continuous typing is a sign of earnest effort—but it is essential to good writing.

Once You Do Sit Down at the Computer . . .

- Be merciless with your prose. If a wonderful sentence does not advance the story, kill it. A smart reporter tucks it away for later. There will come a time when it does fit, after all.
- Do not think readers read you because you are a fine person. Readers have to be seduced. If you have hard material (especially numbers), scatter it in a rational way throughout the text. The same goes for other heavy matter or attributions or anything else that's clunky. You can turn a merely boring story downright stupefying by clustering all that stuff together.
- Let style happen. Some writers (Murray Kempton, Richard Ben Cramer) use long sentences that seem too long unless you see them in context and understand that they carry the dialogue forward inexorably with the kind of momentum that short sentences only break up. If you want a reader to be cruising along with you, let the sentences flow onward without regard for anything somebody has told you about how journalism is the art of writing short sentences

that brutishly tell a tale. If you want them to stop and see something basic in bold relief, stop them. With a short sentence. Short stops the momentum.

Short makes a point.

- Remember that you don't have to tell a reader everything you know. You tell readers what they need to know or want to know or what you have to tell them. A fact does not become important merely because you wrote it in your notebook. You are not notebook-emptying; you are telling a story.

- Avoid mumbo-jumbo. Roy Peter Clark of The Poynter Institute for Media Studies has a great technique for avoiding bad writing on those hateful municipal stories. He suggests imagining you are telling the story to your mother. If you "tell it to mom," it is impossible to write some maggot-gagger like "City Council, by a vote of 5-3, decided last night to accept a $721,388 UDAG grant for waterfront reclamation." Come to think of it, if you "tell it to mom," you will likely avoid all bureaucratic mumbo-jumbo. This will not apply if your mother is the school superintendent, but nobody's perfect.

Besides, if you are thinking about *writing,* it is likely you will be a better *reporter.* People who say they are much better as one or the other are deluding themselves. Without fact, you will write garbage. Without grace, nobody will care about your facts.

The Zen of Newswriting

By Lucille S. deView

[DeView is the writing coach at the *Orange County Register* in California. She frequently leads writing workshops for various media groups, and, at age 80, continues writing "Retrospective," her weekly column on aging that is syndicated by Knight-Ridder/Tribune News.]

> I once had a special bird friend who struggled to sing his song:
> "Whip, whip, whippoor, whippoor." I began pulling for him.
> Come on, now, you can do it. Slower. Think it through. Then
> "Whip-poorwill, whippoorwill." There! See? It wasn't so hard.
> . . . What an odd pair we were, telling each other to be brave, to
> go on.

That is what workshops do: They companion us in our often lonely struggle to make our songs—our writing—come out clear and strong. We long to write with elegance and grace; to fulfill the charge we hear today to be storytellers; to take risks.

One way to accomplish this is to visit the works of writers in other fields.

To paraphrase a famous phrase about a rose, writing is writing is writing. All writers have techniques to share—poets, novelists, nonfiction writers, screenwriters, playwrights, songwriters, writers of children's books. When we cull their skills and apply them to our journalism, the results can be wondrous.

Imagine starting your next story with the surge of action and vitality that you see in films, often before the credits roll. Imagine the thrill of finding metaphors and similes as fresh, bright, lovely, or at times as alarming as those of poets. Imagine borrowing a story structure from a child's bedtime story, a structure effectively simple but not simplistic. As we explore how other writers galvanize their readers, we find ourselves thinking about more sophisticated elements such as foreshadowing, voice, and style. What a creative adventure, one that brings renewed joy to our tasks.

"Joy" is the key word in my writing mantra. And just as laughter is an essential ingredient in learning, so in coaching sessions, I insist we laugh often and loud. This being best done away from the newsroom, we've held a few workshops at a coffeehouse not far from our *Orange County Register* office. After all, many of our favorite authors have done their writing at cafés—so, why not reporters? At the least, I find it conducive to creative thinking to be away from the newsroom. Tensions tend to melt when you're surrounded by kitschy Victorian furniture with doilies on the tables; when you're sipping latté and supping on scones. But let's not relax so much that we forget our goal: to study the techniques of writers in other fields and see what we may borrow from them for our own selfish purposes.

Fiction

It is no surprise that so many novelists have emerged from journalism, including Mark Twain, Ernest Hemingway, and Gabriel García Márquez. A *New York Times* story several years ago described how García Márquez, winner of the 1982 Nobel Prize in Literature, purchased his own newsmagazine, *Cambio,* and, at age seventy-two, joyfully joined its staff. "I want to feel the atmosphere, to be a reporter [again]," he explained. He said he wants the weekly to carve out a niche that will allow it to treat "journalism as a literary genre." He has often asserted his belief that, without being fiction, journalism serves similarly as an effective instrument for expressing reality and providing insights into the nature of our lives. On buying *Cambio* he maintained that what subscribers really want is for reporters "to tell a story, to go back to the time when a reader could know what happened as if he were there himself."[1]

Journalists tend by nature to be voracious readers, but journalist-novelist Pete Hamill says the secret is to be "totally eclectic" in our choices of

---

1. Larry Rohter, "Bogota Journal: García Márquez Embraces Old Love (That's News!)," *New York Times,* March 3, 1999, p. A-4.

reading material. In a *Writer's Digest* interview, he takes the approach of a perennial student, saying:

> When I read a story and it gives me a wallop and I don't know how the hell the writer did it, I go back and look at it and try to figure out how this guy or woman did this to me.
>
> Sometimes it's really hard to figure out if the guy is a deft magician. You're not going to see it right away. How did he do it? How did he saw that woman in half?
>
> When that happens you cheer, and then the craftsman takes over and asks how it was done.[2]

In the introduction to his book *Piecework,* Hamill tells how he put rhythm and tone into his writing by chanting the same phrase jazz drummer Gene Krupa used: "lyonnaise potatoes and *some* pork chops."[3]

Novelists create moods, and so do we. Mood is factual and doesn't require length. A single, short sentence often did the trick for Pulitzer-winner Edna Buchanan, longtime police reporter at the *Miami Herald* and now a novelist. When she wrote, "Bad things happen to the husbands of Widow Elkin," the mood was eerie and the reader was hooked.[4]

Tony Hillerman enriches his mysteries with his knowledge of Navajo customs and ceremonies, hogans and sweat baths, kindness and killers. He knows his territory, knows his people, and his detectives dig hard for answers, as do journalists. Hillerman knows; he was once a reporter.

So was Ernest Hemingway, who said all good books should contain "the good and the bad, the ecstasy, the remorse and sorrow, the people and the places and how the weather was."[5]

Nonfiction

Hemingway makes the case for solid reporting in his book *Death in the Afternoon,* marked by its thoroughness, wit, and unexpected flights of lyricism:

---

2. Tom Callahan,"I Have to Give It Everything I Have" [Interview with Pete Hamill], *Writer's Digest,* 73.9 (Sept. 1993), p. 47.

3. Pete Hamill, *Piecework: Writings on Men and Women, Fools and Heroes, Lost Cities, Vanished Friends, Small Pleasures, Large Calamities, and How the Weather Was* (Boston: Little, Brown, 1996), p. 7.

4. Edna Buchanan, "The Widow Elkin Mystery: 2 Husbands Dead, 1 Missing," *Miami Herald,* July 14, 1985, p. A-1.

5. Ernest Hemingway, *By-Line: Ernest Hemingway: Selected Articles and Dispatches of Four Decades,* ed. William White (New York: Scribner's, 1967), p. 184.

A writer who omits things because he does not know them only makes hollow places in his writing. A writer who appreciates the seriousness of writing so little that he is anxious to make people see he is formally educated, cultured or well-bred is merely a popinjay. And this too remember; a serious writer is not to be confounded with a solemn writer. A serious writer may be a hawk or a buzzard or even a popinjay, but a solemn writer is always a bloody owl.[6]

Lyricism is also a trademark of Diane Ackerman, whose stunning verbs and poetic descriptions massage the senses. In her nonfiction book *The Moon by Whale Light,* she writes:

At sunset, an orange fur lay along the horizon and the sea grew blue-gray. Areas of wet sand, exposed by the withdrawing tide, shone like an array of hand mirrors. Venus appeared overhead, bright as a whistle blow, with the small pinprick light of Mercury at its side. As night fell, the shallows shimmered like ice and the frantic winds began to sound like freight trains. The wind has a large vocabulary in Patagonia. It shushes through the thorn bushes, it rattles the corrugated-metal walls, it flutes through the arroyos; it makes the cliffs sound as if they are being scoured by a wire whisk. A night heron cried *owow*. A whale sneezing loudly sounded as if an iron patio chair were being dragged across a cement floor. In the distance, three whales blew bushes of mist.[7]

Do your verbs pale by comparison? Check them out by putting all your verbs in bold. Read only the verbs. And do the same with your descriptive words; be sure they are specific and concrete.

Metaphors and themes are the tools of the trade for nonfiction writers and journalists. The search for a metaphor to carry the lead—and a theme to weave together the disparate parts of a story—may present a challenge, but the rewards are grand.

In 1988, when Shuttle Discovery was to be launched at Cape Canaveral, Florida, writers uniformly called the craft "the bird." I searched for a more specific description, something more original and suitable, something of my own. (I share with other writers the stubborn determination not to repeat what others have done.) At the same time, I sought a theme to

---

6. Ernest Hemingway, *Death in the Afternoon* (New York: Scribner's, 1932), p. 192.

7. Diane Ackerman, *The Moon by Whale Light: And Other American Adventures among Bats, Penguins, Crocodilians, and Whales* (New York: Random House, 1991), p. 159.

define the magnitude of this particular mission. At last, a treasure trove. My story began:

> On a pristine stretch of Florida beach, Shuttle Discovery waits on its pad, clinging to its orange-brown fuel tank like a giant, gossamer luna moth, at once fragile and strong.
>
> A tense world awaits Discovery's liftoff—the flash of flame, the boiling billows of smoke, the roar louder than the thunder of thunder, the aftershock rumbling underfoot, rattling windows, shaking walls.
>
> Here a people snagged in the starry web of sorties into the heavens beg a return to their proud role as the Kitty Hawk of the Space Age; a return to life after the death of Shuttle Challenger more than 2½ years ago.

I had found my precious luna moth—and a "return to life after death" theme. I visited both elements at the end:

> People feel again that tingle of excitement, that exquisite anticipation honed through the years. . . . Over everything like the faint flutter of a translucent luna moth, float visions of what else might be "out there" in the universe; visions mixed with myths of ancient Greek and Mayan gods who flew heavenward; mixed, too, with memories of the recent glory of that "one step for mankind" on the moon.
>
> What we want most, people from Brevard County say, is to soar again. To rekindle the feeling of being linked with greatness. To recover joy through Discovery.

Songwriting

"Sing me your story," Kate Long tells reporters at the *Charleston Gazette* in Charleston, West Virginia, where she is the writing coach. Kate champions clear, plain sentences in the newsroom and in the songs she writes. Her "Who'll Watch the Homeplace" won the Song of the Year Award from the International Bluegrass Music Association a few years ago. Some of her songs rock, some are jazzy; some make fun, some deal with pain and loss. All have contemporary themes. "Be spare with words," she advised the audience at the 1995 National Writers' Workshop at the *Orange County Register.* "Choose those words that convey the most emotion in the shortest space. Use metaphors and similes to create an effective word picture.

Be on the scene to tell the human interest stories related to the news." In Kate's mind, this advice applies to songwriting, but it directly applies as well to the stories we tell in our daily papers.

Poetry

"One definition of poetry is 'news that stays news'," says poet Peter Meinke, who urges poetry upon journalists. "Reading poetry reminds reporters about what got them into this infernal business in the first place: a love of words, their sound and weight, their look on the page." In an article for *Coaches' Corner* (a newsletter sent to newsroom writing coaches) Meinke says:

> Back in 1582, Sir Philip Sydney wrote that the end of poetry was "to teach and delight," a definition that should apply to journalism as well (poets today tend to skip the first part, journalists the second). But there is no reason for this division: we should be able to find wisdom in poetry and pleasure in journalism as well as the reverse.[8]

Writing poetry was crucial to journalist Terry Anderson during his 2,445 days in captivity in Beirut. Anderson wrote thirty-two poems, though he had never before written poetry. He composed his poems in his head because he was not allowed pencil or paper. In an interview in *Writer's Digest* after his release, he said:

> I went over and over each of the poems, changing and polishing them. They were in my mind. I was beginning to fear I would not remember them, so I began to say them over to myself at least once a day.

When his two companion prisoners were released, he was given one hour in which to write. "I just took the paper and pencil and knelt down on the floor and wrote fast."[9] The poems appear in his book *Den of Lions*.[10]

In my own early reporting days, I often wrote poems in my notebook as a way of talking to myself and more deeply probing the mysteries of the human condition. In a series of poems, "At a Murder Trial," I wrote one about "Emptiness":

---

8. Peter Meinke, "Poetry That Stays News," *Coaches' Corner* (Sept. 1994).
9. Michael Bugeja, "Poetry" [Interview with Terry Anderson], *Writer's Digest* 73.2 (Feb. 1993).
10. Terry A. Anderson, *Den of Lions: Memoirs of Seven Years* (New York: Crown, 1983).

I am covering a murder trial.
It takes all my words.
When there is a recess, I am drained.
I sit outside in the hot noon sun
and read some poems to stuff back some words.
But when it is time to go inside again
I am still empty.

In 1984, when Emily Dickinson was one of three poets chosen for the American Poets' Corner in the Arts Bay of New York's Cathedral Church of St. John the Divine, I wrote this ode to a succinct writer who never used a superfluous word, "To Emily:"

Sweet-face
so glad
you are there.
Secrets
soul-bared
in words spare.[11]

I favor writing short sentences—and, when possible, using sentence fragments to good effect. My favorite example is a 1988 article by Fred Grimm for the *Miami Herald.* I owe him a royalty for all the times I have cited it to writers. His first complete sentence is in the fourth paragraph:

Kermit, W. Va.—Drugs. Bribes. Fraud. Theft. Threats. Arson.
Fixing of juries. Tampering with witnesses. Stealing from poverty programs. Selling of public offices. Buying of police officers. Intimidating enemies. Corrupting elections.
The fire chief setting fires. The police chief selling marijuana. The school board president bribing jurors.
This was a bad place.[12]

---

11. Lucille S. deView, "To Emily," *Christian Science Monitor,* Sept. 7, 1995, p. 17. (The series of poems that included "Emptiness" was published in *Editor and Publisher* under the title "Poems from a Reporter's Notebook.")

12. Fred Grimm, "Convictions End Corrupt Reign in W. Va. County," *Miami Herald,* March 21, 1988, p. A-1.

Screenwriting

David Trottier, author of *The Screenwriter's Bible* and director of the Screenwriting Center in Salt Lake City, stresses getting films—and stories— off to a fast start. He writes: "Somewhere in the first ten or fifteen pages of your script, something should happen to give the central character a goal, desire, mission, need or problem."[13]

An outline will help plan where the turning points (or plot points) in your news stories should appear, for the greatest effect.

Dialogue in screenplays is spare, Trottier says. He cites a scene in which Clint Eastwood's character is asked what kind of childhood he had. His reply: "Short." The lesson for the journalist is obvious. Fewer and more choice quotes rescue many a story and enliven the action, especially when the quotes can be presented in the form of a crisp exchange between speakers.

Foreshadowing is important in news stories and in films. It arouses curiosity and creates suspense. The trick is not to give too much away too fast, Trottier says. Parcel out the information to keep the viewer or reader with you to the very end.

I studied with Trottier at a night class at a community college and have written a screenplay. I've also taken classes in the short story and studied several semesters in a playwrights workshop. I am not alone in my pursuit of other forms of writing. A number of my reporting colleagues at the *Register* regularly take classes in poetry, the novel, screenwriting, even stand-up comedy. And yes, the carry-over into the paper is often noticeable in the writing that appears on our best pages.

Television, Radio

Valerie Hyman, director of the Poynter Institute's program for broadcast journalists, gave these tips to a St. Louis Writers' Workshop audience, and they seem as applicable to newspaper writing as to electronic reporting:

> Tell stories with a beginning, middle, and end—narrative style. End with something strong. Write sentences in this order most of the time: subject-verb-object. Let the people closest to the story tell it. Use officials, observers, and experts for background. Edit out every word of unexplained jargon in your copy. Look for the telling details that capture your experience of a story and write them down. Remember, brevity and clarity come from selection, not compression.

---

13. David Trottier, *The Screenwriter's Bible: A Complete Guide to Writing, Formatting and Selling Your Script,* 3rd Ed. (Beverly Hills, Calif.: Silman-James Press, 1998).

In radio, pictures are painted with words and nimble minds. Writers for National Public Radio are especially gifted in description. My favorite: radio reviews of art exhibits. In one of my workshops, the writers visited a local art museum and wrote essays on a single object of their choice, the better to practice description. They went beyond the scope of the assignment and delved into the moods, emotions, and mysteries of art.

Writers for radio and television have little time to prepare their scripts. Often, they report live. So the next time you are lingering unnecessarily over your copy, imagine you are writing for broadcast. Chances are your decisions will come faster and be the better for putting on some speed.

Stage

Of all the classes I've taken over the years, those for playwrights have had the most profound influence on my writing and my life. My play, "A Summer with Hemingway's Twin," received the 1997 National Play Award from the National Repertory Theatre Foundation. The $5,000 prize and a staged reading of the play in Hollywood fulfilled a youthful dream to be part of the theater world, and it set me on a course of private writing I hope to continue for the rest of my days.

"Show, not tell," is a motto playwrights share with reporters. And the character studies that playwrights develop before writing a line of dialogue could well be used by the writer preparing a profile. In addition to given characteristics, at least several dozen acquired characteristics can be explored, including: grooming, speech (vocabulary, rhythm, pattern, pauses, volume, inflection, dialect, and accent), preferred entertainment and reading, driving habits, body language (loose versus tight, expressive versus restrained, and graceful versus awkward), and sense of humor (amount, style—how manifested?).

Learning to write scene-by-scene is a handy skill for the newswriter. Once, I helped a writer trim a narrative by using the dictum of the playwright: Don't dawdle. When the scene ends, curtain.

Children's Literature

When you read to a child, notice the simple clarity, the inventiveness, the repetition of words and phrases, the tempo. And just as we read aloud to children, so should we read our copy aloud as we write—and do a final reading aloud before we hit the send key. If you catch your breath, you know that sentence is too long! You'll also hear when sentences are awkward or lack variety in length or tone: short, sharp words for tension, rolling sentences with round sounds for more tranquil passages.

Reread your favorite stories from childhood. They'll jog your imagination, your love of adventure, of fantasy. You'll see ways you, too, can help your reader see things, feel things, and be—truly be—in the stories you write. My friend Dennis Jackson, who at the age of thirty-nine developed a debilitating illness, says that he used his time as a shut-in to "read all the children's books I'd missed as a child," and that he "grew to love A. A. Milne's *Pooh* books and every word E. B. White wrote for kids." One of our *Orange County Register* workshoppers, Ron Campbell, read to us from Dr. Seuss (Theodore Giesel), he of *Cat in the Hat* fame. Ron also introduced us to the favorites of his sons—Peter, nine, and Andrew, three—including Maurice Sendak's *Where the Wild Things Are* and Margaret Wise Brown's 1947 classic *Goodnight Moon.*

And . . . Four Workshop Activities

Activity 1. Here's a way to flex your word muscles: Do timed-writing exercises. Try one at your next writers' workshop. Take five minutes in which to write nonstop on a subject the leader announces just before the word, "go." No pauses. No rewriting. No stopping to correct spelling or grammar. Keep that editing hand out of sight. Allow your thoughts to wander. Relax. A few subjects to try: "My favorite Campbell's Soup is . . . "; or, "My first experience at a scene of violence was . . . "; or, "I remember school lunches because . . . "; or, "My favorite dog—or cat—was . . . "; or, "The first time I had a date was . . ." At the end, people read their efforts aloud. You'll be amazed at the sprightly writing that emerges. The lesson here is to learn to trust your first ideas. They give your copy its freshness and vitality. Too often, we censor our ideas and wind up submitting warmed-over third or fourth ideas that are dull or, worse, trite.

Another lesson from timed-writing exercises: Writing is best when we write with the senses—all of them. Sight comes easily, but we seldom write about touch, sound, taste, or smell.

And we forget to draw upon personal memory. When I couldn't find the element I wanted for a column about Crayolas, I did a timed-writing exercise and recalled I once had a Crayola-eating dog. I wrote:

> Beauty, our collie, loved to top off a dinner of leftovers . . . with a heaping helping of Crayolas. . . . Beauty's crime came to light during a spring thaw. We lived in the north country then and winter snows covered whatever fell beside the path, including Beauty's daily bowel movements. When the snow melted, there they were, her brilliantly colored deposits encased in ice; her artistic contribution to the landscape. . . . Rainbows happen.[14]

Another time, my column on superstition was going awry. I fear superstition, but all my examples were lighthearted. When I did a timed-writing exercise, I surprised myself by uncovering the source of my fear. I remembered that when I was young, my grandmother read tea leaves and always found good things in my cup—good news, money, travel. But once she looked in my cup and blanched. She saw a mysterious man in a long black coat, she said, and she feared he was coming after me. I was terrified. I ended my column: "I watched for that stranger for the longest time, but in the end, he came for her. She died that year."[15]

Activity 2. To stretch the imagination, gather some pictures by your photographers but leave off the cutlines about the actual person or event shown. A set of enlarged glossy prints mounted on heavy cardboard works best. Distribute a photo to each writer who must create an event or situation that will suit the photo, though it might be far from what actually happened. Then, in five minutes, have each write a lead based on that imaginary incident. You'll have some laughs, some sad moments, and always excitement about ideas.

Activity 3. Canvas your region and find successful authors, poets, and people who write for other media. Invite them to your workshops to share their writing techniques firsthand.

Activity 4. Experiment with other genres of writing by trying them yourself. Write a scene for a play. Write a poem. Write a comedy routine for TV. Write an essay. Every writer in my workshops must contribute a "Real Life" column that appears weekly in the *Register*. (For some, this is their shocking first experience of essay-writing since college.) The columns are

---

14. Lucille S. deView, "Retrospective: The Many Colors of Fun Now Radiate Scents of Wonder," *Orange County Register*, Sept. 7, 1994, p. E-3.

15. Lucille S. deView, "Retrospective: Superstitions of Youth Are Nothing to Knock-Knock," *Orange County Register*, March 29, 1995, p. E-3.

drawn from a personal experience or observation of the writer. Essays are generally remembrances, epiphanies, parables, pratfalls, insights, lessons learned. Writers are often astounded at the way readers respond to such intimate writing. They identify. They call. They write. They become fans of your writing. The column gives "first-person" writing a good name. And, if things go well, the writer can bring the emotions from the essays into his or her writing to fulfill the need for storytelling at its best.

At the first workshop I held on poetry, we were stunned at the beauty of a poem written by then-sportswriter Matt McHale. I asked for a copy, thinking I might compile a book of poems and other workshop efforts. Matt was too shy to have his poem included.

"Look, Lucille," he said, "my poem doesn't have to have a practical purpose. Think about what it does to you to suddenly realize you are a writer, and that you belong in this world of writers. That does wonders all by itself."

It does.

Literary Theft: Taking Techniques from the Classics

By Lynn Franklin

[Franklin is editor of WriterL, an online writing workshop, and cofounder of *bylines*, an online publisher of literary nonfiction. Her nonfiction novella *Comfort Me with Apples* appeared on *bylines* in 1997.]

> If I have seen further . . . it is by standing upon the shoulders of Giants.
>
> —Sir Isaac Newton, "Letter to Robert Hooke," 1675

Too few journalists appreciate Newton's idea of building upon past discoveries. The emphasis on breaking news focuses attention on the present to the point that it obscures the context of history. Yet deadline pressure is also the best reason journalists should pay attention to history—or, at least, to the history of their literary craft. Reporters simply don't have time to reinvent the wheel.

Although the basic commitment of any nonfiction writer is to the unvarnished truth, the language of the newsroom is fundamentally no different from the language of Shakespeare; a story is a story is a story, whether spun out of the fancies of a Gertrude Stein or the notebook of an experienced reporter. And most of the techniques and devices needed by feature writers or narrative journalists can be taken or adapted from the classic masters of literature.

Literary theft is certainly not a modern notion. The history of literature is rich with innovations that later writers refined or expanded. The first use of a particular device tends to be a prototype. Because prototypes are difficult to read, subsequent refinements of the technique benefit the reader as well as the writer.

Herman Melville, for example, discovered he could add depth to *Moby Dick* by using the color white as a symbol for death and evil. In the course of his experimentation, however, he overused the device, making *Moby Dick* a prototype—and difficult to read. He also tended to beat readers over the head with his symbols. Later authors like John Steinbeck, Virginia Woolf, Edith Wharton, and Jane Kramer built on Melville's technique to increase the power of their works—yet we don't think of them as symbolic writers. Their symbols are more subtly deployed.

In the late 1800s, American psychologist William James described a psychological phenomenon that became the foundation for another new writing technique, "stream of consciousness." James noted that the mind tends to leap from subject to subject in a random, seemingly illogical but in fact associative way. The smell of fresh-baked bread, for example, might trigger the memory of a long-deceased grandmother. James's brother, Henry James, used the insight to experiment with a new type of transition that slipped from point to point not logically but psychologically—in the process inventing the stream-of-consciousness technique of fictional narrative. James Joyce turned this technique into artistic form; William Faulkner polished it. But all three of these novelists were working on prototypes and early design models, which is why their work seemed difficult to their contemporary audience. Today, the technique has been perfected to the point that virtually every capable novelist uses stream of consciousness in a manner so subtle that the technique often seems invisible.

At the end of the nineteenth century, Anton Chekhov—one of the most innovative writers in history—gave new definition to the short story, in the process developing some of the techniques that give modern writing its rapid flow. Chekhov exemplifies the fact that new writing techniques are almost always keyed to the development of the surrounding culture. In this case, the Russian author began his career as a physician, in a time when science was exploding into many specialties and reductionism was being used to define the world at a level that had not previously been thought possible. Astronomers were making fine distinctions in types of stars, taxonomists were busily categorizing plants and animals, and anatomists were taking apart the human body and labeling each piece. It was only natural that Chekhov, when he became a writer, would attempt to do the same with his prose.

In describing the key elements in storycraft, Chekhov built on Aristotle's observation that all good yarns have a beginning, a middle, and an end. Chekhov analyzed each and redefined them functionally as complication, development, and resolution. Then, in that context, he methodically defined the tools in the writer's kit, from foreshadowing to descriptive techniques.

Chekhov was also one of the first writers to condense narrative. One of the reasons Victorian-era books sometime seem so slow and ponderous to today's reader is that they wandered from the plot into meandering, flowery descriptions—it was, after all, a descriptive age. But in this respect Chekhov leaped ahead of his time to eliminate unnecessary passages that impeded the forward flow of his narratives. Later the splendid British short story writer Katherine Mansfield would advance this same effort, declaring that a good story shouldn't have "a single word out of place or one word that could be taken out."[1] Hemingway applied this approach to the actual plot of his narratives. These innovations defined the age of realism in fiction and eventually led to the fast-paced, spare prose we see in many of our finest contemporary novels.

Of course, new writing techniques are forever being developed. Gabriel García Márquez, the celebrated Latin American novelist, recently invented a device that my husband Jon Franklin calls the "interior/exterior transition." Like stream of consciousness, this tool has its basis in psychology and, like Henry James and James Joyce, García Márquez has probably altered the literary landscape. But it will also probably take other writers decades to learn what the technique is and how to use it.

García Márquez's innovation derives from the psychological principle that people often confuse their interior thoughts and imaginings with what is actually happening in the exterior world, especially when they are under extreme stress. We've all experienced the momentary sensation of wondering "did that really happen, or did I just dream of it?" García Márquez used this phenomenon to add realism to his prose. In *The Story of a Shipwrecked Sailor*—based on a real event and originally published as a series of articles in a Colombian newspaper—García Márquez recreated the hallucinations of a sailor lost at sea. He expanded the technique in his novel *A Hundred Years of Solitude,* one of the major books that led to his being named the Nobel Prize laureate in Literature for 1982. Later, Larry McMurtry attempted to translate the technique into the English language

---

1. Mansfield is quoted from C. L. Cline, ed., *The Rinehart Book of Short Stories* (New York: Holt, Rinehart and Winston, 1964), p. 116.

in his immensely popular novel *Lonesome Dove*. Jon Franklin is now working on ways to apply these "interior/exterior transitions" to narrative nonfiction.

Unlike García Márquez, most of us aren't destined to be on the cutting edge of literary history. We simply want to tell our stories in the most powerful ways possible, using the tools that are commonplace in contemporary prose. In this article I'll identify some of the techniques available to us and ways we can apply them to everything from traditional news stories to narrative nonfiction. There's not enough space to delve into the subject in depth, but the basics I'll cover will perhaps give you some fresh ideas for improving your own journalistic copy.

Literary thieves all have their favorite stable of authors worth stealing from, and I certainly have mine. To keep things coherent, I'm going to stick pretty much to a few of those, all of them noted fiction writers. There are numerous excellent writers out there, and they come in all colors and with a wide variety of cultural spins. If you plan to steal, review the literary landscape and select your own models. The ones I've chosen to discuss here are Harper Lee for character and place descriptions; John Steinbeck for symbol, mood, and foreshadowing; Mark Twain for rhythm and descriptions; and William Faulkner for writing on multiple levels.

Surface Techniques

Of all the classic literary tools, the ones that are of most immediate use to journalists are the surface techniques—the ways great writers craft descriptions and create rhythm texture, mood, and other readily apparent elements of prose. These are tools that all journalists need; at some point every one of us must describe, say, a five-car pileup or the quirky way our profile subject lights a cigarette. Unfortunately, most such descriptions read like this:

> A Saturday afternoon in November was approaching the time of twilight, and the vast tract of unenclosed wild known as Egdon Heath embrowned itself moment by moment. Overhead the hollow stretch of whitish cloud shutting out the sky was as a tent which had the whole heath for its floor.[2]

---

2. Thomas Hardy, *The Return of the Native* (New York: New American Library, 1959).

And so on, for another three pages. Another example:

> [My room] had a pinewood floor scrubbed white, with two small bright pseudo-Persian rugs, solid pine furniture, and one reasonably comfortable chair. There was a really beautiful old chest of dark wood with painted panels, a rather inconvenient wardrobe, and a lot of heavy wrought ironwork in the lamp brackets and on the door, which was studded and barred like something from a Gothic cathedral.[3]

And on and on.

You may have recognized the first example here as the opening paragraph from Thomas Hardy's *The Return of the Native* (1878). The second is from one of my favorite mystery writers, Mary Stewart. Though written almost a century apart, the two descriptions are equally boring, moving aimlessly from adjective to simile and back again. Hardy, however, had an excuse for his lapse: He was born before the realists discovered the secret to more effective fictional description.

The secret is a quality called *movement.* It is achieved in part by making your words serve multiple purposes. This means that description can and should do more than just describe. It should set a scene, create mood, hint at character traits. In this way, good description moves the story along.

Compare the previous descriptions with this early passage from Harper Lee's *To Kill a Mockingbird* (1960):

> Maycomb was an old town, but it was a tired old town when I first knew it. In rainy weather the streets turned to red slop; grass grew on the sidewalks, the courthouse sagged in the square. Somehow, it was hotter then: a black dog suffered on a summer's day; bony mules hitched to Hoover carts flicked flies in the sweltering shade of the live oaks on the square. Men's stiff collars wilted by nine in the morning. Ladies bathed before noon, after their three-o'clock naps, and by nightfall were like soft teacakes with frostings of sweat and sweet talcum.[4]

Lee uses as many adjectives and similes as Hardy and Stewart. The difference is that Lee's passage does more than describe the town. It carries the readers back in time. It characterizes both the town and the people who

---

3. Mary Stewart, *Airs Above the Ground* (New York: Fawcett Crest, 1965), p. 65.
4. Harper Lee, *To Kill a Mockingbird* (New York: Warner, 1960), pp. 9–10.

live there. And it sets the pace of the story; like the townspeople, Lee's tale follows a leisurely stroll punctuated by moments of high drama. By serving many purposes, Lee's description moves the story along. It is the single-purpose descriptions that appear static.

It's a bit more difficult to apply these criteria to descriptions of people, but it can be done. As always, you need to think in terms of multiple purposes. Saying someone has brown hair and blue eyes gives only a surface appearance. Adding that the eyes are a cold shade of blue starts to hint of the personality. Simply, the more layers of meaning your descriptions add, the more effective the descriptions become. And this can be as true of journalistic writing as of fiction.

Here's another good example from *To Kill a Mockingbird:*

> Calpurnia was something else again. She was all angles and bones; she was nearsighted; she squinted; her hand was wide as a bed slat and twice as hard.[5]

Not only does Harper Lee tell us something about Calpurnia's physical appearance and personality; she tells us as well about the personality of the narrator. And the description implies action. The narrator Scout clearly has firsthand knowledge of the hardness of Calpurnia's hand.

Classic description enables the reader to visualize a person or a place. But description can also contribute to the story's mood. (The key word here is "also"; descriptions should rarely, if ever, be used exclusively to set mood.) The best writers create mood by paying attention to the texture and feel of the words themselves. The mood of *To Kill a Mockingbird* is reflective, and the texture of sentences like "Maycomb was an old town, but it was a tired old town . . ." creates this mood.

One of the best examples of mood setting is the opening of *The Grapes of Wrath.* In only a few paragraphs, John Steinbeck describes the arrival of the Dust Bowl, establishes the bleak atmosphere of the story, and touches the reader's own feelings of helplessness. He accomplishes this by using concrete, exact language:

> To the red country and part of the gray country of Oklahoma,
> the last rains came gently, and they did not cut the scarred earth.
> . . . The clouds appeared, and went away, and in a while they did
> not try any more. The weeds grew darker green to protect them-
> selves, and they did not spread any more.

5. Ibid, p. 10.

... And as the sharp sun struck day after day, the leaves of the young corn became less stiff and erect; they bent in a curve at first, and then, as the central ribs of strength grew weak, each leaf tilted downward. Then it was June, and the sun shone more fiercely. The brown lines on the corn leaves widened and moved in on the central ribs. The weeds frayed and edged back toward their roots. The air was thin and the sky more pale; and every day the earth paled.[6]

Steinbeck's descriptive passage actually shows movement and change in the scenery; the healthy green corn goes limp, withers, and, ultimately, turns brown. At the same time, the image of slowly dying corn plants creates a mood of need and desperation that continues throughout the story.

Joan Didion achieves a similar effect in the opening of her classic non-fiction book *Slouching Towards Bethlehem:*

The San Bernardino Valley lies only an hour east of Los Angeles by the San Bernardino Freeway but is in certain ways an alien place: not the coastal California of the subtropical twilights and the soft westerlies off the Pacific but a harsher California, haunted by the Mojave just beyond the mountains, devastated by the hot dry Santa Ana wind that comes down through the passes at 100 miles an hour and whines through the eucalyptus windbreaks and works on the nerves. October is the bad month for the wind, the month when breathing is difficult and the hills blaze up spontaneously. There has been no rain since April. Every voice seems a scream. It is the season of suicide and divorce and prickly dread, wherever the wind blows.[7]

Such effective nonfiction description can likewise be found in Tom Wolfe's *The Right Stuff,* Lillian Ross's *Reporting,* and Susan Sheehan's *A Welfare Mother,* to name just a few of the better examples available.

In the above instances, movement is enhanced by making the descriptive passages serve multiple purposes. Another way to add movement to your writing is through the rhythm of words and sentences. Too few journalists think of rhythm in writing, but without it, linguists say, language would be formless and indefinite. Truman Capote claimed that a faulty rhythm could ruin an entire story, particularly if it occurred at the end.

---

6. John Steinbeck, *Grapes of Wrath* (New York: Viking, 1939), p. 1.
7. Joan Didion, *Slouching Towards Bethlehem* (New York: Dell, 1968), p. 3.

Rhythm makes copy easier to read, and in this way it adds meaning to the language.

If you yearn to get more rhythm into your writing, revisit Edgar Allan Poe's stories or poems, and read them aloud. His rhythms are so obvious that even those of us with tin ears can hear them. Then progress to poets with more subtle rhythms. It's a matter of education. Eventually, you'll become aware of the rhythms used by your favorite writers. For me, the passages from Harper Lee, Steinbeck, and Didion all seem memorably rhythmical.

But the author whose prose rhythms strike me the most powerfully is Mark Twain. Ever wonder why he gets away with writing dialect while most of us fall on our faces attempting it? His success, I believe, comes in the way he uses rhythm to make his dialect readable. Try reading *Huckleberry Finn* (1884) aloud:

> Tom's most well, now, and got his bullet around his neck on a watch-guard for a watch, and is always seeing what time it is, and so there ain't nothing more to write about, and I am rotten glad of it, because if I'd a knowed what a trouble it was to make a book I wouldn't a tackled it and ain't agoing to no more.[8]

Thanks to Twain's understanding of rhythm, Huck and Jim and Tom come alive for people living more than a century later.

Truman Capote, Tom Wolfe, and Jon Franklin are among the recent *nonfiction* writers who, in my view, handle rhythm particularly well.

No discussion of description is complete without mentioning the use of figurative language and symbol. We've already seen several good similes: Calpurnia's hard-as-a-bed-slat hand, the teacake softness of Maycomb's ladies. Metaphors and similes should be used sparingly. They should be precise. And they should work on multiple levels. Harper Lee's choice of a bed slat to describe Calpurnia's hands was no accident. If you think about it, a bed slat resembles the paddles used to discipline children. The spankings also hint at violence, and expected violence, between races—and a certain hardness of mind that reverberates perfectly with the story. So the simile works on multiple levels.

Symbols can also add depth to your story, but here's a caution: Symbols are much easier to overuse or use inappropriately. Similes are relatively forgiving, but one bungled symbol can destroy a piece. A symbol should

---

8. Mark Twain, *Adventures of Huckleberry Finn,* ed. Henry Nash Smith (Boston: Houghton Mifflin, 1958), p. 245.

always deepen the story's meaning. It should serve a specific purpose that is consistent with the plot. It should arise naturally from the copy and not be forced into existence. Where metaphors and similes are conscious devices that compare two things, symbols are subconscious ones—and tend to reveal themselves as you write. The reader should not notice that you've created a symbol. It should blend into the story, and recur several times as the story unfolds. Each reference will then build on the previous one, deepening the meaning of both symbol and story.

A clear example of this can be found in chapter 3 of Steinbeck's *Grapes of Wrath*. In three short pages, Steinbeck describes a turtle trying to cross a concrete highway. As it drags its shell through tall grass and wild oats, an oat seed gets caught in its shell. It comes to the highway embankment and must haul itself over the hill. As it crosses the highway, vehicles pass. One veers to avoid it. Another intentionally sideswipes the turtle, flipping it onto its back and sending it spinning to the edge of the road. When the turtle finally rights itself, the oat seed drops from its shell. The turtle proceeds on its way. The passage clearly enough symbolizes the struggles of living, the way humans themselves must overcome obstacles. Fate—symbolized by the vehicles—sometimes passes us by, leaving us unharmed; other times it seems intentionally to make life more difficult. But in the process of living, we spread the seed of new life.

Steinbeck violates several of the recommendations I made earlier. The turtle appears only once in the book. And setting it apart in a separate chapter draws attention to it. Focused as it is on the struggles of that lone turtle, this brief chapter mystifies some readers, but as the narrative unfolds, the significance of the turtle's tale becomes clear. The symbol is subtle and specific enough that it works. Take a look at that chapter—it'll likely give you strong ideas for using symbols in your copy.

Jane Kramer demonstrates how effectively symbols can be used in nonfiction in her book *The Last Cowboy*. Her story follows a modern cowboy as he tries to cope with this dying way of life. As the narrative progresses, Kramer shows the cowboy becoming increasingly frustrated with changes he can't control. Finally, in the last chapter, she describes the cowboy's angry castration of a neighbor's bull that has strayed onto his land—an act that symbolizes the cowboy's own feelings of inadequacy and impotence.

One of the biggest pitfalls in writing descriptions is the tendency to fall into cliché. Most of us know to avoid phrases such as "cold as ice" or "it was a dark, stormy night." But we often don't realize that we can actually see the world as a cliché and how that affects our writing. In this day of television sitcoms and action videos, far too many writers notice only the stylized gestures and habits portrayed in most visual media. Surprise is illustrated by the widening of the eyes; fear by a trembling hand; sorrow by a single tear. The world is richer than this. Yet modern writing seldom depicts the sensual wealth available to us. Georgia O'Keefe described this problem memorably when she wrote: "Nobody sees a flower—really—it is so small—we haven't time. . . . So I said to myself—I'll paint what I see—what the flower is to me but I'll paint it big and they will be surprised into taking time to look at it."[9]

To write good descriptions, we need to take the time to see—really see—the world around us, to notice detail that our readers don't have time to see. And not just see, but feel, hear, smell, taste. . . . The world we describe is alive with sensory detail that subtly influences our thoughts and emotions, but that most people don't consciously notice. It is this detail, however, that can make your copy come alive.

Here, for example, is a passage from *Huckleberry Finn,* where Huck stands on the riverbank watching a man chopping wood on the other side of the river:

> You see the ax flash and come down—you don't hear nothing; you see that ax go up again, and by the time it's above the man's head, then you hear the *k'chunk!*—it had took all that time to come over the water.[10]

Most people don't consciously notice the delay in sound when it travels a distance. By describing this phenomenon, Twain brought the observation into the reader's consciousness and, in the process, made the scene much more real in the reader's mind.

Foreshadowing

One technique that the best journalists use to add power to their work—but one that you seldom hear mentioned in a newsroom—is foreshadowing. It often makes the difference between a great story and a merely good one. Foreshadowing builds suspense by providing hints of what is to come. It is a technique that has been used by storytellers since long before Homer was born. Shakespeare, in the early acts of his plays, typically foreshadowed his endings:

---

9. O'Keefe is quoted in *One Hundred Flowers,* ed. Nicholas Calloway (New York: Knopf, 1987), p. 2.

10. Twain, *Huckleberry Finn,* p. 100.

> I fear, too early. For my mind misgives
>   Some consequence, yet hanging in the stars. . . ."[11]

By today's standards, of course, this description of Romeo's fears (in Act I) may seem too obvious; Shakespeare did tend to be heavy-handed with his foreshadowing, but his wasn't a modern audience. As with movement, today's audiences expect more subtlety than earlier generations did, and modern writers must make the necessary adjustments. But the thing that hasn't changed is the ability of good foreshadowing to build suspense and prime the reader's subconscious for later events. Foreshadowing is another instance in which good copy says more than one thing, and so it, too, tends to quicken pace and intensify meaning. Ultimately, when the story fully unfolds, the foreshadowing enhances the emotional satisfaction the reader feels at the narrative's end.

Foreshadowing is one of the hardest things for journalists to learn. Partly, that's because it's just difficult to achieve in its own right. On top of that, we are emphatically taught to write stories using inverted pyramid structures that preclude any use of foreshadowing of an ending that's all too evident before any narrative is even launched. Foreshadowing also involves a mixing, or piggy-backing, of information that runs against our composition teachers' admonition that we should sharply separate different subjects. If you're writing a term paper about beekeeping, for example, the composition-class rule calls for you to devote one section to bee anatomy, a separate one to the workings of the hive, and so on. This is subject organization and tends to produce dull prose—though, admittedly, it is a structure that most college freshmen need to master. Real stories, however, are action-based. This means they are chronological, which automatically forces us to weave subject matter. Foreshadowing is a critical part of this process.

Most writers are familiar with Chekhov's description of foreshadowing: "If in the first chapter you say that a gun hung on the wall, in the second or third chapter it must without fail be discharged."[12] Though this is a good example, it lends itself to misinterpretation. It implies that the writer should use the gun later in the story simply because he'd introduced it in the first chapter. From the writer's point of view, foreshadowing is the reverse of

---

11. William Shakespeare, *Romeo and Juliet*, I.iv.106–07, in *Shakespeare: The Complete Works,* ed. G. B. Harrison (New York: Harcourt, Brace & World, 1968), p. 481.

12. Chekhov is quoted in Donald M. Murray's *Shoptalk: Learning to Write with Writers* (Portsmouth, N.H.: Boynton/Cook, 1990), p. 149.

Chekhov's statement: If you're going to have someone fire a gun late in your story, then you need to mention that gun earlier—if, indeed, that gun plays a meaningful part in your narrative. Foreshadowing can be, in fact, a form of "backwriting." The writer goes back through the copy and adds foreshadowing to prepare the reader for later events. (Backwriting can also yield symbol and metaphor.)

An easy way to observe good foreshadowing at work is to go to your video store and rent *How to Steal a Million Dollars,* the old film starring Audrey Hepburn and Peter O'Toole. Like many romantic comedies, the plot is simple: Hepburn and O'Toole's characters lay plans to steal a statue from a burglar-proof museum. What makes this movie exceptional is the attention paid to setting up the final scene. Every single item that O'Toole uses to steal that statue was foreshadowed somewhere earlier in the film. In doing this, the screenwriters demonstrated their understanding of Chekhov's advice about storytelling: Any device that you're going to use at the climax or resolution of your story likely needs to be mentioned earlier. This is related to the "character rule," which says that every major character in the story should be introduced by the time the complication is made clear.

Have you ever read a mystery in which the criminal turns out to be someone newly introduced in the narrative? Or in which the hero suddenly flies into a judo stance—and we had no idea he *knew* judo? Those are examples of what happens when you don't foreshadow; the reader stops thinking about your story and starts wondering "Huh, where did *that* come from?" You've lost the impact you've worked so hard to create. It is for this reason that writers often work on their elements of foreshadowing *after* they've written the final scenes. Generally, by this point, you've written an entire draft. When you get to the ending, you'll be able to tell what needs to be foreshadowed earlier.

For example, is there a secondary character who says something that helps your main character resolve a problem? If so, you need to introduce that individual earlier and foreshadow whatever trait it is that leads that person to say that specific thing at the end. Does your main character herself have a particular skill that assists in resolving the story complication? Again, you need to foreshadow that skill.

This does *not* mean that you are going to give away the ending. Think of foreshadowing as setup. The best foreshadowing is subtle and is woven into the story—often in multiple ways. In this fashion, foreshadowing helps build tension and gives resonance and power to the story.

One of the best literary examples of well-done foreshadowing is Steinbeck's *Of Mice and Men.* If you'll recall, the story follows George and

Lennie, two drifters who wander from job to job. Lennie is a large, retard-
ed man who is unaware of his own strength. George tries to keep Lennie
out of trouble, but at the story's end, Lennie accidentally strangles a
woman. Rather than have Lennie taken to jail or an asylum, George shoots
and kills him.

Steinbeck begins foreshadowing that ending in the very first scene.
George catches Lennie carrying a dead mouse in his pocket, and Lennie
swears "I didn't kill it. . . . I found it dead."[13] George makes Lennie throw
it away and promise he won't do "bad things" like he'd done at the ranch
they'd just left. So we've got an image of death and the idea that Lennie has
done something "bad" at an earlier job. (The mouse is also, of course, a
powerful symbol—another example of multiple use.)

Some of the foreshadowing in *Of Mice and Men* seems pretty obvious
to anyone who studies it. But the reader isn't studying—she is reading faster
and faster and faster. As the story proceeds, George makes further reference to the bad things that Lennie does. Then Lennie accidentally kills a
puppy. This further bit of foreshadowing creates tension; the reader subconsciously knows that something awful is going to happen.

But perhaps the most effective piece of foreshadowing in the book is a
scene that occurs in the bunkhouse. A ranch hand named Carlson con-
vinces old man Candy it's time to shoot Candy's ancient dog, essentially to
"put him out of his misery." Candy doesn't have the heart to do the deed,
so Carlson takes the dog outside. The scene proceeds:

> A shot sounded in the distance. The men looked quickly at the
> old man. Every head turned toward him.
>
> For a moment he continued to stare at the ceiling. Then he
> rolled slowly over and faced the wall and lay silent. (54)

Later in the story, George and the others discover the dead woman's body.
Candy watches George go off with the group to search for Lennie. Staring
down at the dead woman, Candy mutters "Poor bastard." Then,

> The sound of the men grew fainter. The barn was darkening
> gradually and, in their stalls, the horses shifted their feet and rat-
> tled the halter chains. Old Candy lay down in the hay and cov-
> ered his eyes with his arms. (108)

---

13. John Steinbeck, *Of Mice and Men* (New York: Bantam, 1958), p. 6. (Further page references to this novel will be cited parenthetically in my text.)

Candy's lying down and covering his eyes echoes the earlier scene in the bunkhouse in which, after hearing the shot that killed his dog, he showed no emotion but, instead, rolled over and visually blocked out the world. It's the reader who, at this point, begins to feel the emotion.

Meanwhile, George finds Lennie sitting by the same pond we saw in the original scene. Lennie has clearly forgotten all about killing the woman. George pulls out his gun and hesitates, much as Candy hesitated before making the decision to have his dog shot. But unlike Candy, George finds the nerve to shoot his own "pet":

> And George raised the gun and steadied it, and he brought the muzzle of it close to the back of Lennie's head. The hand shook violently, but his face set and his hand steadied. He pulled the trigger. The crash of the shot rolled up the hills and rolled down again. Lennie jarred, and then settled slowly forward to the sand, and he lay without quivering. George shivered and looked at the gun, and then he threw it from him, back up on the bank, near the pile of old ashes. (117)

The scenes with Candy and his dog foreshadow both George's ultimate actions and his grief. One might say that the story consisted of all the foreshadowing being brought together in a single act—though, of course, Steinbeck did it in reverse order. The foreshadowing also made it possible for the writer to render the entire climax as action, without having to pause to describe George's thoughts. Yet the reader feels the pain. So in the closing scene, when Slim leads George back to the ranch, the reader subconsciously understands that George was Candy's "poor bastard."

Because you won't—and sometimes can't—know what you need to foreshadow until you've completed at least a rough draft of a story, foreshadowing very often becomes a product of backwriting. Look at the end of the draft and ask which elements are most important to that ending: Was it the character's ability to adapt? His or her need for love or attention? Or, perhaps, the character's courage? Which elements, in short, made the ending possible? Once you've decided *what* to foreshadow, you need to go back through the story and add foreshadowing details and references. If, for example, your character's courage is essential to the ending, you'll need to show the character making—or struggling to make—small courageous decisions earlier on.

Keep in mind that when you foreshadow something once, you open the reader's mind to it. Every time you foreshadow it again, it becomes deeper and more symbolic. So to obtain the maximum impact, try to foreshadow the most important elements of your ending multiple times. Good writers develop a sensitivity to this.

More about Writing on Multiple Levels

The best stories—the ones that create experiences that evoke strong emotion in the reader—tend to work on multiple levels. The action, or plot, takes place on the surface level. Below that is the symbolic or psychological level. And below that, the rhythmic level (the *pacing* of the narrative).

The surface level is pretty obvious. In *Of Mice and Men* the surface story is about George's trying unsuccessfully to protect Lennie—and his eventual decision to shoot him.

The symbolic and psychological level is more complex. Candy and his old dog represent the relationship between George and Lennie; Lennie is essentially George's pet. At the end of the story, George puts his pet out of its misery. Psychologically, *Of Mice and Men* is about responsibility and the enormous emotional toll that comes with love.

In order for journalists to write their nonfiction stories on this psychological level, they must actually report on emotions and thoughts. Just as a political writer looks for nervous ticks, shifting eyes, and other signs of evasion, the narrative writer learns to read the signs that provide clues to people's inner lives. The literary journalist, for example, makes note of the things that Tom Wolfe called "status life": everyday gestures, poses, styles of walking, manners. But, more importantly, the narrative writer interviews subjects about their thoughts and feelings. Most people, of course, aren't introspective enough to immediately answer direct questions such as, "How did that make you feel?" or, "What were you thinking?" But if the writer asks smart, relevant questions, the subject will think about them and will eventually provide an answer. You'd be amazed at how often people will call you back and enthusiastically answer a psychological question you'd posed days earlier.

The psychological level works on a broader level as well; there will be an overarching psychology for the story itself. For example, if it is a tale of loss and subsequent growth, the psychological level might focus on an individual's struggles to overcome pain, to find the strength to carry on. Similarly, a story about the injustice of the court system might be the psychological story of an individual learning to live in a world that isn't always fair. Such a story might show the individual learning to overcome the inevitable anger. Identifying the overarching psychological level will tell you where to focus your interview questions.

The third story level involves the rhythm or pacing of the narrative. Just as words and sentences have rhythm, the story narrative itself changes tempo, flowing from slow to fast rhythms and back. Generally, moments of peak action or emotion have a staccato rhythm; sentences or phrases are short and crisp, adjectives minimal. Preparatory narrative tends to be more melodious with longer sentences and more adjectives. Compare the following two descriptions, again taken from *Of Mice and Men:*

> [1] A few miles south of Soledad, the Salinas River drops in close to the hillside bank and runs deep and green. The water is warm too, for it has slipped twinkling over the yellow sands in the sunlight before reaching the narrow pool. On one side of the river the golden foothill slopes curve up to the strong and rocky Gabilan mountains, but on the valley side the water is lined with trees—willows fresh and green with every spring, carrying in their lower leaf junctures the debris of the winter's flooding; and sycamores with mottled, white, recumbent limbs and branches that arch over the pool. (1)

> [2] The little evening breeze blew over the clearing and the leaves rustled and the wind waves flowed up the green pool. And the shouts of men sounded again, this time much closer than before. (115)

The first description is from the opening of Steinbeck's novel. Notice the long sentences and flowing rhythm. If the words were put to music, the rhythm might be a fox trot or a waltz. Just as in symphonic music, the more leisurely rhythm not only sets up the early, preparatory scenes but also contrasts with the fast-paced rhythms that occur at peak moments. The second description—taken from near the book's end, just before George shoots Lennie—consists of short phrases and a more staccato beat. In such high-tension scenes, a more leisurely rhythm would jar the reader and destroy the emotional impact Steinbeck had set up.

While I've taken these two examples from this novel's beginning and end, you'll find alternating slow and fast rhythms throughout the narrative as you move from setup to action and back. (Remember, however, that even when you're slowing the rhythm, you must still have movement; otherwise, you'll lose your reader.) Generally, as you near the story's end, the average rhythm and pace increases. Just as the frenzied music in an action movie's chase scenes raises the viewer's emotional level, so the quickening of the rhythm in the climax of a narrative increases the reader's heart rate. Such is the power of rhythm, which, at the base level of the symphony of story, subtly or not so subtly colors all that is above it.

William Faulkner was a master of symphonic prose, and one of the best places to see these three levels at work is in his short story "Barn Burning." Even if you've been unable to fathom some of Faulkner's longer works, you should take a look at this piece, which, for all its simplicity, creates reverberations among all three levels. The story is about an easily offended migrant worker who takes revenge on his employers by burning their barns. The story is told through the eyes of one of his sons. Brilliantly crafted, the tale elicits strong emotion in the reader without resorting to sentimentality or purple prose. In one scene, for example, the boy and his father are walking up the street to the home of their new employer. The boy has fallen behind and is observing his father:

> Watching him, the boy remarked the absolutely undeviating course which his father held and saw the stiff foot come squarely down in a pile of fresh droppings where a horse had stood in the drive and which his father could have avoided by a simple change of stride.

A few moments later, the boy's father marches into the employer's house, tracking horse manure all over the white rug. As he confronts the employer's wife, his son looks on:

> His father had not spoken again. He did not speak again. He did not even look at her. He just stood stiff in the center of the rug, in his hat, the shaggy iron-gray brows twitching slightly above the pebble-colored eyes as he appeared to examine the house with brief deliberation. Then with the same deliberation he turned; the boy watched him pivot on the good leg and saw the stiff foot drag round the arc of the turning, leaving a final long and fading smear. His father never looked at it, he never once looked down at the rug. The Negro held the door. It closed behind them, upon the hysteric and indistinguishable woman-wail. His father stopped at the top of the steps and scraped his boot clean on the edge of it. At the gate he stopped again. He stood for a moment, planted stiffly on the stiff foot, looking back at the house. "Pretty and white, ain't it?" he said.[14]

---

14. William Faulkner, "Barn Burning," in *Selected Short Stories of William Faulkner* (New York: Modern Library, 1961), pp. 11, 13.

On the surface level, the scene is simply the migrant worker paying a visit to his new employer and, on the way, accidentally stepping in horse manure. On the psychological level, the scene is about the worker's contempt for his employers and his passive-aggressive ways of terrorizing them. On the rhythmic level, the tempo alternates between a slow and fast march. Notice how, in the above passage, the rhythm changes pace. Faulkner uses short sentences and phrases to describe the father standing in the room. But as soon as the man turns around to wipe the manure into the rug, Faulkner slows the rhythm; the reader can actually feel the father wiping his feet on the carpet. That act is accented by the writer's then picking up the tempo, returning to shorter phrases and sentences and ending with a quote which, for all purposes, is a single crash of cymbals.

Nowhere does Faulkner state out loud that the father is an angry man, that he resents the wealthy. He doesn't need to; the man's actions, his "undeviating course" for the horse droppings, the subsequent movements in the house, capture the man's psychology. In the process, we, the readers, feel the son's shame, humiliation, and mounting rage. This is why stories written on multiple levels are so powerful.

The finest nonfiction writers also commonly work on all the three levels I've described. To name but one example, Cynthia Gorney is particularly adept at writing on multiple levels and has demonstrated this in scores of compelling feature articles written over the years for the *Washington Post,* the *New York Times Magazine, Mother Jones,* and other publications. She can evoke emotion even in what appears on the surface to be a simple travel piece. (If you can lay hands on her story "Trail of Fire," featured in the *Washington Post* back in the 1980s, you'll see a master at work.)

The truth is that most experienced writers subconsciously work on the three levels—they just don't appreciate the power of the instrument they're playing and perhaps don't have full control. By consciously writing on multiple levels, you can shape your stories more expertly, and your batting average for really effective pieces will improve.

—

I've touched on a sampling of the ways by which journalists can steal technique from classic writers. All of these particular techniques are relatively easy to translate from fiction to nonfiction. Since journalists by nature are realistic writers, the simplest classic authors for them to steal from are those in the realist tradition. Steinbeck's descriptive passages could easily be nonfiction. The techniques of Twain, Hemingway, F. Scott Fitzgerald, and Edith Wharton also translate fairly easily.

But don't be afraid to steal from other good writing as well. As you make your selection, keep two criteria in mind. For one, choose writers whose sound you like. You don't necessarily have to agree with their message. You just need to appreciate the way they say things. And secondly, select writers who've had an impact on their civilization. Simply put, if you're going to steal, steal from the best.

In the process, don't forget holy books. Hemingway once bragged that he'd stolen everything there was to steal in the Bible, but he was exaggerating; there are many more ideas and techniques to be found and used there. Because of the cultural differences, it may be more difficult for a Westerner to steal from the Koran, but I've no doubt it can be done. Anything that has lasted, that has shaped religions or civilizations, is certified to be powerful.

Everyone steals what can most be used. Just for the record, the Newton quote I started with was not his original idea. He stole it from Lucan, a Roman poet who died in A.D. 65. Lucan's original quote was: "Pygmies placed on the shoulders of giants see more than the giants themselves."[15] We don't have a record of where Lucan stole the idea.

But as for the act of theft itself, T.S. Eliot probably said it best: "Immature poets imitate; mature poets steal."[16]

---

15. Lucan is quoted in *Bartlett's Familiar Quotations,* 15th Ed. (Boston: Little, Brown, 1980), p. 118.

16. T. S. Eliot, "Phillip Massinger," in T. S. Eliot, *The Sacred Wood: Essays on Poetry and Criticism* (London: Methuen, 1964), p. 125.

Business Writing That Screams "Read Me!"

By Tom Silvestri

[Silvestri is vice president in charge of Media General Inc. community newspapers in Alabama, South Carolina, Virginia, and Florida. Previously, he was an award-winning business editor at the Richmond, Virginia, *Times-Dispatch*.]

We were three weeks into the launch of a new Monday section when one of my bosses stopped me after the morning meeting and said, "I've got some ideas on Metro Business I'd like to show you, particularly on the writing."

"Sure," I responded. "Do you need me to gather up the staff for a meeting?"

"No," he said. "I'll just drop by your desk sometime after deadline."

Until that day, most reactions to the new publication had dealt with artwork, design, and general appearances. Illustrations for the cover had been banned because the first issue featured one that looked like an editorial cartoon. Poorly conceived formats had been redone. Theme pages had been tweaked so related information could be better packaged. White space, particularly between the folios and headlines, had consumed discussion at many postpublication meetings.

Not much had been said outside the department about the *writing*. That worried me.

Despite the expansion of coverage and all the innovations, Metro Business was banking its success on how well the writing attracted readers who normally shunned the business page. These were readers who would volunteer for experimental root-canal surgery or clean out a Port-A-John with a toothbrush rather than admit they enjoyed the prose from local business reporters. Many of the nontraditional readers were working women, recent college graduates, minorities, and others who didn't frequent Main Street. To them, business news was a wasteland of tortured sentences filled with numbers, jargon, acronyms, and self-serving propaganda from corporate spin doctors, as well as a country club of sorts with some bizarre admission standards that involved your bank account, your contacts, and your pedigree.

Shortly after 2:00 P.M., I could hear my boss's distinctive footsteps rounding the corner, headed for my desk. In one motion, he plopped down a folded copy of a newspaper, swung around for an intended quick exit, and said simply, "Here's what I was talking about."

It was a two-day-old *Wall Street Journal.* Two stories had big blue circles around their headlines: column 6, where the *Journal* parks its thorough stories on recent news, and the middle column, where some of the finest offbeat stories appear.

"We need more stories like these," he said. "That's what Metro Business should run."

That was it. The critique was over: Read the *Wall Street Journal.* Copy the *Wall Street Journal.* Be the *Wall Street Journal.* Thanks, boss.

We won't get into my reaction or that of my reporters who watched the exchange. Let's just say it was nuclear.

When I tell this story at business writing workshops, complete with an imitation of handing the folded-over, marked-up *Journal* to an unsuspecting editor, it usually draws a large laugh.

But I add a different setup line: "Don't do this to your staff."

Don't walk up to business writers at your small- to medium-size daily or weekly newspaper and nuke them with the blanket statement: "Do this: Be like the *Wall Street Journal.*"

It's too easy, too shortsighted. It's also not fair.

True, the *Journal* is the best model for business journalism. But it has luxuries that reporters and editors at community publications can never afford:

- The time to take months to research (yes, research), report, write, rewrite (yes, rewrite), edit, and polish (yes, polish, too);
- The resolve to publish only excellent work and run stories because they are ready and not just because editors have to fill up pages;

- The strength of a large, worldwide staff that ensures a steady pipeline of material and plenty of people to throw at news without robbing or disrupting other sections;
- The prestige that opens doors to information from sources eager to be associated with the best; and
- The confidence to mix levity with seriousness, innovation with the routine, and front-page scoops with pages and pages of tiny type chock-full of numbers.

The *Journal* has it all. So when the workshop-goers laugh at my Metro Business story, they are acknowledging the pain of forever being compared with the profession's leader. At least in the *Journal's* case, readers expect it to be a good read. Readers will tell you that, at most community papers, business news stories are usually boring, incomprehensible, not relevant to their lives, and full of insider passages and quotes that could be summed up with this label: "For us to know and you to find out."

Is that right? Of course not. That's one of the pitfalls of business journalism. But in that injustice comes our opportunity. We can write business stories that scream "READ ME!" by getting out of the long shadows of the *Journal* and establishing a new breed of business pages in local or community newspapers. The formula is simple:

- Acknowledge the importance of business news;
- Eliminate what "turns off" readers to the business page;
- Adopt hallmarks to guide your reporting;
- Addict yourself to *structure* as the essence of good business writing; and
- Encourage what "turns on" business-page readers.

The Magic of Business Writing

It always struck me as odd that business writers go to business writing workshops to be reassured that business writing is special. Are we such ugly ducklings in our own newsrooms?

We shouldn't be. The successful revamping of business sections that attracted new readers and advertisers in the 1980s should have taken care of that insecurity. After more papers added supplements like Metro Business and beefed up staffs to cover the economy, major employers, utilities, the workplace, and technology, business stories started showing up regularly on page one.

And rightly so. Business sections are a newspaper's window to the community's power brokers, the money that greases growth and progress, the financial lifelines that keep local economies alive, and the classes that define the haves and the have-nots. The stories to be told by business writers involve action-packed drama, inspiring rags-to-riches accounts, gut-wrenching tales of the little guy battling an unforgiving system, the fine line between success and failure, the uncertainty of conflict, and the crucial decisions that decide the fates of entire communities. By riveting attention on pocketbook issues, business sections command the attention of every wage-earner wondering how to spend, save, and predict the next recession or growth spurt. By writing with the consumer in mind, business reporters assemble giant puzzles that inform readers what their pieces really mean.

When business stories land on page one, they have the potential to shake up everyone. "Whoa!" the reader reacts. "What's *this* doing on the page reserved for serious government, crime, education, and medical stories, sometimes mixed with a feature about people?" *Why, reader!* the front should be saying, *It's an important story just for you.* Once the readers realize that the story speaks to them, that it's a report with information they can use, it makes them want more. The magic of the business story is that, on its own page, it's information or news, but on the front page, it's a reader-grabber and showstopper.

Business stories belong on the front page. That's really the first business page. If you are a business writer or editor, this is your mission.

Business Page Turn-Offs

What would happen if we spoke the language of the kind of business stories that cause readers to run screaming from the section? It might sound something like this exchange between two friends:

BUB: Hey, BA, what's going on? Haven't seen you in a while. How are you?

BA: Not so good, frankly.

BUB: Oh, no. Tell me.

BA: You didn't hear about my company?

BUB: I read something about changes at Acme, but I had no idea you were involved.

BA: Let me tell you, it's been no picnic!

[Something weird takes over. BUB and BA become talking business news pages.]

BUB: Give me the full 10K Report.

BA: My primary income source filed for either Chapter 7, Chapter 11, or Chapter 13 after deciding, based on a feasibility study, that our product line had downsize growth potential in a turbulent market.

BUB: Wow! I had no idea Acme's gross receipts and operating income weren't on the uptick, especially with same-store volume. Didn't your bottom line grow by 58 percent in five out of the last fifteen years to three-quarters of a million dollars in one of three sectors after adjusting for inflation?

BA: Those were the days! I can remember our grand opening during which we formally unveiled our state-of-the-art facility thanks to government-issued tax incentives. It was a real economic opportunity for our valuable personnel. Human resources loved it.

BUB: So, what disrupted the income stream and cash flow?

BA: First, it was a controversial hostile takeover in which our closely held manufacturing base was almost swallowed by an international conglomerate bent on expanding its niche in the global marketplace.

BUB: Man, I bet the writedowns would have been six figures.

BA: Fortunately, scrutiny ensued. First came the SEC, then the IRS. Followed by the FBI, FCC, SBA, the RTC, Nasdaq, and the NYSE. The Dow and the S&P went crazy, especially after inflation fears were triggered by lower-than-anticipated CPI, GDP, and PPI figures. It was all over AM & FM.

BUB: So, what happened? Did you get interactive?

BA: We rightsized to an efficient level so we could focus synergy on developing to be a market leader. Then, enplanements and deplanements maximized at the international airport complex, allowing us to beat back the outside threat and shift into a proactive mode. We posted a slight profit of zero point zero zero zero two percent.

BUB: So, it turned into a win-win situation?

BA: Not exactly. I was outsourced and had to go to an outplacement firm. They told me that I'm really an entrepreneur and that small business was the engine of a healthy economy.

BUB: You're such a results-oriented player. Let me know if you need assistance in networking.

BA: Thanks for your input. I remain cautiously optimistic as I pursue other interests.

That script serves as prelude to my Top Ten list of *Business Page Turn-Offs:*

1. Lemon Drops: Bad Packaging, Poor-Quality Art, Dull Headlines, and Weak Leads. Page designers and layout teachers often refer to headlines, visuals (photos, illustrations, and graphics), raised type, and other devices as "reader entry points." They are the aspects of the page that draw the readers' attention, compelling them to *read* the stories. More so than any other section, business pages live and die on packaging. (Please, do not bring up the *Wall Street Journal* here.) When the page is a lemon, sour readers will skip the section. That's why reporters need to work closely with section editors to make sure all the ingredients of a well-designed package are ready for publication. The business writer who fails to factor page design as part of completing the assignment is missing a key point: Writers should own the layout, just as they should the writing, because story and design must grab and pull in the busy reader.

For the writer, the next crucial step is the lead. Business stories must have powerful openings. If it's a straight news lead, quickly get to the point and then explain its significance to as wide a group as possible. Before crafting a lead, business writers should imagine a bored, skeptical audience yawning, "Why should I care?" or, "So what?" If the lead calls more for a feature approach, the writer must produce an indisputable best example that illustrates the story. Too many setup leads fail because the person isn't interesting enough. The editor's request to get people in the story is taken literally: Any person will do as long as he or she is in the opening. "When" leads are just as troublesome. "When Harold Newman was a boy playing in a sandbox, he never knew he'd grow up to become a captain of industry. Now 40 years later, Newman heads an international construction company that's building more than sand castles." The same lead would have worked had Newman been a novelist, pirate, or convicted bank robber. Avoid the temptation.

2. Agony of Defeat: No Game Plan, No Control. Business sections should know what they are doing days, weeks, and months ahead of publication. Don't try to wing it each day. The reader will know the difference between a rush job and a well-thought-out plan. Your job is to know what you *want* to do tomorrow, next week, and into the future. Without planning, business writers and editors merely rake up the leaves that have fallen each day and put them in a pile called the daily section. For starters, news budgets or digests should be written down and shared with everyone in the department and, for that matter, the rest of the paper.

You will not approach quality until you compress the routine—selecting formats, uploading the stock pages, combing the wires, and building a local report—into the shortest period, to free up more time for creativity and innovation. When the routine steps eat up all your day, you are left with process. That's a dead end. By squeezing quality time out of the routine, you can experiment, tinker, and try new ways. Remember: Creativity breeds passion.

3. Dead Ends: Single-Source Theory. Companies with bad news aren't dummies. They will usually send the press release—if they send one at all—at 5:00 P.M., knowing you'll have to swallow the company line on what happened because they've gone home. So, you go with the company's version without question and write: "While the loss was unexpected, Chairman David Miller said Acme was positioned for a bright future: 'I'm confident today's action will put us on the right course'." It sails through the editor, and you run the story without checking with anyone else. The result? You learn the next day that the "action" taken by the company included filing for bankruptcy. You call the company and complain that that wasn't in the press release. Its response: "You didn't ask." The company is right.

A single source is particularly dangerous in business stories because so many people have a slice of the overall story. To quote only one unfairly skews the story. How big is that slice? Another no-no is to quote somebody about someone else without checking it out further. Person A describes the actions of person B. You print it. Guess what? Person B's version is different, and he's upset. You lose.

4. Circle Pegs in Square Holes: Long Stories That Run Tuesday through Saturday and Then No Depth on Sunday. Why do business writers think length equals importance?

It doesn't.

Then why do we put long stories in the paper on the days readers have the least time to read them? Save the in-depth stories for Sunday and "Get Ten" the rest of the week: Ten inches out of thirty-inchers and ten inches out of twenty-inchers. Length is a weekend thing. If the story's so good, give me the highlights on Wednesday and come back Sunday with the full picture. Don't fight the obvious.

5. Lost Causes: Jargon, Alphabet Soup, B.S., Ghost Towns. Business jargon requires translations. It's a foreign language.

Alphabet soup acknowledges that every group or agency has its own acronym. String a few out in a story, and it becomes deadly. Acronyms are tough to read, tough to remember, and for many readers, nothing more than Morse Code. We know what happened to the telegraph.

Inoculate your stories against the spread of B.S. Don't let fluffy, inflated quotes slip into your story; they cheapen it. Few people will believe the comments of corporate spin doctors, anyway. Their statements don't even sound human. "We're cautiously optimistic about the future as ABC Corp. uses synergy to please stakeholders." Say what?

Ghost towns are stories without people. It's usually why readers fail to visit business news sections. Let's face it, business is about people. To be accurate and worthwhile, business stories should have plenty of people in them. Go to architecture school if you want to concentrate on buildings and institutions.

6. *Doing a Number: Too Many Statistics.* On the seventh day, God didn't rest. He created a graphic to hold numbers. That's where they belong. To make English out of numbers or to try to get them to flow in copy is wasted effort. Any sentence with more than three numbers numbs the mind. Put the numbers in accompanying charts, graphics, maps, and boxes, and let the text stick to words. The next time you write a number like $768,954, stop and say it out loud. Slow road, right?

7. *MIAs: The "So What?" Paragraph.* Next to the lead, the most important part of a story falls typically in the third-to-sixth paragraphs. It's the context, or the "nut paragraph." When it's missing, the reader struggles to get a handle on the story. The "nut" tells readers why the story is important, why they should care. This "So what?" paragraph can add historic perspective ("most important step in 30 years"), significance ("biggest test this community has ever encountered"), relevance ("the latest in a series of offers"), unusualness ("marks the departure of a pioneer in state government"), or dramatic effect ("the tax increase is expected to cause additional white-flight in a city that's been hard-pressed to keep its middle class"). When the story appears on page one, the "So what?" paragraph can further justify what the editors were thinking in putting the piece out front; bluntly, it says why the story deserves such play.

The "So what?" paragraph can also be a good check on whether the writer understands his or her own story. Red flag: Story arrives without "nut paragraph." Writer and editor spend thirty minutes trying to write one without success. The conclusion is clear: More reporting is needed.

8. Nothing But Air: Doing Only Telephone Interviews. Interviewing over the phone provides only one sense: sound. That's okay if you are interested only in a string of quotes to fill out the story. By getting out of the office to conduct interviews, to actually talk with your sources in their homes, offices, or places in the news, you add sights, smells, other sounds, and sometimes tastes and emotional aspects to the story. If someone tells you on the phone, "We're doing the best we can," you're getting a simple conclusion. But secure the quote while watching the person's eyes and the actions of those around him, and you're getting more: you're getting a complete picture.

9. No Study of Studies. It's an incomplete story if you report the results of studies, surveys, and reports without asking, "How do you know?" Victor Cohn in *News & Numbers* (Iowa State University Press, 1989), John Allen Paulos in *A Mathematician Reads the Newspaper* (Basic Books, 1995), and Philip Meyer in *The New Precision Journalism* (Indiana University Press, 1991) all urge reporters to probe what's behind the numbers being presented to them. In the case of statistics, ask: How do you know? Have you done a study? What kind? What numbers lead you to your conclusion? How were your numbers obtained? Were they derived from a random sample or from a collection of anecdotes? Does a correlation suggest a casual relationship, or is it merely coincidence? How confident can we be of them? Are there other ways to tally any figures presented? How valid, how reliable, how probable are they? Compared with what?

Sticking to the executive summary attached to the survey isn't reporting. It's typing.

10. Garbage In, Garbage Out: Press Release Journalism. Business reporters should never come close to relying exclusively on press releases. Very simply, the people who issue them often distort information. *Why* do they do this? Because . . .

- They are themselves in the dark about the real information you need.
- They seek to hide the truth, the whole truth, and nothing but the truth.
- They think we won't publish without them.
- They're doing to us what their bosses do to them.
- It's their way of getting back at you for disturbing their naps.
- It's easier for them to make up stuff.
- It's tough to defend the indefensible.
- It sounds more impressive than what actually goes on at their company.

- If it's a choice between giving out the real story and protecting their fannies, it's no contest: Fannies 1; Your Story, 0.
- And, you don't pay their salaries.

Remember these reasons the next time you sit typing their work under your byline.

Three Hallmarks of Good Business Coverage

Making assumptions can be an occupational hazard when covering business. So, no one should assume every newspaper's Business News Department adheres to certain hallmarks. Don't ask me to assume. Here are my foundation hallmarks:

***Hallmark No. 1:* Regularly take inventory of your market.** During the year, Business sections should confirm what they should know about their markets. What they find out should guide their coverage. For starters, if the major employer in town does not show up fairly regularly in stories, then something is wrong. At least once a year, you either list or check to find out:

- Top employers in your area?
- Latest Census data on local population, income, households, and employment?
- Performance of publicly traded local companies? (Review quarterly, if possible.)
- Major franchises in your area?
- What products are being made in your community?
- The top nonprofit organizations?
- The top retailers?
- Sales of new cars and the top dealers?
- The top sellers of real estate, builders of homes, and issuers of mortgages?
- Where do businesses get financing?
- What businesses have moved into your community, and why? Which ones have moved out, and why?
- Any trends evident in local bankruptcy courts?
- The community's movers and shakers?
- Business people on community and charity boards?
- What clues to the news exist in your own newspaper's marketing reports?

Hallmark No. 2: **Commit to a strategy that there are two sides to every story.** It keeps you out of trouble. You are only asking for problems when you let someone quote someone else or refer to a person's beliefs and thoughts without checking with him or her. Always go directly to sources. Do not take the easy way out and let someone speak for another person. This is particularly true for family-run businesses where the person out front doing the talking may not be the best source. A partnership means more than one person is involved. And if you can't get the information from a small business or family owner, there are always workers, suppliers, and those who service the company.

Warning: Do not settle for, "No comment," or, "A spokesman could not be reached for comment."

Editors and reporters need to ask one question over and over: *How do you know that?* When I have asked that question, I have always gotten a good handle on the sourcing, reporting, and how much further to check the facts. Also, editors should not divorce themselves from the gathering of information. Fact gathering is not just a reporter thing.

Hallmark No. 3: **Always have a plan.** For your story. For your beat. For your section.

Evaluate it regularly. Adjust to the news by playing to important stories first. And conduct weekly sessions in which the staff bats around ideas so that you're usually looking at a "to-do" list of ten to fifteen stories.

Have a backup plan. A worst-case scenario plan. A plan for good times, for bad times, and for times when nothing changes.

A Major Secret Is Structure

Story structure can be more important to business reporting than the actual writing itself. That might be an overreaching statement. But selecting a structure that efficiently organizes a reporter's material can guarantee a quality report faster than it takes the writer to decide the tone, voice, and length of a piece. Deciding up front the form of a story allows the writer to concentrate on the best way to explain what the reader needs to know. The form also can be the writer's outline, which is the best first step to writing coherently and thoroughly. Structure acts as a traffic cop at a busy intersection of material. Avert those painful collisions.

Some recommended forms:

- *Lead by Example.* Open the story with the best example, person, or experience that typifies the main thrust of the story. Follow with a sharply written transition that tells the reader why the example was selected. Summarize the story's key points. Follow in that order with detail. Weave the example throughout the story or return to it at the end. Warning: It's got to be the *best*. Weak examples will be viewed as a shallow gimmick.

- *Chapter and Verse.* Steal the techniques that work for novelists. Break the story into distinguishable parts and label them as "chapters." Open by summarizing the story's key points, introducing key characters, and setting the scene. Then tell the story chapter by chapter. Make sure each chapter ends in either suspense or in anticipation of the answer appearing in the next part. Two main directions are possible: Start with the result and then work through how the characters arrived there; or, start at the beginning and end up in the present.

- *Toast with a Champagne Glass.* Use the shape of a champagne glass to structure your stories. Open with a summary that fits the inverted pyramid (that's the part holding the champagne). Then, after a brief transition, go directly into a chronological account of what happened. Use time to move the story along (that's the stem of the glass). End with a big finish (or, a look at what is ahead).

- *Know Your ABCs.* Start with a forceful lead. That's point A. Add a nut paragraph that makes clear the story's importance. Follow that with a brief summation of other points you will be covering, in order of importance: B, C, D, E. Then, elaborate further on point A, and proceed through B, C, D, E, explaining each in detail. Now, the reader knows your ABCs.

- *Lists.* Some stories are better rendered as simple lists than as knock 'em–shock 'em prose. Do not get in the way of presenting information when it can be easily labeled or organized. For example: Instead of writing a story on why a company decided to build a new headquarters, simply *list* their reasons for doing so, the reasons they might have had for not doing so, and then what reasons won out. Another example: Instead of writing a story on a company's relocating to your town, list the factors that were considered in making the move. Use lists, especially when there are clear conclusions or aspects of a story. Among the most logical: Top Ten lists. A cliché, you say? Then, go ahead and write it the old-fashioned way, and make your reader earn it.

- *House of Examples.* Imagine a house with four to six windows in front. Think about structure in terms of putting a different face in each window to represent the aspects of the story. Your house, or story, is not complete until each window is occupied. In turn, each person plays a part in the story. For example: Your story is about businesses working with schools to improve public education. One window has the face of a business that has had a successful partnership; another face is sad, that of a business where the arrangement didn't work; another is somewhat puzzled, representing the long time it takes for such an experiment to take hold; an upstairs window shows a different face, representing a suburban business that's gone into the urban core to work with young students; another window has a face where the eyes almost look like dollars signs, reflecting a rich business interested in giving something back to the community; and the last window is actually the back of a head, which represents a business that wants no part of the project. When you go through all the windows, you understand the whole story after first seeing the parts. The structure also forces the writer to explore the many sides, or faces, that a trend might have.

Structure keeps the writer on track and pulls the reader aboard. Think about it before you make the first keystroke.

Business Page Turn-Ons

Business writers on local or community newspapers have an overriding mission: Inform by turning on the reader. Start by making difficult material easier to read. Keep your language simple, familiar, and tight by avoiding jargon, by using common rather than academic, stuffy, or pedantic language, and by removing unnecessary words.

Here's my Top Ten list of *Business Page Turn-Ons*:

1. Helping Out: Define, Explain, Clarify. Keep to one idea per sentence. Transform ideas into actions. Be concrete rather than abstract. Provide context by stating a clear point, followed by a clear statement of significance.

The business writer's tool kit should be built around three items: a dictionary-like memory (okay, store them on the computer) of the terms, labels, code words, names, and acronyms that populate "business-speak"; a decoder ring of sorts that pushes stories to explain and consistently answer the question, What does it mean?; and a magnifying glass so that stories are put in the proper context, and numbers, statements, and predictions are brought into focus.

If you have to use a technical term, define it immediately. But keep in mind it's better to describe than merely to define.

2. Be a Hard-liner: Hard News, Hard-edged, Hard Facts, Hardheaded.
Writing means breaking news, going beyond the hype and the media kit, getting around the stonewalling, and persisting until the news's significance is so clear that the readers are consuming every word—your words. The good writer with weak facts disappoints. The once-promising story reads well, lulling the hard-pressed editor on deadline to ship it. But on closer review, the story is nothing more than cotton candy for the mind: chew, chew, chew, and readers remain hungry. Some business pages lose their soul when they become softball entertainment sections. Not good.

Business news is hardball. Readers expect it, so do not disappoint. Build your story and section on scoops, insights, and news that sits on hard, razor-sharp facts. Leave the typing exercises to the high school classrooms.

3. Sure Reads: Cars, Foods, Toys, Ways to Make Money. Every business writer should have a backup plan for stories during slow times. Do not waste your efforts interviewing yet another owner of a nameless, faceless new business that is destined to fail. Here's a correlation you can take to the bank: Bland business pages have no stories on what we drive and eat, what entertains us, or what makes us rich. In the rush to fill space, we fail to include obvious topics that interest our readers: the latest trends on cars; the news about how we get our food; the toys that children will be screaming for come Christmas; and success stories on investors who found a way to beat the system or score big on a hunch that paid off handsomely.

When you think about what interests readers, you cannot go wrong with cars, food, toys, and money.

4. Wrap It Up: Package, Package, Package. Small businesses know that marketing and promotions are vital to a product's or service's success. Good is not enough if you are not drawing attention to your selling points. Apply that logic and formula to a business page. Stories that arrive sans artwork, design ideas, or a plan risk failure. Packaging news means each major story should be accompanied by a potentially dominant photograph, an explanation or information graphic, a suggested headline, headshots of key people quoted, and suggested quotations that could be highlighted. Identifying the parts well before deadline goes a long way toward designing a package that will attract the reader's eye. Keep a scorecard for each story. But good design doesn't happen by itself. It requires action.

5. Show the Reader the Money. Speak directly to readers, and if the story has a direct effect on them, consider showing that in your lead. Every business story, every business page, should contain a section that shows readers the money: cost to taxpayers or consumers; cost to municipality; how much it costs to make the product or create the service; the value of the project; the difference between profit and cost; monthly bills; and retail versus wholesale. Business writers should regularly ask: How much did it cost? What did you pay? How much did you make? What's the investment? What's the return? Business stories that miss the money miss the mark.

6. Just for Effects: Set an Example (or Several). Writing coaches urge newspaper reporters to become storytellers. End journalese, they assert, by using narratives to install the writer's voice in telling stories. To do that, business writers need to power or pepper their stories with *examples*:

- People who typify the subject.
- Experiences to document what happened.
- Different results to a planned event that show the benefits, the detriments, and the lack of change.
- Predictions on how a proposal would play out.

7. Mix It Up: Do Something Special Each Day. Plan for something each day and do not wait for news to occur. Map out an interesting story for the weeks and months ahead. Let only significant breaking news bump it out of the way. You know you can adjust to news. But making up each day's report on deadline can get old and tiresome, for your business news staff as well as readers. Think about stories that excite the reader, and pencil them in.

Or take this route: Identify the topics of significance in your community. Then, match them to a day in the week. For example: Monday is personal finance, Tuesday is energy, Wednesday is transportation, Thursday is the workplace, Friday is leisure, Saturday is homes, and Sunday is new jobs. Then, write under those banner topics on the assigned day. Or, another way: Monday is the newsmaker profile, Tuesday is new business profile, Wednesday focuses on one company, Thursday looks at jobs, Friday explains how a product is made, Saturday spotlights a new subdivision, and Sunday details the story of the week. By *selecting* topics you want in the paper, you drive the reporters to dig deeper to find news and explore trends. Reexamine your selections quarterly so that your ideas remain fresh. Keep a box that tells the reader what the rotation will be. When you change, explain it to the reader.

8. Take the Big Challenge: Satisfy Seniors, and Attract Youths, Minorities, and Working Women. Think about those groups as you write your stories and map out your sections. They are often outsiders to the business pages, representing new readers. But they will not stay with you until their faces and comments, and their interests and business activities, regularly show up.

9. Cross-Pollinate: Treat Business with the Touch of a Botanist.

Readership surveys routinely rank business sections by the frequency of readers' turning to the section on a day-to-day basis. Business usually lags behind local news, lifestyles, and sports. Puncturing that perception of business news might require a merger with other sections to capture their readers.

Link up with the sports section for stories on team finances. Venture into entertainment news with the scoop on just how thoroughly movie theaters depend—in financial detail—on that overpriced popcorn for their livelihood. Examine religion through the money needed to support a parish or congregation. Merge with local news to rank the top taxpayers that happened to be commercial businesses. Dig into a state legislature story by examining economic development deals in terms of how much it costs taxpayers to attract each out-of-state job. Tackle transportation by spotlighting the shortcuts through neighborhoods that truckers take to save money and time.

When these types of stories show up in the business section, they arouse reader curiosity and have a better chance of stopping the nontraditional scanner than would the ubiquitous—but necessary—earnings report. Widen the business page's perspective and show off angles that other sections would not touch because it's a business story. Turn *Yuck!* into *Yes!*

10. Common Bedfellows: Add Local Voice to Significant Wire Stories.

When building your daily budget, look first to what is happening on the wire. Making the connection between your community and the world around you gives the business section the best of both worlds. Too many local sections fight the news wire in an attempt to get one more local byline. Guess what? The reader is looking for a story he heard on the radio and television. Find a way to get it on the page by finding the local angle in the national story. Surely a strike by General Motors worries a local dealer. When the Asian economy takes a nosedive, someone local has to feel it. And if there is no connection, tell the readers so. At least they know you've checked it out.

That's a turn-on, too.

Managing the Murky Middle

⌒

By Carl Sessions Stepp

[Stepp is senior editor of the *American Journalism Review* and the author of *Editing for Today's Newsroom* (1989) and *The Magic and Craft of Media Writing* (2000). He has served as a writing and editing coach at more than thirty newspapers, including the *Washington Post*. He teaches journalism at the University of Maryland.]

As an editor, coach, and teacher, I have talked with thousands of writers over the years, and I maintain a kind of running "top ten" ranking of the comments they make.

High on the list is this one: "I often spend half my writing time on the lead. Once I'm satisfied with it, the story just seems to flow from there." For a long time, I nodded in agreement when someone would say that. After all, I write that way too. And I staunchly believe that a hefty investment at the front end of the process (spending more time organizing and getting started, for example) does accelerate the whole enterprise.

I think it was when I began to judge journalistic contests that I started having second thoughts. The more carefully and thoughtfully I read, the more I noticed that my biggest complaint about stories was disorganization—lack of direction, lack of cohesion, lack of the kind of structural

This essay was adapted from a presentation I made at the 1995 National Writer's Workshop in Columbia, South Carolina, and from my book, *The Magic and Craft of Media Writing* (Lincolnwood, Ill.: NTC Publishing Group, 2000).

integrity that defies a reader to stop reading. Too many stories seemed to be just a sort of miscellaneous collection of marginally related tidbits and factoids rather than a unified narrative or news tale. To use the wonderful old phrase, they consisted of "a beginning, a muddle, and an end."

Granted, the topic and the lead are vital elements to writing, and I don't begrudge the time and effort expended on them. But the true craftspeople in print journalism also recognize that the beginning is simply that—just the beginning. There's a great deal more work to do afterward.

I am not going to propose that we spend *less* time at the front end. I'm advocating *more* time and attention to the secondary stages of the writing.

It is always risky to recommend anything to journalists that costs them time. Time remains their most precious asset. Virtually every writer I know lusts for the chance to spend more time reporting, organizing, writing, and rewriting. But deadlines loom, and today's production demands make it seem fancifully naïve to propose spending more time on much of anything.

I therefore acknowledge the risks of recommending any solutions that cost time. But I'm going to do it anyway, and I will defend doing so on three grounds.

First, I defend it in the ideal. Our first goal is to consider ways to improve writing. Taking more time is one top way. Time by itself, of course, doesn't guarantee excellence. But it is fair to say that in most cases the quality of the final product is related to the time and effort spent. As writers, we shouldn't become defensive about that fact. Great writing tends to take more time than we think—more time than publishers, editors, and readers think, too. If writers don't defend that position, who will?

Second, I defend the notion that it is practical for writers to redistribute their time. Writers should look for ways to save time elsewhere that can be applied to the act of writing. If you can't expand the actual amount of time devoted to a single story, then the only solution is to rearrange your use of existing time. Better time-management techniques help. Becoming a better interviewer, for instance, means you can get more and better information in less time. Becoming a more efficient outliner means you can organize your stories more quickly. Better organizing tactics allow you to spend less time sweating over leads. And so on. If you constantly get better at your work, you should find yourself saving some time.

Third, I offer the most pragmatic defense of all: Pick your shots. If you can't spend more writing time on every story, then do so on some stories—on the most important ones, the most sensitive ones, the ones where extra writing time matters most. I will agree that not every writer can spend extra writing time on *every* story . . . if you will agree that every writer should be able to spend extra writing time on *some* stories.

So, let's dispose of the time argument and move on.

Where the Trouble Begins: Paragraph Two

We will assume we have an interesting topic and an engaging lead. It is right there—at the second paragraph—that serious trouble often erupts. We labor over the lead, sometimes for hours, occasionally for days, if time allows. Then we write it, and roll on. It's like a notebook-dam bursts, and words come flooding out, paragraphs begin washing by in an eye blink. The second paragraph may never get a second thought.

But we need to slow down. The second paragraph plays a crucial role in maintaining the readers' interest and escorting them into the body of the story. A lousy second paragraph—one that lets go of a reader who has been grabbed by the lead—can undo all that effort invested in our perfect lead.

Read some newspapers and magazines, and you'll find several recurring problems with second paragraphs:

- *The second paragraph is really the runner-up lead.* Writers have a congenital desire to tell everything first. They fall in love with their material and can't decide whether the main point is that the City Council suspended the police chief or raised parking ticket fines. The easy way out is to put one point in the lead, the second one in the next paragraph. To a writer, this makes perfect sense. To a reader, it is a logic killer. By definition, a reader who gets to paragraph two has been engaged by paragraph one and wants to find out more. By changing the subject, we break the connection that has been established and provide a splendid opportunity for the eye and mind to wander elsewhere.
- *The second paragraph repeats the lead.* Writers also sometimes fall in love with different ways of wording things. So they use one way in the lead, then another formulation in the second paragraph. Or they inject a direct quote that merely retells the lead in different words. It's okay to repeat main points in paragraph two (in fact, we should do that as a reader service), but we need to be careful that we add important material and don't merely rehash what the reader already has been told.
- *The second paragraph drops back to background too soon.* I once read a story about police storming into a government meeting to arrest and haul off an elected official. Its lead was engaging. But its

second paragraph, instead of building on that dramatic confronta-
tion, sank immediately to background, way back to the beginning of
the dispute that led to the arrest. What I wanted to know, instead,
was, *What had happened?* Had the official resisted . . . departed
silently . . . apologized contritely . . . blurted a confession . . . exited
with dignity and a witty retort? Had the police used handcuffs . . .
shoved the official . . . behaved like intruders at the symphony? Had
the audience reacted . . . burst into tears . . . shouted insults? The
background was needed, and fairly soon, but not in paragraph two.

A good second paragraph in a typical news story avoids these problems:

- *By building on the most compelling point in the lead* (it should
  amplify, with additional insight and detail, the point or action that
  has engaged the reader in the first place);
- *By adding, whenever it's possible, the essential how and why to the
  story* (leads tend to focus on who has done something important or
  what newsworthy thing has happened—and a logical next step, for
  readers, is an explanation of how that thing has happened or why the
  story matters); and
- *By possessing a strong structural connection to the lead* (for example, you might repeat the name of the key person in the lead, employ
  a pronoun with a clear reference to the lead, or use a synonym for
  the key concept).

The Middle Becomes Muddle

Now where are we? We have a good idea, a strong lead, and a compelling
and amplifying second paragraph. Typically, the first section also will
include our best quote on the main point and perhaps one or more paragraphs of detail further supporting the lead. Here, if we aren't careful, the
middle begins to muddle. Afloat in midstory, having spent most of our
thought and energy on the lead and its ancillaries, we have a tendency to
write faster and faster, dropping in thoughts as they occur to us. What
began as a well-focused story can quickly turn into a jumble.

Two techniques to help you stay on track are the *interior outline* and
what I call the *kickoff paragraph.*

1. The Interior Outline. I once attended a church where the minister
began every sermon, after a brief introduction, with the words, "Point num-

ber one." His sermons always had three points, and he unfailingly introduced them as "point number one," "point number two," and "point number three." You couldn't get more direct than that.

Most of us write stories that have several points, even if we don't announce them with this preacher's wording. Most but not all of us prepare some sort of beginning outline, whether it takes the formal shape of Roman numerals and letters or the more common form of a list. But we also need an interior outline.

Interior outlines organize the body of the story. Typically, they comprise three to five points, ordered logically and arranged in blocks. Some careful writers can develop the interior outline as part of the main outline before they begin writing. But my experience is that it helps to return to outlining after you have completed the lead and introductory segment of your story. Having written the lead, you now see the story differently. You have overcome what most writers feel is the hardest writing challenge—the lead—and are free to concentrate on the story's innards.

The process shouldn't take much time. Consider how you have framed the story in the lead, and then determine what major points need coverage and in what order. Jot them down, in order, with any subpoints or supporting matter that you need. And decide, if possible, on your ending. Some writers have trouble envisioning the actual ending at this point, preferring to let it emerge during the momentum of writing. That's fine. If you don't want to settle on an exact ending, you do need to know the overall point you are heading toward. Otherwise, you fly with no direction.

2. The Kickoff Paragraph. Once you have an interior outline, you can craft your kickoff paragraph. Think of it as the lead to the *body* of the story. It is transitional in nature, linking the main section to the middle and ending. Kickoff paragraphs can take many different shapes, but all generally share certain virtues. They move from what is already known to what is coming; they specify or at least hint at every major point that is to come; and they present points in the same order as they will be developed in the body.

Take the common example of a school board story. The lead isolates the main point, say, that anti-drug programs will begin in elementary schools next year. The introduction will deal with the decision, the pros and cons, quotes from the combatants, and so forth. The kickoff paragraph then leads us into the rest of the story.

If the story has multiple points, the kickoff paragraph becomes a roundup. It should begin with the known, perhaps something as simple as, "Besides the new anti-drug program . . . ." Then it itemizes:

> Besides the new anti-drug program, the board also raised teach-
> ers' salaries by 5 percent, adjusted boundaries for two middle
> school districts, and rejected a citizens' challenge to current high
> school history textbooks.

Or, if the entire news story is about one main action, such as the controversial anti-drug programs, then the kickoff paragraph might take a different form. For example, it might introduce a contextual look at how the new
program came about:

> The decision climaxed a six-month controversy during which
> some parents' groups lobbied for the anti-drug education, oth-
> ers resisted imposing it on tender elementary pupils, and board
> members personally visited dozens of classrooms in nearby
> school districts using similar programs.

Even in other journalistic genres such as feature stories or profiles, this
kickoff paragraph remains important. It tends to come shortly after the
"nut paragraph" (which tells why the story is being offered and what its
broader context is), and it typically previews in order the points to come.
Let's say, for instance, that you have profiled a local professor whose
research has won a major prize. The lead might focus on the turning point,
the moment the professor realized her central experiment had paid off. By
paragraph four or five, the nut paragraph would summarize the story's
thrust, perhaps that a lifelong devotion to science, sometimes at the risk of
ridicule and frustration, underlay the professor's triumph. The introduction completed, the kickoff paragraph might then signal the rest of the story
as follows:

> Prof. Boynton's passion for science began with the tiny bottles
> of chemicals she bought with her childhood allowance, and it
> sustained her through graduate training, a frustrating stint in
> industry, and a second career as a professor that almost aborted
> during her first ill-fated research project.

Clarity, Clarity

So far, so good—solid topic, lead, second paragraph, interior outline, and
kickoff. Our paramount concern, as always, remains accuracy. Beyond that,
the newswriter's foremost worries boil down to two: drama and clarity. The
first means, make it interesting; the second means, keep it understandable.

I will leave it to others to address the necessity of drama, and I'll concentrate on clarity here—on the fact that, even with a strong foundation and interior outline, we do not necessarily avoid the muddle. Here, I like to introduce the notion of the writer as mechanic or construction worker, lugging a toolbox or wearing one of those holster belts with assorted wrenches and pliers dangling from the pockets. As a writer you are a professional technician, gifted with a set of tools and techniques that you stand ready to employ as needed. Here are some of the tools you can use to maintain an orderly, accessible flow through a story's middle:

- *Interconnections.* Think of how the pieces interlock in a length of chain. Each one physically connects to the piece before it and the piece after it. We can apply this same principle to writing, by ensuring that each paragraph contains some grammatical connector to those before and after it. Because it creates a seamless and logical flow, this technique makes it harder for people to stop reading. Among the best interconnecting devices are pronouns, synonyms, and repeated key words. Transitional words and phrases also work: for example, chronological terms (first, next, then, after the vote, etc.) or locator terms (nearby, across town, in the next room, etc.).
- *Previews.* If a section or subsection will take more than a handful of paragraphs, then write a preview paragraph that introduces it and makes clear its range and scope. Readers need these paragraphs to help them see the general boundaries of the territory they are entering.
- *Wrap-ups.* Wrap-ups are the opposite of previews. They come at the end of a long or complex section and offer readers an opportunity to pause, catch up, and take stock of what they have learned so far.
- *Signposts.* When you drive through unfamiliar landscapes, you regularly encounter helpful signs: slippery when wet, curve ahead, watch out for falling rocks, don't feed the bears, and the like. Readers, too, benefit from such guidance. One of the most useful things you can do as a writer is to share with your readers the intelligence you have about what is coming up. In a phrase or a sentence, you can signal that a key turning point is about to befall your protagonist, that the next section is complicated and full of statistics, that the tone of the adventure is about to change dramatically. The longer the story, the more signposts you should scatter along the trail.
- *The buddy system.* Ever been on a hike or a field trip with a bunch of kids? Then you know the value of the buddy system, where individuals share responsibility for one another and things occasionally

come to a halt to count heads. Writers should consider themselves to be their readers' buddies, and should pause from time to time so everyone can catch up. Here's where we've been, here's where we're going, here's a review of the story so far.

- *Scenes and connective tissue.* A classic organizational device is to use scenes to slow the action and show your points. Scenes are often presented in present tense, a semblance of real time, with a minimum of writer intervention. For clarity, then, they are interspersed with connective tissue. Connective tissue tends to speed things up, by summarizing, condensing large gaps of time between scenes, letting the writer intervene with material the reader needs in order to appreciate or evaluate the scenes. (Similarly, quotes and illustrative details or examples should be strategically placed, as often as possible attached directly to the article's dramatic high points.)

Just Good Writing

No matter how well an article is organized, it ultimately comes down to a series of words shaped into sentences. As craftspeople, writers recognize the cumulative importance of this miniature architecture. Good words make good sentences, and good sentences make good stories. A strong story tends to be a collection of good small parts.

Here are some guidelines I have found helpful over the years, for constructing clear and interesting sentences:

- Keep most sentences short (under twenty-five words), but vary the pace. In general, use shorter sentences when explaining complex material. Longer sentences work well when the material isn't heavy with data—for example, in quotes where someone is expressing feelings.
- Hold most sentences to one main idea. It is not really the number of words that makes a sentence difficult, but the number of ideas. This is not a matter of "dumbing down" your copy. It is easier for readers of all intellectual abilities to understand material that is presented one idea at a time, in orderly fashion. Stories that throw out too many ideas at once can confuse us all.
- Stash the hot words in the hot corners. The main points of emphasis in sentences and paragraphs are their corners—the beginning and the end. Concentrate your most potent words there.
- Express your main point in the main subject and verb of a sentence rather than in clauses and phrases. Central characters should show up in the subjects, important actions in the verbs.

- Begin sentences and paragraphs with familiar ideas and references to what has already been written. End sentences with new information or more complex data. If you are changing subjects, do so toward the end of a sentence or paragraph.

And a Little Magic

Writing is in part a craft, and thus it profits from attention to detail and from laundry lists such as the ones I've presented above. Bringing your left-brain discipline to bear on an article's middle almost guarantees a better story. Middles are so often overlooked that even a modest attention tends to improve them noticeably.

But writing is also in part magic, the bounce that comes from free thinking and inspiration, those bolts from the great beyond. So let your creative, right-brain side help, too. Think about the body of your story. Imagine what you want it to become. Draw diagrams to help you discover and connect the points like branches to a tree trunk. Devote a portion of your noodling time to your interior outline, your kickoff paragraph, the components of the body of your copy.

You will be rewarded—though no one wins awards for writing a great middle. There are honors for intrepid reporting, prizes for great headlines, and kudos for winning leads. Middles barely get a notice. But that is why they are dangerous. Given the concentrated energy required elsewhere, writers and editors tend to neglect the middle. This neglect begets stories that are disorganized, meandering, wordy, turgid, out of focus. The consequence is simple: People stop reading.

A good middle holds the audience won by a great lead. It gets readers to the meat. It keeps them on the page. Don't let a murky middle drive off your hard-won readers.

SpellCheck and Beyond:
A Strategy for Revision

By John Sweeney

You have this writer's fantasy. In some dream world, perhaps next Monday when you finally get it together, you will pound out leads so lyrical that they make people stop and stare. The rest of the story will dance off the keyboard in rhythms so appealing that strangers burst into dramatic readings at the coffee counter. Images pour forth so vividly that teenagers forsake video games for reading. And the ending is so natural, so satisfying, that editors throw away their pencils and just wave the story through.

Some day. Perhaps.

In the meantime, you sweat it out. You misspell "parallel," misuse "anxious," and garble every third sentence. Just like the rest of us.

You have two choices. Wait for that dream world. Or get better, step by step, word by word.

To do that, you need discipline and a plan.

"Discipline," Florence King wrote, "is never a restraint. It's an aid. The first commandment of the romantic school is: 'Don't worry about grammar, spelling, punctuation, vocabulary, plot or structure—just let it come.' That's not writing; that's vomiting, and it leads to uncontrolled, unreadable prose. Remember: Easy writing makes hard reading, but hard writing makes easy reading."[1]

But what about the plan?

Our only hope is to have a revision strategy. It must go beyond just clicking the SpellChecker. It must be thorough and flexible at the same time. It must be thorough enough to let you revise from structure to paragraphs to sentences to words. It must be flexible enough to let you chop and cut as you race deadline.

Every writer makes mistakes, misses the point, or, from time to time, falls asleep at the keyboard. It's time we acknowledge that, and develop a revision strategy. It would flow from three assumptions:

- Assume you have made mistakes in your copy.
- Assume you are unclear.
- Assume you can do better.

But a revision strategy is built on knowing one thing especially well: knowing who you are, as a writer. Know your weaknesses. Know what you will do in the heat of the moment, when the writing juices flow freely and the muse whispers in your ear. Know your bad habits and sloppy shortcuts. We all have them.

You may spell poorly. In that case, find a good dictionary and use it. Get familiar with SpellCheck programs. Tape a list to your computer terminal of words that you frequently misspell.

You may not understand punctuation. Find a simple guidebook and work your way through it. I did just that as a seventeen-year-old airman working on an Air Force base newspaper. My chain-smoking, hard-talking editor-sergeant didn't take kindly to my frequent guesses about commas and quotation marks. He advised me, "Fix it, boy." So I did, with an inexpensive copy of Harry Shaw's *Punctuate It Right!*[2] I stayed in the barracks every night for a week learning about colons, semicolons, and question marks. Victory. I still have my copy of Shaw. It sits on my shelf, a silent trophy.

A revision strategy cannot be based on gut feelings. It must be part of your routine to be effective.

---

1. Quoted in *Advice to Writers,* ed. Jon Winokur (New York: Random House, 1999), p. 106.
2. Harry Shaw, *Punctuate It Right!* (New York: Barnes & Noble, 1965).

Here are a half-dozen additional ways to build a strategy that will help as you revise both breaking news stories and long-term projects.

Find the Big Thing

Ask yourself: What was my *point*? Did I make it? Many articles suffer from a lack of focus. You must say one thing. Decide early on what that one thing is. Then check to see if you said it. No shame is attached to rewriting. Make it your rule: Never turn in an article that does not have one discernible major point.

Be sure, also, that you back up that point in the text. Where is the "news" in the article—is it where it should be? Did you talk with the people affected by the action? Did you get to the decision-makers? And the expert who added context? Are the quotations to the point? Do they advance the story?

Do the Right Thing

- Is your article accurate? Is it fair?
- How do you know what you are saying is true?
- Is the article as complete as it can be?
- Are the quotations accurate and fair?
- Did you give those criticized an opportunity to respond? Did you treat them fairly?
- Did you explain unsuccessful efforts to reach sources?
- Did you identify your sources?
- If you used anonymous sources, did you explain why?
- If the story were about you, would you consider it fair?
- Did you avoid stereotypes?

Get the Words Right

- Did you avoid clichés? Set phrases come from set thinking. Set phrases are usually disconnected from their original meanings.
- Do your words often enough stimulate your readers' senses? The more they make readers see, hear, or feel something, the more exciting the writing is.
- Do your words say what you mean? As a guard against staleness, take your images literally. For instance, what would your readers likely see if you wrote that "civic leaders *ripped* apart the state's traffic analysis"?

And what image might be generated by your lead that says a city official "*blasted* the Council's dinner meetings"? Is that what you intended? Or did you simply treat those words as dead images? Are "rip" and "blast" just another way of saying "criticize"?

- Have you avoided loaded language? Be wary of loaded words. They can mean more than you want to say. Dictionary definitions only go so far. The verb "funneled," for example, means to pass some thing through a funnel or funnel-like construction. But to say the money that came to politicians was "funneled through two political action committees" is to say this was a little more than the usual contribution. Many readers would think the money was funneled because contributors didn't want the public to know. Is that what the writer had in mind? Perhaps not. But it's likely that readers might come away with a vague notion of something sordid.

Get the Mechanics Right

- Have you followed the *Associated Press Stylebook*?
- Have you checked the grammar? Usage? Punctuation?
- Have you checked for problems with libel or privacy?
- Have you checked the numbers? Have you done the math?
- Are all the locations, names, and titles correct?
- Are the dates and references in order?

Read for Your Readers

Once you've finished your draft, read back through it quickly, ignoring typos and grammatical goofs and concentrating on *whether or not the story makes sense.* (Read it as your reader will, straight-through.)

Then go back over it again, this time slowly. Read it out loud. Hearing every word. Listen to the sound of the language, the words, the sentences. Are you tripping over your words? Then your reader will, too. Are you running out of breath in the middle of a sentence? Then your reader will, too.

What is the tone of the article—does it sound like a human is speaking? Will the reader see a *face* behind the words? George Orwell once said readers will often do that, imagine a face behind the page. That habit persists even after they've seen photos of the author. "What one sees," Orwell wrote, "is the face that the writer ought to have." What face does your reader see when she reads your words?

Test Your Sentences

Journalists must often revise in haste, relying on luck and habit. Luck philanders. Habit can be trained to be faithful. Here are two habits that can help you on deadline:

- *Circle every preposition.* If you find three or more prepositional phrases in a sentence, rewrite it. Likewise, circle all forms of the verb "to be," and replace them with action verbs, if you can. Chances are good that you'll find the prepositional phrases and the "to be" verbs lingering side by side. That shifts the action from the verb to the prepositional phrases. Make sure the reader knows who is performing the action and what the action is.[3]
- *Check how many ideas you have in a sentence.* It should be just one. Take that as a guide: Say one thing in a sentence. Then it won't matter (as much) how many words are in the sentence. People will still be able to understand it. Theodore M. Bernstein came up with that advice for *New York Times* reporters in 1954.[4] It still holds for reporters today.

Look on these suggestions as a start. Develop your own strategy for revising. Learn to add to it as you learn the craft. The important thing is to do it.

Otherwise, that writer's fantasy will remain just that—a fantasy.

---

3. See Richard A. Lanham, *Revising Prose* (New York: Scribner's, 1979).

4. Theodore M. Bernstein, *The Careful Writer: A Modern Guide to English Usage* (New York: Atheneum, 1977).

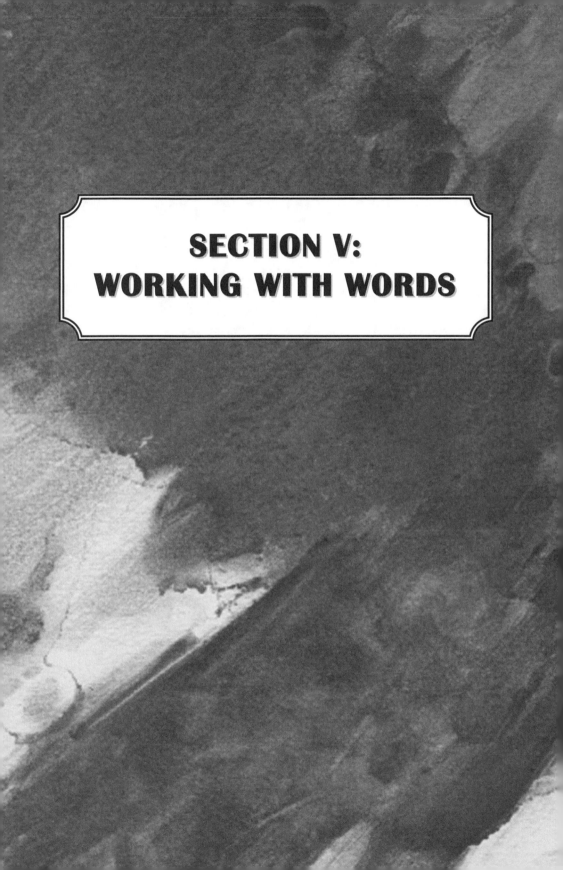

SECTION V:
WORKING WITH WORDS

These Things We Can Count On

By J. Taylor Buckley

[Buckley is a long-time reporter, columnist, and writing coach for *USA Today*. He was that paper's founding managing editor of the "Money" section, and later served as a sports columnist and as the paper's first full-time Moscow correspondent.]

Rene J. Cappon is renowned among Associated Press reporters for his keen editing eye. In his book *The Word* he rails at "threadbare phrases" and "Words to Swear At" used by reporters who are too lazy to seek fresh ways of saying things. One of his short chapters lists several hundred linguistic "misdemeanors" he has spotted in his long career as an editor. I've kept my own list, which I call my "ALWAYS" list, of Very Predictable Expressions I see used by reporters. Here's a sampling:

- Economies, particularly local ones, always *sag,* even though money is always *pumped into* them.

- Budget cuts are always *draconian.*

- Government budgets are always *unveiled.*

- Votes in Congress are always *crucial.*

- Committee chairmen and chairwomen in Congress are always *powerful.*

- Battle lines are always *drawn.*

- Deadlines are always *around the corner.*

- Races are always *tight.*

- Grips are always *icy.*

- Reality is always *harsh.*

- Power lines never fall; they're always *downed.*

- Fires always *rage;* smoke always *billows.*

- Rain always *fails to dampen the spirits* of parade-goers.
- Thunderstorms always *travel in bands,* as do rioting teenagers.
- Tornadoes always *hopscotch* through counties. Storms in the plains always *rumble.* Hurricanes are always *brewing.*
- People always *dig out* after snowstorms, *thaw out* after ice storms.
- Truces and labor agreements are always *hammered out.*
- New products are always *rolled out.*
- Security is always *beefed up.*
- Disaster victims are always taken to *makeshift morgues.*
- Investigators always *sift through* wreckage.
- School buses (any kind of buses) always *plunge off* the roadway.
- Ships always *steam* from one place to another. Those with holes in their hulls, if able, always *limp* into port.
- Takeoffs by malfunctioning aircraft are always *aborted.*
- Plane crashes, especially those involving celebrities, are always *fiery.*
- The deck of an aircraft carrier is always measured in *football fields.*
- Lawns are always *well manicured.*
- Funds are always *earmarked.*
- Prep schools are always *prestigious.*
- Bullets are always *pumped into* one's head or torso.
- Machine guns are always *toted,* as in "machine gun–toting guards." They are never *wielded* or *brandished.* It's knives that are always *wielded* or *brandished.*
- SWAT teams always carry *high-powered rifles,* never pistols, low-powered rifles, or just rifles.

- Neighbors of crime victims are always *shocked and saddened,* while neighbors of mass murderers are always *shocked and appalled.* But how do they know their neighbor is the murderer?

- Murderers are always *loners who kept to themselves.*

- Car chases, especially those involving the police, are always conducted at *high speed,* and almost always at least one car *careens.*

- The bodies of teenage women sexually victimized and murdered are always found *scantily clad,* while older women in similar circumstances are always found *partially nude.*

- Denials of wrongdoing are always *vehement.*

- Mistaken identity, like beer, always comes *in cases of.*

- Elusive thugs are always *wily.*

- Details are always *sketchy.*

- Felons who receive subpoenas or errant motorists who get tickets are always *slapped with* them.

- Suicide victims are always *despondent.*

- Death is always *sudden, unexpected,* or *premature.*

- Failing newspapers always *die,* just as failing businesses always *close their doors.* No enterprise just closes or shuts.

- The family farm always *goes on the auction block.*

- The shots one must get after being bitten by an animal suspected of carrying rabies always come *in a painful series.*

- Cigars are always *chomped,* rarely, if ever, smoked.

- A wait-and-see attitude is always *adopted.*

- Debates are always *spirited;* arguments are *heated.*

- Negotiators are always *cautiously optimistic.*

- Contract talks that stagnate or drag on always go into *marathon sessions* that end in *11th-hour settlements.*

- Crisis-induced press conferences are always *hastily called.*

- A newsmaker caught fending off obnoxious reporters and ridiculous questions is always said to be *keeping the media at bay.*

- Among the performers in any media circus are always the ever-present *hordes* of photographers.

- Running backs always *find daylight* after blockers create *a hole big enough to drive a truck through.*

- Errors made by baseball players are always *costly.*

- Teams that win in tournaments, especially high school teams, always *came to play.*

- Rookies always come in only one color: *green.*

Speaking of Metaphor

By Jeanne Murray Walker

[Walker has published five volumes of poetry. Her plays have been performed in London, Boston, Washington, and other cities. Among her many honors are a National Endowment for the Arts Fellowship, the Calladay Award, and the prestigious Pew Fellowship in Poetry. She frequently leads writing workshops.]

Try talking without it. Try thinking without it. Without it, try convincing your neighbor to move his fence. You can't. At once a paradox and the path to clarity, surprising and obvious, funny and serious, metaphor is power. It lives in the babble of lunatics, the sentences of judges, the language of street gangs, the augury of prophets, the come-on of advertisers, the wisdom of poets, the gossip of office workers. It lies deep within the heart of every language. We can neither entirely explain it nor obliterate it, and anyone who masters it can master a good deal more. It is worth thinking about carefully and using skillfully. It is worth examining no matter what you write, journalism or poetry.

Next time you stroll through a mall, notice how many stores are named with metaphors. For some reason hair salons seem particularly clever at this. Consider *Hair to Please, Julius Scissor, Plan A Head, The March Hare,* and *A Cut Above.* Then there are the names of secondhand stores:

John Frederick Nims (1913–1999) was the first teacher who made sense of metaphor for me, and I want to acknowledge my debt to him for some of the ideas in this essay.

Second Hand Rose, for example, and *Play It Again, Sam.* The store own-
ers, I assume, bank on this little kick of surprise to make me remember the
next time I need a haircut or thrift shop jeans.

Anyone who pushes a help button on a computer knows plenty about
metaphor. Twenty years ago, I thought waiters brought *menus.* And I
thought *files* were where I kept last year's income tax forms. *Boot up* meant
preparing to go out into the Minnesota winter. People who invented computer language actually lifted most of the terms from other parts of their
lives. There is *home,* for example. There is *entering* and *exiting.* There is
searching and *merging* and *formatting.* There is the *soft return* and the
hard return (as, for example, the return of the prodigal son). At a computer show not long ago I spotted a poignant sign that read, "Memory Bought,
Sold, and Exchanged." When I started learning how to use a computer, I
thought all this was profoundly odd, but after fifteen years, I am in danger
of forgetting that the words ever meant anything else. Sitting at my computer now, I think it's a tragedy worthy of a country-and-western song:
"Home Is Just the First Page of a Document."

It's a short leap from computers to science, where experiments are
changing the shape of knowledge every day. Without metaphor many of
our recent discoveries would remain nameless. Take, for instance, the
famous experimental observation that a photon of light can appear either
as a particle or as a wave, depending on how the experiment is set up.
Angela Tilby, a science writer for the BBC, describes this odd phenomenon in her book *Science and the Soul.* Under one set of experimental conditions, she reports, the photons arrive looking "much the same shape as
a stream of bullets would make if fired from a rather rickety machine-gun."
Under another set of experimental conditions, the pattern looks "more
like the pattern that sea waves would make if they rolled in to a jetty with
two gaps in it, reformed, and then crashed up against a line of floating
buoys."[1] Prominent in this description of the experiment is metaphor. No
wonder. It's not that Tilby wants to simplify for readers, but that there is no
language except metaphor to describe these experiments. The unseen
parts of the universe must be described metaphorically.

In fact, science supplies the example, *par excellence,* of the way the
human mind is forced to resort to metaphor to think. The crisis of new
data and the need to explain that data is occurring not only at the sub-
atomic level but at the level of deep space with unimaginably large dis-

---

1. Angela Tilby, *Science and the Soul: New Cosmology, the Self and God* (London: SPCK,
1992), p. 147.

NEW ROCHELLE PUBLIC
LIBRARY
CHECK-OUT RECEIPT

Title: One scandalous story
: Clinton, Lewinsky, and thi
Item ID: 31019152869262
Date charged: 4/3/2010,
14:19
Date due: 4/24/2010,23:59

Title: The journalist's craft
: a guide to writing bette
Item ID: 31019153053049
Date charged: 4/3/2010,
14:19
Date due: 4/24/2010,23:59

RENEWALS:632 7878X1700
during business hours
Visit us online @ www.nrpl.
org
Thank You

tances, speeds, and sizes. For example, the men who receive data from Voyager as it hurtles through darkness are *not* playing it again, Sam. Far from reconfiguring familiar images, they're sometimes pondering information no human has ever seen. They can only make sense of it by comparing it to what happens on earth.

What Is Metaphor?

A metaphor, really, is an equation. $X = Y$. But unlike most equations, metaphor has a built-in absurdity: that X is also *utterly other than Y*. It is this very two-faced aspect of metaphor that makes it arresting. When two things usually stored in separate categories are forced together, I don't know what happens in the minds of other readers, but in mine a little explosion of awareness goes off. *Oh, of course!* I think, and I feel pleasure.

As an example of how metaphor works, it's worth looking at one of Charles Simic's poems. It is little more than a list of equations; the *right* ones, it must be noted, and brilliant ones, but still, remarkably, equations. Here's the first section of Simic's "Bestiary for the Fingers of My Right Hand":

> Thumb, loose tooth of a horse.
> Rooster to hens.
> Horn of a devil. Fat worm
> They have attached to my flesh
> At the time of my birth.
> It takes four to hold him down.
> Bend him in half, until the bone
> Begins to whimper.
>
> Cut him off. He can take care
> Of himself. Take root in the earth,
> Or go hunting with wolves.[2]

It's easy to visualize a fat, stubby thumb as the loose tooth of a horse. But at the risk of belaboring the obvious, a thumb is not in any other sense like a tooth. It does not feel hard or grind hay or smell the way a horse's tooth might. Of course, that's exactly the point. When X and Y are so different, the one similarity that might be imagined between them is unlikely to have

---

2. Charles Simic, *Selected Poems, 1963-1983* (New York: George Braziller, 1990), p. 32.

occurred to the reader, and therefore, it comes as a lightning strike. The next metaphor, *a rooster to hens,* switches the game abruptly from visual to more philosophical comparison. In the same way, each metaphor in this poem shifts the ground under the reader, creating a new comparative category, creating repeated surprises.

Every one of these metaphors appeals to our senses. By the time I'm into the second line, my body is already affected by what I'm reading. If a writer can get me to see or touch or taste or feel the Y, I am already going along with him. So metaphor is a strategy that appeals to the body in order to persuade the mind. Metaphor lives in the kitchen—and in the basement and in the hardware store—rather than in the library.

Wizards of Metaphor

Children seem to be the natural wizards of metaphor. Picture a drawing of a house with two windows for eyes, a door for a mouth, and scribbly smoke for hair. Not only are children's drawings alive with metaphor, their everyday talk is, too. One of my young friends who baby-sits regularly asked her young charge to point to her nose. The child pointed to the right place. Then, pointing to the bridge of her nose, she said, "And this is my nose's spine."

Poets sometimes write in startling and simple equations that sound like they might have come from a child. One poet who does this brilliantly is Nancy Willard. Consider this, her "Carpenter of the Sun":

> My child goes forth to fix the sun,
> a hammer in his hand and a pocketful of nails.
> Nobody else has noticed the crack.
>
> Twilight breaks on the kitchen floor.
> His hands clip and hammer the air.
> He pulls something out,
>
> something small, like a bad tooth,
> and he puts something back,
> and the kitchen is full of peace.
>
> All this is done very quietly,
> without payment or promises.[3]

---

3. Nancy Willard, *Carpenter of the Sun* (New York: Liveright, 1997), p. 19. The poem "Carpenter of the Sun" is reprinted here with the permission of Nancy Willard.

The matter-of-fact tone of this poem makes its claim—that a child can repair the sun—seem credible. And, in fact, most parents understand perfectly well what Nancy Willard means. When my children were young, there were days when gloom might have overwhelmed me except that as I watched them playing, the sun seemed healed and everything was full of peace.

Lisel Mueller is another master of the quiet, childlike voice, but her poems sometimes bare their fangs, as is the case here in "Small Poem About the Hounds and the Hares":

> After the kill, there is the feast.
> And toward the end, when the dancing subsides
> and the young have sneaked off somewhere,
> the hounds, drunk on the blood of the hares,
> begin to talk of how soft
> were their pelts, how graceful their leaps,
> how lovely their scared, gentle eyes.[4]

The point of this poem is not, surely, animals, any more than animals are the point of Aesop's fables. Rather, Mueller's poem sets up a metaphor for the sort of gratuitous cruelty that we don't like to admit goes on in human society. In this poem the child's innocent voice becomes a strategy for sneaking up on knowledge we don't want to have.

When children use metaphor, it is often to articulate something they have noticed for the first time. It seems to be among our first and most powerful tools for thinking about the world.

Language Is Metaphor

Language, itself, is a collection of metaphors, or words that stand in for things. One points to a bug and exclaims "Beetle!" but the word is not the thing. No fact could be more obvious than that, but like many obvious facts, the metaphorical nature of language constantly seems to slip out of our minds.

The minute a word has been invented to stand for a thing, it becomes useful for other purposes. Take *beetle,* which in the first instance means a

---

4. Lisel Mueller, *Alive Together, New and Selected Poems* (Baton Rouge and London: Louisiana State University Press, 1996), p. 72. "Small Poem About the Hounds and the Hares" is reprinted here with the permission of Lisel Mueller and of Louisiana State University Press.

bug. It has been borrowed to make the term *beetle-brow*. *Beetle-brows* are eyebrows that protrude like beetles. Similarly, your *belly* is literally the region under your ribs, while the *belly* of a ship metaphorically lies under the ship's ribs. *Ribs* is also, of course, a metaphor. In fact, many objects are named for parts of the human body, perhaps because we humans are so obsessed with ourselves. There's the *elbow* in a pipe, the *foot* in verse, the *ear* of corn, and the *heel* who won't give you the time of day. There's the *foot* of a mountain, the *neck* of a vase, and the *joint* where you hang out at night.

Idioms Are Metaphor

A whole other level of metaphor in language comes more sharply into focus when we turn the microscope on idioms. I heard an economics reporter on National Public Radio the other day say that the president of a corporation, by reducing the health care benefits of his workers, was "trying to get the last squeal out of the pig." A reporter for a local paper wrote that in Hawaii, "tourism has a large footprint." Such colorful phrases are constantly being invented, frequently on the street, frequently by kids. A metaphor springs to life, catches on, lives a short, healthy life as an idiom, and then, mercifully, it dies.

Or it should. On its way out of the language, an idiom might hang around for a while, inhabiting the status of *cliché*. Think, for instance, of people "having a whale of a good time." Think of how profits can "go south," making an investor who is already "on the edge" finally "go round the bend," more than likely in the difficult "dog days of summer," and end up on "the junk heap of life." These clichés have lost so much energy by years of overuse that it's easy to forget they are metaphor. Their first ability to surprise us with their aptness is worn out because we don't see or touch or taste them as physically real any more.

I suppose the very invisibility of the Y term in clichés is responsible for the hilarious ways people sometimes force mixed metaphors together, as in the case of the physicist Richard Feynman who wanted to explain that no one knows why photons act both as waves and particles. He said, "Do not keep saying to yourself, if you can possibly avoid it, 'How can it possibly be like that?' because you will go down the drain into a blind alley from which no one has yet escaped."

This leads me to remember a wonderful parody on mixed metaphor by the poet Catherine Carter, in her "Poem from Sussex County":

That boy's just about as crazy
as a bedbug. Let me tell you
she sent him forty times around
Robin Hood's barn, and he just keeps coming
back for more, tangles up his feet
in her hair, and no knowing
what color it is this week. She lies
like a dog on a rug,
and he just grins, happy as a pig
in shit, can't find his own ass
with both hands and a flashlight.
Tell you, she fucks him
every which way but happy, he goes
round that barn like he's on his way
to a fire—or maybe he's been there
already and likes the smell
of the smoke—but one
of these days he's just going to shut
that barn door and won't ever come out
no more.[5]

Metaphor as a Whole System

Beyond the phrase level, there is a more complex aspect of metaphor. It is what Eva Hoffman is talking about in her autobiography, *Lost in Translation*.[6] She reminds us that we each construct reality out of a web of images and meanings that we are taught when we are young. The speed of modern communication and travel tends to dislocate each of us from this original set of images. It's possible that you moved, as I did, from a small town to the city. Maybe you have forsaken the religion of your childhood. Maybe you no longer inhabit the Italian or Swedish or Irish neighborhood where you learned how to behave and talk. In any case, there's no doubt that your old ways of seeing and expressing the world have been challenged. You may have been forced to abandon the images you originally understood and loved. If so, you are translating from X to Y.

I have been reading a book that tells of the first incursion by Europeans into the Waorani Indian tribe in Ecuador. In the 1950s, a Waorani named Dayuma fled her tribe to avoid being speared in a massive revenge vendetta.

5. Catherine Carter's "Poem from Sussex County" is printed here with her permission.
6. Eva Hoffman, *Lost in Translation* (New York: Dutton, 1989).

While working for a Spanish patron, she became acquainted with Rachel Saint, a missionary, who wanted to learn the Waorani language. Slowly Dayuma taught Rachel the Waorani dialect. Whatever stories from the Bible Dayuma heard, she converted to Waorani images. There used to be a lot of sheep in the Hebrew culture, for example, so sheep show up reasonably often in the Bible, but because Dayuma had never seen any, she translated *sheep* as *deer*. Dayuma eventually led Rachel through the jungle into the Waorani tribal territory, where she lived for many years. Under Rachel's influence, many members of the Waorani tribe accepted Christianity, which is different for them than it is for a Western culture. In the transaction, Rachel, too, was changed. She began to eat smoked monkey and yuca, to speak in the Waorani dialect, and to revel in her open-air bamboo house. So deeply did Rachel Saint translate herself into Waorani that, at her request, when she died, she was buried in the clearing outside the church in tribal territory.[7]

Though in a less dramatic sense than Rachel Saint or Dayuma, most of us are trying to make ourselves clear in a strange tongue. The diversity on the streets of America and the barrage of ethnicities and cultures we see on film and television guarantee that few of our original systems of belief and expression remain intact. We are always, at some deep level, uprooted, at least in imagination, and translating from one metaphorical system to another.

Metaphor as Argument

How could this be true if metaphor were only decoration, as it is sometimes made out to be? There are people, in fact, who think of metaphor as nice and pleasant and ornamental. In this view, it can do no harm, and, of course, no good, either. It might as well be a Victorian doodad stuck on a modern building. But metaphor is neither that innocent nor that helpless in constructing meaning. It is the I-beam that holds up the whole load.

That is, metaphor, if it does anything, argues.

The argumentative nature of metaphor becomes more clear in poems where the poet chooses one metaphor and sticks with it. Extended metaphor, as it is called, reveals a whole, coherent system of thought, a deep and complicated way of looking at the world. This is the way Emily Dickinson uses extended metaphor, for instance, in her poem "Because I Could Not Stop for Death":

---

7. Ethel Emily Wallis, *Dayuma: Life under Waorani Spears* (Seattle: YWAM Publishing, 1996), pp. 110–15.

Because I could not stop for Death,
He kindly stopped for me;
The carriage held but just ourselves
And Immortality.

We slowly drove, he knew no haste,
And I had put away
My labor, and my leisure too,
For his civility.

We passed the school where children played,
Their lessons scarcely done;
We passed the fields of gazing grain,
We passed the setting sun.

We paused before a house that seemed
A swelling of the ground;
The roof was scarcely visible,
The cornice but a mound.

Since then 't is centuries; but each
Feels shorter than the day
I first surmised the horses' heads
Were toward eternity.[8]

Dying, Emily Dickinson argues, is taking a ride with a gallant but head-strong carriage driver. That is, The Action of X = The Action of Y. In this poem, Dickinson's extended metaphor argues the various aspects of similarity between death and a carriage ride. I, for one, buy it. By the end I almost can believe she is speaking from beyond the grave, though I know that when she wrote this poem she hadn't yet experienced death.

In Dickinson's poem, metaphor insists on a level of meaning that lives beyond the visible, that is referred to by the visible. It makes the invisible

---

8. Dickinson's poem was titled "The Chariot" when it was published in *Poems by Emily Dickinson*, edited by Mabel Loomis Todd and T. W. Higginson (Boston: Roberts Brothers, 1896), pp. 138–39. When Thomas H. Johnson's edition of *The Poems of Emily Dickinson* was published in 1955 (Cambridge, Massachusetts: Belknap Press of Harvard University Press), this new fourth stanza had been added to the poem:

Or rather—He passed Us—
The Dews drew quivering and chill—
For only Gossamer, my Gown—
My Tippet—only Tulle—

world palpable. And by doing so, it transforms material reality. Metaphor is a matter of vision, not ornament, a matter of argument, not decoration.

Metaphor and Simile

Metaphor is a term that was used in the English Renaissance to cover more than two hundred rhetorical figures that make different kinds of comparisons. It would be nice to know exactly how to formulate all those figures, but that information is not easily available. Comparisons these days tend to be divided into two categories. What we now call *metaphor* is the strongest form of comparison because it omits the explicit acknowledgement of mere similarity between X and Y—through the use of "like" or "as"—and instead insists, for example, *The sun is a thumbtack piercing the sky.* That is an assertion.

The form of comparison that uses "like" or "as" is called *simile: The sun, like a thumbtack, pierces the sky.* Now the violence is at one remove. The writer is not making the paradoxical claim that the sun *is* a thumbtack, only that the sun at the moment seems in some sense to be *like* one. Simile is both less drastic and less powerful than metaphor because it compromises with reason and admits that the equation is only apparent, not actual.

In both simile and metaphor, the first term—the X—tends to be the one commented upon. The second term—the Y—is the meaning the writer is arguing for. Y is a way of explaining X. Y is the dangerous term, the term that locks in the polemic. If the sun is like a thumbtack, that's one kind of day. If the sun is like a yellow M&M, that's altogether different. You'd better be right about it. It can't be both.

Whatever the formulation, whether as a metaphor or as a simile, comparison seems to be of almost obsessive interest to contemporary people, perhaps more to adolescents than to adults. Anywhere you go, you can hear references to virtual reality, which seems, sometimes, to have taken the place of everyday life. Furthermore, the casual conversation of young people is studded with the word *like.* Stand in line at a rock concert sometime and eavesdrop on a conversation: "He, *like,* walked right over to me and, *like,* started in with the whole thing. *Like* I mean who's going to believe what he, *like,* SAID?!" It's hard to know exactly what the adolescent means by using *like* this way. Maybe she doesn't herself know. Maybe *like* is a mere placeholder, a way of passing time while she's thinking of the next phrase. I don't know. But I do wonder why she would use *like* (instead of the old faithful *uh!*) if comparison isn't somehow crucial?

The Need for Metaphor in Newswriting

Comparison does not only furnish a strategy that is foundational to all thought; because it grabs readers by their senses, it is also a fabulous technique of argument. So it proves invaluable in writing editorials or opinion columns, and, indeed, in all different forms of newswriting.

If you can persuade a reader to feel a breeze on the back of his neck or to taste cold watermelon, you have a better chance to make that reader agree with you about the X part of your comparison (say, an argument about the schools, or an analysis of an economic problem) than if you appeal to him with abstractions. And because of its tendency to self-consciously double back and reflect on itself, metaphor can create a variety of tones, from pure smart aleck to self-searching, philosophical inquiry.

Metaphor is particularly important in writing about science, which grows daily in importance. Because of a growing rift between science and everyday reality, there is now, more than ever, a crucial need for writers to translate laboratory discoveries into comprehensible stories. Science and technology are surging forward precipitously, driving more and more deeply into abstract, theoretical regions, leaving an uncomprehending population behind. Most of us spend our days trying to get our cars started, raising our children, doing our jobs. We are, in other words, caught in one "reality," while scientists are moving into another.

Reality is a fragile concept, as Einstein pointed out in an essay called "Physics and Reality." As he wrote, "the eternal mystery of the world is its comprehensibility."[9] Popularizers increasingly will be the ones who have to accomplish this comprehensibility, translating between realities, making each side plain to the other. It has been said, and I believe it is true, that a great deal rests on what journalists do in this regard. Many choices that we, as a society, make in the twenty-first century will emerge out of our understanding of scientific and technological discoveries. I would argue that it is helpful for journalists to think consciously of metaphor and to learn to control it as a tool in the process of clarifying choices.

Journalists also are being called upon to translate cultures the way Dayuma and Rachel did. More of us fly. We fly farther and faster. But travel writing is not the only kind of reporting that requires an ability to translate from one culture to another. Political writing, which often involves negotiations between cultures, requires the ability to see several cultures clearly and to translate between them. Because world economies are also increasingly tied together, economic news also often requires translation.

---

9. Albert Einstein, *Essays in Physics* (New York: Philosophical Library, 1950), p. 18.

Using Metaphor to Organize a Story

Extended metaphors can be used brilliantly to organize certain kinds of stories. In March of last year, I heard a story on NPR's *All Things Considered* about how people in Hinkley, Ohio, turn out to wait for the return of the buzzards. The day of their homecoming isn't long after the swallows come back to Capistrano. The comparison between the two birds, perhaps, is obvious. What might not have been so obvious to the writer when he chose the subject was how moving the story would turn out to be. Although buzzards are not nature's most beautiful birds, they have apparently chosen the town of Hinkley as their own, and the town officially honors them with a day of ritual clothing, feast, and songs. Why? The buzzards take over the job of burying the dead. They leave everything cleaner and more alive. They are as welcome, according to the news story, as the swallows are in Capistrano.

I recall seeing a story in the *New York Times* that used extended metaphor in another way. The story claimed that the economic euphoria that had been driving up the U.S. stock market during the previous several years was like the euphoria in Japan that had led to the economic crash there. It's a bubble here, the writer then claimed, just as it had been in Japan. And it would soon burst. Whatever you think of that economic analysis, the writer managed to avoid the sort of abstraction that tends to put a lot of readers to sleep when they turn to the business section of their daily newspaper. Although I suppose a bubble isn't a particularly original comparison with a country's out-of-control economic expectations, as a reader I did what the writer wanted me to do. I pictured a soap bubble; I found myself involved. When will it pop, I wondered?

—

The first step toward learning to use metaphor effectively in your own writing is to practice and be conscious of it around you.

I will conclude with something I call "The Metaphor Kit," an assortment of exercises designed to help you learn to create more expressive metaphors as you write stories.

The Metaphor Kit:
Tips for Writing Metaphor

1. How does a writer invent a comparison? No one knows how a mind comes up with comparisons, but it seems pretty clear that practice can improve your ability. Inventing comparisons will probably go better for you if you think of it as a form of play. You write down everything you can come up with, and then you cross out the comparisons that seem too close, too farfetched, or not relevant. Alex Karras, legendary defensive lineman for the Detroit Lions in the 1950s, was nearly blind without his glasses. But he was not allowed to wear them while he played professional football. One day, a reporter asked Karras how he could tell where the ball was once it had been snapped and players began rushing by. Karras replied that he just grabbed everything, and if it wasn't the ball, he threw it away. That's how you make metaphor.

2. What are the various forms of comparisons? First, of course, there are the two famous figures, *metaphor* (X = Y) and *simile* (X is *like* Y), which don't need more explanation. But there are other ways of formulating comparisons. In fact, a quick look at modern poetry reveals that there are as many different ways of making comparisons as there are ways to win a lover. Here are examples of a few:

- The Y can go on at some length: *Each day is an empty pail I fill and carry to the kitchen.*
- X can act like Y without being called Y: *I unlock handcuffs with a stem of grass.* The grass is a key.

- Or a metaphor can be buried in an adjective that modifies X: *By midnight, the carnal rain has swamped us.* The rain has a body, so it must be something other than rain.
- The Y can appear in a prepositional phrase: *There he stands on the verandah of Mozart's Third Concerto.* The Concerto is a house with a porch.
- The Y can be missing entirely. *I have never worn any shoes but those in which to bring fire.* Shoes suggest a whole way of life that from the beginning dictated that the speaker had no choice but to bring humans fire.
- The Y can be personified by the X. *Midnight, with his hangdog face, is on the prowl again.*

3. What exercises can help a writer learn to use comparisons?
You will likely discover a number of ways to practice making metaphors. Here are three exercises that I've found especially useful:

Comparisons in the Language: To write a figure that makes a comparison, you need first to be able to recognize one. Scan newspapers, listen to the radio, watch billboards, read poetry. Look for comparison. Identify it. Appreciate it. Pay attention to the way it's formulated. Keep a journal that catalogues various metaphors according to the ways they are constructed.

For practice, sit down with paper and pencil and think of what the following X's would be if they weren't themselves but were something else. Give yourself one minute to write *as many* Y's as you can for each X. Let yourself go. Nothing is too crazy for this kind of brainstorming exercise. You can cross out the inept or silly entries later.

A peony	A dripping faucet	A fat woman's hips
A ringing phone	Old garden shoes	A rake
Dusk	A lottery ticket	A mosquito

Idioms: Make a list of idioms and think about where they came from. Here are some examples:

- He won't get to first base.
- He's out in the cold.
- He's beside himself (with worry).
- He's in a blue funk.
- Give him a hand.
- Blood is thicker than water.
- Once in a blue moon.
- Take a leaf out of his book.

Extended Metaphor: If you want to get better at thinking up extended metaphors, do the same thing. Look for comparisons around you. Try to distinguish between one-shot metaphors and metaphors that imply similarity between whole systems. It is basically a matter of seeing the relationship between the *meaning* of one thing and another.

If you want practice inventing extended metaphors, try thinking of situations in politics, education, family life, the law, sports, and other categories in journalism and everyday life that might be compared to the following:

- One aspect of a zoo (the lion cage?)
- One aspect of a symphony orchestra (the drum section?)
- A tornado
- Looking through a telescope into outer space

Rhythm's Cousin, Cadence

By Dennis Jackson

[Jackson has edited four books of essays on D. H. Lawrence and served as editor of the *D. H. Lawrence Review.* He has written for newspapers, magazines, and journals and serves often as a writing coach for various media groups. He is Director of Journalism at the University of Delaware.]

Sportswriter Mitch Albom once told a Wilmington Writers' Workshop that "the key to good writing is rhythm." A year later in the same setting, columnist Leonard Pitts said, "When I write, I hear a rhythm."

Neither elaborated.

It's such an elusive thing—we struggle for words to describe the rhythms we hear in nature (sloshing lake waters) or music (reverberating gamelans), or the ones we see in paintings or other visual arts. Most reporters cannot define *rhythm* after they've accomplished some of it in stories. And few editors are able to tell reporters how to generate it when it's missing.

Albom and Pitts are surely right to put premium value on rhythm in their own good writing. But, here, I want to focus not so much on rhythm as on its cousin, cadence. I want to show the relation cadence has to what one writer calls the "psychological geography" of sentences. This all boils down to the things we can do inside sentences to achieve rhythm and, more crucially, to signal *significance* to readers.

I began thinking about cadence in journalistic writing in 1993, when I heard Donald Drake tell a Writers' Workshop how much his long narrative news stories in the *Philadelphia Inquirer* are influenced by his knowledge of plays and dramatic structure. Drake coaches young reporters at his paper to envision a narrative as a series of dramatic "scenes" and to view the ends of each section of a story as a "curtain line." In effect, he's talking about the need in a story for internal moments of drama, for stresses or cadences in the writing that will alert readers to those passages' special meaning.

Drake's remarks intrigued me because I was then reading Philip Stevick's book *The Chapter in Fiction,* which focuses often on the power of cadence. Stevick observes that most chapters in a good novel reinforce a sense of conclusion by "various stylistic and substantive devices which, in certain positions, enable the chapter to seem to end and which can be called, by analogy with music, cadence." A chapter achieves a powerful sense of *finality,* he says, "by means of the substance and the syntax of its cadence."[1] I realized Drake was talking about the same thing but was applying it to the ways *journalists* can signal drama and meaning by using those same "stylistic and substantive devices" to achieve cadence.

Stevick identifies thirteen types of cadences that novelists use to end chapters. Many of them can occur as well in long newspaper or magazine stories.

For example, Philadelphia reporters Huntly Collins and Shankar Vedantam used what Stevick calls an "anticipatory cadence" in a 1996 story that tracked the competitive hunt by the Merck pharmaceutical firm for protease inhibitors that could be used to treat AIDS.[2] Two early sections of their story each end with an anticipatory cadence—one that simply encourages readers to look forward to what's coming next:

> In Atlanta, Tom Blount, a tall, forceful man with a commanding presence, was worried about his lover.
>
> Blount had just found out that Jim was infected and was determined to keep him alive. That was what love was about. He quit his job as an architect and became a full-time AIDS activist.
>
> At the time, none of these people knew much about the politics or the science of AIDS. But their lives, and the lives of many people they knew, would be changed by the research just beginning at Merck.

●

---

1 Philip Stevick, *The Chapter in Fiction: Theories of Narrative Division* (Syracuse: Syracuse University Press, 1970), pp. 40–41.

2. Huntly Collins and Shankar Vedantam, "8 Years and $700 Million Later, How a Better Drug Was Found," *Philadelphia Inquirer,* March 17, 1996, pp. A-1, A-22, A-23.

The cadence comes in that last sentence, as readers are encouraged to anticipate the elaboration of how this new research will change lives. That sentence serves for that section as a curtain line.

The next eight-paragraph portion of the story ends this way:

> On March 26, 1990, Merck began to test its experimental protease inhibitor in dogs.
>
> About the same time, another pharmaceutical company, Hoffman-La Roche in Nutley, N.J., announced that it had discovered a protease inhibitor drug of its own. It would be called saquinavir.
>
> The race was on.

●

Again, just before the bullet, the reporters achieve what Drake calls a "curtain line," creating a sharp sense of cadence with that blunt declaration: "The race was on." Readers anticipate getting to watch that race, as the drama further unfolds.

Piano-Playing, Motown Song-singing, Foot-tapping, Hand-clapping . . . and Writing

Stevick noted that his thoughts on cadence in prose came by way of an "analogy with music." Two well-known newsroom writing coaches, Donald Murray and Roy Peter Clark, have similarly highlighted the helpful analogies we can draw between the structure of musical pieces and the structures—both small and large—of our prose.

Murray won the 1954 Pulitzer Prize for his editorials and has since written a shelfload of books about writing. He says that, as he works, he often listens to classical music:

> [I] think the great composers have taught me a lot about writing by osmosis. The text is heard by the reader after all and to place that quality in the text, the writer has to hear the draft as— before?—it appears on the monitor screen. Writers are in the music business.[3]

That idea—*Writers are in the music business*—has been underscored in recent years by a series of piano-playing, Motown song-singing, foot-tapping,

---

3. Donald M. Murray, *Writer in the Newsroom* (St. Petersburg, Fla.: Poynter Institute of Media Studies, 1995), p. 26.

hand-clapping Revival-cum-Writing Workshops conducted around the country by Roy Peter Clark, the Poynter Institute's effervescent senior scholar. Clark sings and plays the piano, airs and compares tapes of Otis Redding's and Aretha Franklin's renditions of "R-E-S-P-E-C-T," and uses these performances to make his point that, in our search for words to describe what we do as writers, we often borrow from the grammar and lexicon of musicians. We speak, for example, of a story's *tone,* of its having *rhythm* (or not), of its having *cadence.* We praise writing that "sings."

But just as we borrow musical terms to describe and appraise what we do while sitting at newsroom keyboards, musicians themselves often borrow from the language of writers as they strive to articulate things that happen in music. Note, for instance, the words *sentence, period, punctuation, comma, phrase,* and *tone* used in the following definitions of cadence, each taken from books about music.

First, there's this definition from *A New Dictionary of Music:*

> CADENCE, a progression of chords . . . giving an effect of closing a "sentence" in music.[4]

And in *The Enjoyment of Music,* in a section titled "The Structure of Melody," Joseph Machlis examines the pattern of this well-known tune:

Lon - don Bridge is fall - ing down, fall - ing down, fall - ing down,

Lon - don Bridge is fall - ing down, my fair la - dy.

You will notice that this melody divides itself into two large halves. . . . Each of these halves is called a *phrase.* In music, as in language, a phrase denotes a unit of meaning within a larger structure. Two phrases together form a musical *period.*

Each phrase ends in a kind of resting place that punctuates the flow of the music. Such a resting place is known as a *cadence.* The first phrase of *London Bridge* ends in an upward

---

4. Arthur Jacobs, *A New Dictionary of Music,* 3rd Ed. (Harmondsworth, England: Penguin, 1973), p. 58.

inflection, like a question. This is an inconclusive type of cadence, indicating, like a comma in punctuation, that more is to come. The second phrase ends in a full cadence that creates a sense of conclusion. The vigorous downward inflection on the word "la-dy" contributes to this decisive ending. (. . . [N]ot all final cadences move downward.)

. . . [The melodic line] gives the impression of having reached its goal. If you will hum the last phrase of several well-known tunes such as *The Star-Spangled Banner, America,* and *Auld Lang Syne,* you will notice they all end on a tone that produces this effect of finality.

. . . *The Farmer in the Dell* presents an ascending first phrase which is answered by a descending second phrase:

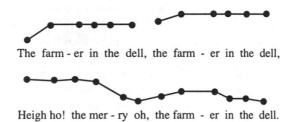

The farm - er in the dell, the farm - er in the dell,

Heigh ho! the mer - ry oh, the farm - er in the dell.

And then Machlis adds, in a statement that can be applied as meaningfully to *writing* as to music:

> The melody moves forward in time, now faster, now slower, in a rhythmic pattern that holds our attention. . . . Without the rhythm the melody loses its aliveness. Try singing *London Bridge* or *The Farmer in the Dell* in tones of equal duration, and see how much is lost of the quality of the pattern. Without rhythm, the melody could not be organized into clear-cut phrases and cadences.[5]

Indeed, if our *prose* moves forward "now faster, now slower, in a rhythmic pattern," it will hold our readers' attention as well. Without rhythm, our writing likewise loses "aliveness" and—with its "tones of equal duration"—

5. Arthur Machlis, *The Enjoyment of Music: An Introduction to Perceptive Listening,* 5th Ed. (New York: Norton, 1984), pp. 8-9.

cannot be organized in the reader's mind into clear-cut phrases and cadences. All our sentences begin to read like . . . all our sentences. Readers drift away.

Tonality

Even more critical than the lack of rhythm, however, is the absence of cadences, of *stress points* in our writing. Cadence is crucial because it has so much to do with the matter of *voice*—or, to borrow a musical term, *tonality*—in our writing. It is voice that gives the stamp of authority and authenticity to what we write. Near the start of her beguiling little volume, *One Writer's Beginnings,* Mississippi short story writer Eudora Welty addresses the importance of voice in prose.

> Ever since I was first read to, then started reading to myself, there has never been a line read that I didn't *hear*. As my eyes followed the sentence, a voice was saying it silently to me. . . . It is human, but inward, and it is inwardly that I listen to it. It is to me the voice of the story . . . itself. The cadence, whatever it is that asks you to believe, the feeling that resides in the printed word, reaches me through the reader-voice. I have supposed, but never found out, that this is the case with all readers—to read as listeners—and with all writers, to write as listeners. . . . The sound of what falls on the page begins the process of testing it for truth, for me.[6]

Notice how Welty links cadence to "the reader-voice." And how she defines cadence as "whatever it is that asks you to believe, the feeling that resides in the printed word." Her point is that, through the creation of cadences, we prompt our readers to re-create a voice, a "reader-voice," in their *mind's ear* (which allows them to *hear* what we're writing as if it were being spoken to them).

Donald Murray underscores the value of this task in *Writer in the Newsroom,* where he asserts that voice "is the single most important element after accuracy" in journalistic writing:

> It is voice that attracts and holds the reader. . . . [E]ffective writers put that heard quality into the writing. They write what they can speak, what sounds right. They write with their ears, tuning

---

6. Eudora Welty, *One Writer's Beginnings* (New York: Warner, 1985), pp. 12–13.

their voice. It is voice, more than any other element, that marks excellent writing. The music of the writing reveals and reinforces meaning, communicates trust and the attitude of the writer toward the meaning.[7]

They're Just Cousins

On the few occasions I've heard editors and reporters use the word *cadence,* they've used it interchangeably with *rhythm.* But these are not the same thing. They overlap. One is part of the other. But they are not the same.

Rhythm is achieved largely through *stylistic* means; for example, through

- Alternating long and short units of prose (by swelling and then contracting sentence lengths or internal sentence elements, even varying syllabic lengths of words);
- Breaking up passages with effective punctuation and pauses;
- Using grammatical parallelism; or,
- By making other such stylistic modifications.

Cadence can be achieved partly through these rhythmic modulations, but cadence involves content as well as style. It's a happy wedding of syntax *and* substance. Cadence results in your story when you place the right things in the right places at the right times.

My earlier extract from Machlis's book indicates how songwriters, in songs such as "London Bridge," seek cadences that will "punctuate" the flow of their music. Poets likewise must create such "punctuation," especially for poems that have rhyming words in emphatic end-of-line locations. Prose writers don't face as intense a pressure to generate these "resting places" that Machlis mentions, these cadences that signal *how* the writing is to be sounded or read. But, as Eudora Welty suggests, good prose writers nonetheless remain keenly sensitive to the stress points that can help generate "reader-voice" and the sense that certain phrases are meant to convey special meaning.

A writer can achieve cadence in many ways. For the purpose of discussion, I've isolated five of the primary techniques:

---

7. Murray, *Writer in the Newsroom,* p. 23.

1. Through an accumulation of coordinate elements within a sentence.
2. Through the use of "emphasis points" in sentences and paragraphs.
3. Through the manipulation of sentence lengths (and by swelling or contracting clauses or phrases within sentences).
4. Through the use of grammatical parallelism in adjoining sentences or paragraphs. Or,
5. Through the ways we "branch" free modifiers in sentences. (Free modifiers are clauses or phrases that we add to the base clause of a sentence in order to modify it.)

My examples below come from diverse genres, but all these techniques can be used successfully in journalistic writing.

Creating Cadence through an Accumulation of Coordinate Elements

The first chapter of the Book of Job is flush with reports of illnesses, thefts, natural disasters, sabotage, and murder—just the average sort of "news" fare found on page A-1 of our daily papers. Job suffers afflictions, his camels and oxen and asses are stolen, lightning burns up his sheep, his servants are killed by miscreant Chaldeans, and his sons and daughters are blown away by a "great wind from the wilderness."

> Then Job arose, and rent his mantle, and shaved his head, and fell down upon the ground, and worshipped.

The words "and worshipped" convey a strong sense of a climax to this portion of Job's tale. That cadence is formed by the substance (he *worshipped*) and the syntax. The writer swells the prose units from the three-word statement "Then Job arose" . . . to the four-word units "and rent his mantle, and shaved his head" . . . to the six-word unit "and fell down upon the ground," and by then clipping the last unit in the series back to just two words, "and worshipped," we get that cadence. Cadence is rhythm. But it is more: It is finality or closure; it is content; it is a drumbeat that resonates significance to your readers.

Creating Cadence through Use of "Emphasis Points"

Because much of the tonality of our prose comes from the words we stress, a good writer must know how and where to apply that emphasis.

Most young reporters I've met over the past quarter-century in classrooms or newsrooms do not understand this. They haven't yet captured the cadence of their voice in their writing. They haven't learned how to make the *sound-shape* of sentences and paragraphs reinforce meaning. Within a given story, there's scant difference between their *most emphasized words* and their *least emphasized words.* Consequently, much of what they write in Monday's story sounds like much of what they write in Tuesday's story.

These young reporters—and a surprising lot of professionals whose stories I read daily—frequently create what I call *IT-must-be-around-here-someplace* leads. These writers know what the news should be for their leads but don't know where to put it. They often cast primary news into subordinate sentence structures or into unemphatic grammatical or syntactical positions. They circle around their "news," hiding the main point within layers of unemphatic verbiage. The reader surmises: "IT must be around here someplace!"

So, I constantly remind young reporters about the two chief kinds of emphasis points in a sentence—(1) grammatical and (2) positional.

Grammatical emphasis means, primarily, that the subject and verb of the base (or main) clause of your leads and other pivotal sentences in a story should be *key words,* crucial, colorful, news-delivering words.

Noam Chomsky and other linguists have told us that humans are genetically programmed to identify grammatical patterns, that by the time we are eighteen months old, we're usually able to speak in logical sentences. We learn to speak through subjects and verbs: "Mommy feed. Baby eat." It makes sense that, in our sentences that count the most, we should try to make the best possible use of these words—subjects and verbs—that count the most grammatically.

Positional emphasis is another way of stating what Strunk and White urged, decades ago: "Place the emphatic words of a sentence at the end."[8] Joseph Williams elaborates on this in his book *Style,* as he focuses on what he calls a sentence's "psychological geography":

> Emphasis is largely a matter of controlling the way a sentence ends. When we maneuver our most important information into that stressed position, the natural emphasis we hear in our mind's ear underscores the rhetorical emphasis of a significant

---

8. William Strunk, Jr., and E. B. White, *The Elements of Style,* 2nd Ed. (New York: Macmillan, 1972), p. 23.

idea. But the sentence will seem weak and anticlimactic if it ends with lightweight words. . . . Sentences should move toward strength.

. . . How you manage the words that appear in that concluding stress position goes a long way toward establishing the energy that your readers hear in the voice that your writing projects."[9]

So, to sum up, here are two ways to maximize your use of *emphasis* spots in what you're writing:

1. Readers look in the early part of a sentence for your *topic,* your grammatical subject and its verb, so you lend clarity to your prose by presenting that topic early and directly.
2. Readers assign special emphasis to words they hear in their *mind's ear* at the end of sentences or paragraphs. Words placed there sound the most resonantly and linger longest in the reader's mind. So you benefit by saving a memorable phrase for that end spot.

But . . . how *do* you get key words into the subject-verb position and at the same time save other special words to create a cadence at the sentence's end?[10]

It can be tough. Things will butt heads: One news element will work against another. Sometimes, you just have to violate one or another of these guidelines concerning emphasis sites. Obviously, you cannot labor over every sentence, trying to make it follow these guidelines. But you can strive at least to construct *critical* passages—your lead, your "nut paragraph," the story's best moments of drama, the climax of narrative sections, your kicker—so that important words fall both into subject-verb slots and at the *end.*

This information on the "psychological geography" of sentences becomes especially useful when you're trying to *revise* an important passage where you have sentences or paragraphs that you know are not working to maximum strength. In many cases, you won't know what words you want to deploy as cadence words until you've finished your rough draft and are reading it aloud. Then, if you decide you didn't get the right words

---

9. I draw my quotes here from two different editions of Joseph M. Williams's book *Style: Ten Lessons in Clarity and Grace.* My references are to the third edition (New York: HarperCollins, 1989), p. 154, and to the fifth edition (New York: Longman, 1997), pp. 146–47.

10. The admonition to place emphatic material at the end of sentences (and paragraphs) does not apply to many hard news leads. There, the chief emphasis typically shifts back to the *front* of the lead sentence or paragraph because attributive tags so often appear at the end, muffling whatever cadence could fall there.

under the right stress in certain places, you might consider revisions that will draw more on the power of emphasis points.

Here, for instance, is a sentence from a 1994 Associated Press news story that is in need of such revisions:

> The drama began after Paul Broussard, 38, a deputy who had been suspended a day earlier when his estranged wife, Andrea Baden Broussard, obtained a restraining order against him for beating her, shot and killed the woman, then ran across the street to the courtyard of an Alexandria bank.[11]

What goes wrong here?

1. For a start, the sentence (because of its structure) seems too long, at forty-nine words. (Hour-long episodes of TV's *Law & Order* have portrayed less felonious activity than the writer packs in here.)
2. The reporter makes poor use of both grammatical and positional emphasis points. The subject and verb of the base clause ("drama began") report no substantive news. The emphatic terminal position is wasted on scenery—as three consecutive prepositional phrases take us "across the street / to the courtyard / of an Alexandria bank." Those are what Joseph Williams calls "lightweight words," anticlimactic at best in a sentence filled with so much "drama."
3. The mid-branching suspensive element ranges on far too long, losing the reader in the maze of "38, a deputy who had been suspended a day earlier when his estranged wife, Andrea Baden Broussard, obtained a restraining order against him for beating her."
4. The subject and verb lie too far separated in the noun clause that forms the object of the preposition "after." The reporter asks too much of readers, to expect them to mate that subject ("Broussard") with its verb ("shot and killed") after twenty-six words have intervened.

It would be nice to say such syntactically disturbed sentences appear only rarely in our daily papers. It would be nice, but not true. Scrambling to make deadline, reporters will scroll around a screen searching for larger structural weaknesses while failing to heed the flaws that bedevil their smaller units of writing.

---

11. Chevel Johnson, "TV station criticized for airing a suicide," *Philadelphia Inquirer,* Sept. 17, 1994, p. D-13.

Here's another sample taken from the AP wires, this one a news lead by a reporter (Howard Benedict) who has made especially keen use of emphasis points:

> Space Shuttle Challenger exploded into a gigantic fireball 75 seconds after liftoff today, killing its crew of seven, including schoolteacher Christa McAuliffe.[12]

The sentence introduces its topic immediately in the base clause's subject and verb—"Space Shuttle Challenger exploded," and then branches its modification off to the right, ending with the free modifier, "killing its crew of seven, including schoolteacher Christa McAuliffe."

That terminal stress is smartly used. The reader will almost certainly identify most strongly with the young schoolteacher whose story had riveted the press for months before the launch.

The sentence's structure could be reversed, depending on what the writer wants to stress. It could've read this way:

> Seven Astronauts including schoolteacher Christa McAuliffe were killed today when Space Shuttle Challenger exploded just after liftoff into a gigantic fireball.

This lead still reports that seven astronauts—among them the schoolteacher—died, but now the primary stress (at the end) is on the dramatic nature of the event, the Challenger's explosion into that spectacular fireball.

It all depends on what you select to emphasize most, as you construct your sentence. This is not inconsequential, as author Joan Didion has observed: "To shift the structure of a sentence alters the meaning of that sentence, as definitely and inflexibly as the position of a camera alters the meaning of the object photographed."[13]

Creating Cadence through Manipulation of the Lengths of Prose Units

Though by all reports St. John of Zebedee was unschooled as a writer, he (or his translators) clearly recognized the power of the short sentence. In

---

12. Quoted from an Associated Press report filed from Cape Canaveral, Florida, by Howard Benedict, p.m. cycle, Tuesday, Jan. 28, 1986, from the Lexis-Nexis Academic Universe database.

13. Didion is quoted in Donald M. Murray's *Shoptalk: Learning To Write with Writers* (Portsmouth, N.H.: Boynton/Cook, 1990), p. 160.

the New Testament Book of John (chapter 11), he narrates how Jesus brings his friend Lazarus back to life. Lazarus's sisters summon Jesus to help their ailing brother, but by the time Jesus reaches Bethany, Lazarus has been dead four days. Here's St. John's "spot" news coverage of what happened next:

> Then when Mary was come where Jesus was, and saw him, she fell down at his feet, saying unto him, "Lord, if thou hadst been here, my brother had not died."
>
> When Jesus therefore saw her weeping, and the Jews also weeping which came with her, he groaned in the spirit, and was troubled.
>
> And said, "Where have ye laid him?" They said unto him, "Lord, come and see."
>
> Jesus wept.

Obviously St. John, as well as King James's staff of translators, knew that a short sentence, isolated in its own paragraph, can create powerful cadence. The writer here gears down, each verse growing shorter than the one before, until we hit that dramatic final statement: "Jesus wept."

Richard Ben Cramer is another writer who respects the energy of short sentences. He demonstrated this in a 1979 *Philadelphia Inquirer* story "A Walk in No Man's Land," which helped him win the Pulitzer Prize for international reporting. He gathered information for his story by walking boldly through a "no man's land" in Lebanon between the poised guns of Israelis and Palestinians. His story opens this way:

> RAS EL BAYADA, Occupied Lebanon—It is eerily still in no man's land, a two-mile testament to the lesson that people are as much a part of the landscape as houses and fences and fields.
>
> Here, eight miles from Lebanon's southern border, between the last Fatah commando checkpoint and the spearhead of the advancing Israelis, the chickens come out to meet you on the road. It has been 48 hours since grain was scattered for them in their yards.
>
> Here, everything is frozen in time, like a Pompeii without the lava. Crates of oranges are stacked, unattended, next to empty houses. Telephone wires dangle broken and useless from their poles. An open spigot pours an endless stream of water onto a swamp that was once a garden.

Here, the mere whoosh of a breeze through the leaves can make you sprint for cover, scanning the sky for warplanes until you dive into the orange groves . . . only to emerge a moment later feeling foolish and shaky from the rush of adrenalin.

To be sure, there is noise and plenty of it. There are real planes and antiaircraft guns nearby. Artillery blasts thudding on the hillsides make the sheep bleat as they scatter and the frogs wail in the ditches.

But it takes man's noise to break the stillness—a child's cry, an engine, or a laugh. And without man, the eeriness is unrelieved in this world between two worlds.[14]

The story continues through another thirty-one paragraphs. I've done a bit of finger counting through the whole of the story to come up with the following statistics:

- Number of words in Cramer's story: 1,055
- Number of sentences: 85
- Number of paragraphs: 37
- Average number of words per sentence: 12.4
- Average number of words per paragraph: 31
- Longest sentence: 43 words
- Shortest sentence: 2 words
- Longest paragraph: 55 words
- Shortest paragraph: 9 words
- Number of sentences over 30 words: 5 (6 percent)
- Number of sentences with 10 or fewer words: 37 (43 percent)

It may seem pedestrian to parse Cramer's prose into such numbers, but they tell us things that, in some cases, may not be so obvious as we read the story. Clearly his sentences (which average 12 words) and his paragraphs (31 words) are impressively short, even by journalistic standards. Nonetheless, his story never falls into an artificial staccato-type rhythm, into the sort of "bad-Hemingway" prose that stories featuring such short units sometimes devolve into. Nor does Cramer's prose ever seem to sweat, though a series of short sentences packed tightly together can often do that. (Short sentences—with their frequent full-stop periods—can slow down the pace of reading more so than long sentences can.)

---

14. Richard Ben Cramer, "A Walk in No Man's Land," *Philadelphia Inquirer,* March 17, 1978, p. A-1 *ff.* Reprinted in *The Pulitzer Prize Story II,* ed. John Hohenberg (New York: Columbia University Press, 1980), pp. 134–39.

Though Cramer's sentences average only 12 words each—and 43 percent of them are 10 words or under—there's still impressive *variety* in the lengths of his prose units. For example, the lone sentence in his fourth paragraph stretches into 43 words, and his paragraphs range from 9 to 55 words long.

Cramer's prose falls close to the "Easy" category on Rudolf Flesch's readability scales in *The Art of Readable Writing,* a 1949 book that strongly influenced the development of modern journalistic style.[15] Here's the mathematical chart Flesch used to measure the "readability" of prose:

DESCRIPTION OF STYLE	AVERAGE SENTENCE LENGTH	AVERAGE NUMBER OF SYLLABLES PER 100 WORDS	ESTIMATED SCHOOL GRADES COMPLETED	ESTIMATED PERCENT OF U.S. ADULTS
Very easy	8 or less	123 or less	4th grade	93
Easy	11	131	5th grade	91
Fairly easy	14	139	6th grade	88
Standard	17	147	7th or 8th grade	83
Fairly difficult	21	155	some high school	54
Difficult	25	167	high school or some college	33
Very difficult	29 or more	192 or more	college	4.5

Some numbers in this chart are outdated, but as we begin the twenty-first century, good newspaper prose is still characterized by much of what Flesch proposed in the late 1940s. After World War II, newsprint was scarce and high-priced. So the AP and UP wire services and many newspapers enthusiastically took up the readability formulas that Flesch and other communication specialists were developing. Flesch devised "reading ease" scales, based on a finger-count of a passage's number of words, average sentence lengths, number of syllables per word, and so on. His readability formula encouraged reporters to write concise, simple sentences, using familiar, short vocabulary.

But Ray Laakaniemi is oversimplifying in his more recent *Newswriting in Transition* when he extends Flesch's principles to declare outright that

15. Rudolf Flesch, *The Art of Readable Writing* (New York: Harper & Brothers, 1949), p. 149.

"Journalistic writing is precise and short."[16] Even Dr. Seuss (Theodore Giesel)—who spent his career writing for children—recognized that "Simple, short sentences don't always work. You have to do tricks with pacing, alternate long sentences with short, to keep it vital and alive."[17]

You can get away with writing long sentences in journalistic prose . . .

- If they're gracefully constructed and deliver their meaning readily (that is, if they're front-loaded with a subject and its verb, and if their free modifiers are placed at the end);
- If you're writing features (where you can often generate a long, readable sentence more easily than you can in writing hard news);
- If you're writing chronological narrative (in anything—news, features, or sports); and
- If you need a long sentence to establish the sort of conversational flow that results from alternating long and short units (for the sake of variety).

In short, long sentences help us perform those "tricks with pacing" that Dr. Seuss mentioned, and thus they comprise a vital part of how we create cadences and voice.

Creating Cadence through Use of Grammatical Parallelism

You're likely aware of the technique of grammatical parallelism featured in so many Walt Whitman poems. You've also heard it used with maximum effect by Dr. Martin Luther King, Jr., in his 1963 March on Washington speech, when he hammered out his most passionate points in the seven consecutive sentences that each began "I have a dream. . . ." King there masterfully employed grammatical parallelism and repetition, and manipulated his sentence lengths as he created rhythms and cadences that underscored his primary points.

The question is, can we translate these kinds of rhetorical techniques used in poems or public discourse into what we write for our *Daily Bugle*?

Yes, in some stories we can. Grammatical parallelism might seem self-consciously ludicrous in an account of Friday's synagogue fire or a mugging

---

16. Ray Laakaniemi, *Newswriting in Transition* (Chicago: Nelson-Hall, 1995), p. 134
17. Dr. Seuss (Theodore Giesel) is quoted in Donald M. Murray's *Writing for Your Readers: Notes on the Writer's Craft from "The Boston Globe"* (Chester, Conn.: Globe Pequot Press, 1983), p. 116.

at the Acme. But notice how effectively Cynthia Gorney used precisely the same techniques King used, as she wrote a *Washington Post* news feature about her 1979 interview (the first anyone had done) in Soledad prison with Robert F. Kennedy's assassin, Sirhan Sirhan:

> The heavy midmorning light of the Salinas Valley comes through the conference room window. The window is barred. The pane is tattersalled with lead, so that even if shattered the glass would cling in place in shards. Sirhan wears a white T-shirt, blue jeans and a solid prison-issue belt around his narrow waist.
> He says he did not eat breakfast.
> He says he was too nervous to eat.
> He says he would like to make it known that he is remorseful, that he believes it was wrong to have killed another human being, that he feels sorrow at having murdered a father and husband.
> He also says he has been in prison long enough. Sirhan Sirhan, who wrenched aside the 1970s with the force that history gives only to political assassins, wants to go home.[18]

Gorney's deliberate use of grammatical parallelism in the paragraphs that begin "He says he . . . . He says he . . . . He says he . . . . He also says he . . . ." becomes integral to the way she builds rhythm and delivers meaning.

The variation and manipulation of Gorney's sentence lengths particularly impress. After the four initial sentences of 14, 4, 19, and 17 words, she gears back to two single-sentence paragraphs of 7 words (He says he did not eat breakfast) and 8 (He says he was too nervous to eat), before swelling to a one-sentence paragraph of 36 words. Her final paragraph here includes sentences of 10 and 21 words. So she achieves good variety of sentence lengths—from 4 to 36 words—and avoids lulling readers to sleep with sentences that fall too frequently and monotonously into the 17- to 32-word range. Her variation of sentence lengths helps her achieve effective rhythm, and, more importantly, to strike resonant cadences.

Gorney manipulates sentence lengths to guide readers toward her meaning. After punching out two short sentences ("did not eat breakfast," "was too nervous to eat"), she expands to that 36-word sentence that includes three noun clauses beginning with "that"—

18. Cynthia Gorney, "Sirhan," *Washington Post*, August 21, 1979, pp. B-1, B-3. Reprinted in *Best Newspaper Writing 1980*, ed. Roy Peter Clark (St. Petersburg, Fla.: Modern Media Institute, 1980), p. 24.

> . . . *that* he is remorseful, *that* he believes it was wrong to have
> killed another human being, *that* he feels sorrow at having mur-
> dered a father and a husband.

(Even within those clauses there's further swelling: from 4 words in the first
clause to 12 each in the next two.) She moves from the trivial ("did not eat
breakfast," "too nervous to eat")—to the poignant ("feels sorrow at having
murdered a father and a husband"). After that swelling 36-word sentence
about his remorse, she punches out a short 10-word statement: "He also
says he has been in prison long enough." That sentence is like a short-trav-
elling uppercut that leaves a boxer wobbling. Gorney is *slanting* her story;
there's an unmistakable edge that weights her prose against Sirhan. We
hear her *voice,* her stress points, and what we hear is unmistakable: Sirhan
wants out of prison, and Gorney knows she has been granted this exclusive
interview so he can voice that argument.

All this she further underscores with the last sentence in the passage:
"Sirhan Sirhan, who wrenched aside the 1970s with the force that history
gives only to political assassins, wants to go home." The mid-branching
adjectival clause ("who wrenched aside. . . .") is suspensive; it creates a fairly high-tension syntax as it delays the delivery of the final knockout punch,
that 4-word climax that completes the base clause: "Sirhan . . . *wants to go
home.*"

Gorney maximizes her use of terminal emphasis positions in sentences
and paragraphs to create forceful cadences and deliver her story's essential
points. In a nutshell, Sirhan

> . . . did not eat breakfast.
> . . . was too nervous to eat.
> . . . feels sorrow at having murdered a father and a husband.
> . . . says he has been in prison long enough.
> . . . wants to go home.

That's 32 words—out of the total of 136 in this passage. But those are *the
key words* that tell her story.

Creating Cadence through the Ways
We "Branch" Free Modifiers

"Free modifiers" are nonrestrictive structures that we add to the base clause
of a sentence in order to modify it.

Here's an example:

> Hoover watched Kennedy warily, *sensing a possible new foe in the charismatic young senator from Massachusetts.*

The italicized free modifier[19] is "nonrestrictive"—it can be deleted without destroying the syntactic completeness of the sentence. We typically set these modifications off from the base clause by using a comma or dash.

Here are some further defining features of free modifiers:

- They can include noun, verb, and adjective clusters; subordinate and relative clauses; and prepositional phrases.
- We call them "free" because they can be moved around in a sentence.
- They specifically modify the subject of the nearest verb but often seem to modify the whole base clause rather than just the subject.
- Most begin either with an –*ing* present-participle form of a verb; with an adjective; or with the past participle form of a verb.

Here is why they are so important: The clarity, rhythms, and cadences of our writing depend in crucial ways on *where* and *how* we add these free modifiers to sentences.

We can *branch* them from a sentence's base clause in three directions. Attached to the front of the base clause, the free modifier is called "left-branching":

> *Aware that he was facing a hostile press,* Richard Nixon chose his words carefully.

A "mid-branching" free modifier—interposed between the subject and the verb of the base clause—delays completion of a thought and thus creates syntactical suspension:

> Richard Nixon, *aware that he was facing a hostile press,* chose his words carefully.

A "right-branching" free modifier is one placed after the base clause, allowing the writer first to state a topic and then to refine or modify it—sometimes at great length—in the dependent construction that ends the sentence.

---

19. I have italicized the free modifiers referenced in the excerpts throughout this section.

> Richard Nixon chose his words carefully, *aware that he was facing a hostile press.*

When we speak of left, mid, and right branches, we're simply talking about the *direction of modification* in our sentences. (We can and often do write sentences that "branch" in more than one direction.)

I'll illustrate these various types of branches further, commenting as I do on how they affect—or effect—what Joseph Williams calls the "psychological geography" of a sentence.

Left-Branching Sentences. There's nothing innately wrong with using sentences that branch modification to the left. But such constructions delay your subject and verb, thus often delaying your delivery of *meaning* to the reader. Consequently, when you construct such a sentence, you need to be aware you're doing so, and you should have a special reason for it.

Here are two examples where long left-branching modifiers are made to work *for* the reporter, generating rhythm and building toward an impressive cadence at sentence's end:

First, Red Smith's lead from a 1975 column about the Ali-Frazier fight in Manila—

> *When time has cooled the violent passions of the sweltering day and the definitive history is written of the five-year war between Muhammad Ali and Joe Frazier,* the objective historian will remember that Joe was still coming in at the finish.[20]

Undoubtedly, that left-branching free modifier significantly affects the sentence's rhythm and cadence. Frazier lost the fight, but Red Smith wins with this forty-two-word sentence that leaves such a memorable noun clause in the terminal emphasis position: "that Joe was still coming in at the finish."

Second, a paragraph from a 1995 story by *Philadelphia Inquirer* reporters Carol Morello and Marjorie Valbrun, about the O. J. Simpson murder trial verdict—

---

20. Red Smith, "Joe was still coming in," *New York Times,* Oct. 1, 1975. Reprinted in *The Pulitzer Prize Story II,* ed. John Hohenberg (New York: Columbia University Press, 1980), p. 300.

> In Atlantic City casinos and Center City beauty parlors, from a spa in Langhorne to an assembly line that shut down for a moment in Northampton Township, from the Court at King of Prussia to the classrooms of University City High, everyone paused to ponder one last time the case that has riveted America.[21]

The writers branch their modification to the left, and build to a strong final emphasis on "the case that has riveted America." The left-branching construction seems justified, and the sentence seems clear.

But these reporters flirt with danger. They test their readers' patience with a fifty-four-word sentence. They string in front of their base clause a series of prepositional phrases that range for forty-one words before the subject and verb appear ("everyone paused")—and that's perilously long to hold a reader in syntactic suspense. There *has* to be a big payoff, in a sentence so constructed. In this one, there is—after all, this *is* the case that for more than a year "has riveted America."

Red Smith and the two Philadelphia reporters expertly control their readers, calculatedly employing long left-branching modifications to set up sentences that build to a compelling cadence.

But less experienced writers often use similar left-branching arrangements without being aware of their frequency or length, doing so at the expense of clarity and communication. In some cases, these writers unknowingly fall into a *habit* of confronting readers with front-heavy, left-branching sentences that make their prose more challenging than it needs to be.

An example: Several years ago, I judged the Enterprise Reporting entries in a New Jersey Press Association competition. One reporter for a daily paper submitted eight related news stories. Here are the leads for six of them:

> 1. TRENTON—*While the state proceeds to turn over control of the 26 motor vehicle agencies to private hands, and a plan to privatize inspection stations rolls along,* a third possibility to allow private driver training schools to issue driver's licenses cleared an Assembly committee last week with little notice or fanfare.

---

21. Carol Morello and MarjorieValbrun,"Reactions Show Racial Divisions in the Philadelphia Area," *Philadelphia Inquirer,* Oct. 4, 1995, pp.A-1 *ff.*

2. TRENTON—*Through information collected over two days of testimony and a probe of its own in 1965,* the State Commission of Investigation detailed numerous problems besetting the private agencies, ranging from agent truancy to major security breaches.

3. TRENTON—*Despite a flat denial from a Whitman administration spokesman that the governor's office is actively participating in selecting private agents to run motor vehicle agencies,* a candidate for the Cherry Hill post disclosed he has discussed the job with the governor's deputy chief of staff.

4. TRENTON—*Stopping short of a requested full-scale investigation,* the State Commission of Investigation nevertheless decided Wednesday to monitor the planned private conversion of 22 state-run motor vehicle agencies, the Times has learned.

5. TRENTON—*Though mandatory state police background checks and security clearances are still lacking,* five recruits selected by the Division of Motor Vehicles began training Monday to take over as agents in DMV facilities targeted for private conversion.

6. TRENTON—*Despite repeated insistence by top officials that the administration has imposed a formal selection process for hiring private agents to operate state-run motor vehicle agencies,* an affidavit filed by one supervisor recruited for the job appears to suggest otherwise.

These leads were written over the course of months, but notice the sameness of their construction. A bit of numbers-crunching makes clear some of the stylistic habits this reporter needs to alter:

- The six leads contain 240 words (an average of 40 per lead);
- Of those 240 words, 113 (47 percent) are cast in "left-branching" modifiers; and
- On average, the subject word in the six leads falls 21 words deep in the sentence.

Because of their structure, these leads seem too long. They tend to hide their news in the unemphatic middle of the sentence. The reporter is depending too much on dependent constructions (almost half the words) to convey meaning.

The first lead ranges for fifty words—too many, usually, for a reader to have to assimilate in a news lead. Local readers would likely find interest in these stories (the reporter's editors thought them newsworthy enough to submit them for an enterprise reporting award). But the leads' left-branching modifications delay disclosure of their *subject* words (on average buried exactly in the unemphatic middle of these sentences), causing readers to have to *search* for whatever the chief news is.

That search seems especially imposing in a news lead.

So, if you're using a left-branching sentence, have a purpose in doing so, especially if you extend that "branch" for more than, say, eight to ten words. Generally you're wise to keep such constructions short, to convey readers as immediately as you can to the subject-and-verb meat of your sentence.

Mid-branching Sentences. Similar guidelines apply to "mid-branching" constructions, which also delay the reader's progress through your sentence. Here's one such construction used in the lead of a 1992 news story:

> New Jersey's waste-hauling industry, *which was brought under state regulation 20 years ago to pry it out of the grip of organized crime,* will be set free April 14.[22]

The subject there is separated from its verb by a nineteen-word, mid-branching free modifier. In this lead, that doesn't seem particularly problematic. But an obvious hazard of using such a suspensive mid-sentence branch is that it can divorce your subject and verb for too long a stretch. You need to be wary of how long you can hold the reader's attention while you *suspend* the grammatical completion of a sentence. In general, you're tempting fate in journalistic prose if you're writing many sentences with mid-branching structures.

Right-Branching Sentences. A right-branching sentence accumulates material *after* the basic idea has been stated, continuing to define or amplify the main clause after it has been grammatically completed. The most attractive reason for generating such a sentence is simply that you can pack more into it, managing all the while to keep it clear and accessible.

Look, for example, at this sentence:

---

22. John J. Fried, "N.J. Waste Haulers Set Free," *Philadelphia Inquirer,* April 6, 1992, p. D-1.

> Jackie Robinson challenged the racism that dominated all pro-
> fessional sports, *forcing whites to acknowledge his athletic
> skills, encouraging blacks to follow him into mainstream sports,
> all the while claiming he was "just another fellow playing a
> game" he loved.*

Configured in other ways, that sentence could become an impassable
swamp for readers. It's long, and it covers a lot of ground, conceptually. But
it remains readable because the reporter has branched modification to the
right, using that series of "-ing" present participles to keep the sentence
flowing along. The base clause immediately declares the subject-verb-direct
object core of the statement: "Robinson challenged racism." Then the
right-branching free modifiers elaborate on that statement and lead to the
forceful declaration that Robinson wants a world where anyone—of any race
or color—can be "just another fellow playing a game" he loves.

So What?

Branching more of your sentence modifications to the right will not in itself
make you an outstanding writer. It likely will make you a more readable
journalist.

Roy Peter Clark declares in *The American Conversation and the
Language of Journalism* that "[t]he right-branching sentence is the staple of
effective journalism in the modern era."[23] It is so because it allows reporters
to write comparatively long sentences that remain easy to read.

A sentence front-loaded with a subject and verb immediately tells the
reader what you're writing about. That frees you to concentrate in the rest
of the sentence on generating a memorable cadence at the end. As
cadences accumulate through your story, they go a long way toward infus-
ing it with whatever energy, authenticity, and voice it will project.

In the *mind's ear* of your reader, those cadences will form the drum-
beats that signal significance.

---

23. Roy Peter Clark, *The American Conversation and the Language of Journalism*
(St. Petersburg, Fla.: Poynter Institute for Media Studies, 1994), pp. 10–11.

A "StyleCheck" for Your Writing

By Dennis Jackson

In the decades since word processors infiltrated newsrooms, we've watched software programs becoming increasingly sophisticated, to the point that one media professor recently declared these programs "full-fledged partners in the writing process."[1]

That seems a little too happy too early.

It is true, thanks to SpellCheck programs, that editors no longer have to ferret out from careless reporters' copy all the miscreant appearances of such creations as "recieve," "priviledge," and "sophmore."

Stylebook software programs will—as you write—tell you whether "hanky-panky" has a hyphen (it does) or whether "hell" deserves a capital "H" (it doesn't, but "Hades" does). I still miss the old *UPI Stylebook,* which insisted on this distinction: "A *burro* is an ass. A *burrow* is a hole in the ground. As a journalist you are expected to know the difference." Today, if a journalist doesn't know that difference, some software "partner" may come to the rescue.

Certain grammar-checking programs will even scan your stories for punctuation and grammatical errors and the presence of clichés, jargon, or passive voice verbs.

---

1. James Glen Stovall, *Writing for the Mass Media,* 4th Ed. (Boston:Allyn and Bacon, 1998), p. 30.

These programs are yet to be trained to trot over to the courthouse to cover a trial, or conduct a bedside interview with the guy whose canoe slipped over the falls. Software programs likewise remain clueless about most substantive matters of *style,* the things you do (or don't do) in your writing when it comes to features such as rhythm, cadence, or voice.

It would be good if some such "GdProse" program did exist, something that would flash signals telling you to "speed up your pace," "use a short sentence to highlight the drama here," or "create a stronger cadence as this sentence ends." When that sort of thing begins occurring on our screens, *then* these software programs can be sworn in as "full-fledged partners in the writing process."

In the meantime, I've designed a little "StyleCheck" program that I call "The Count-All-the-Peas-in-the-Pod Method."

It's digital only in the sense that you'll have to count things, like the number of words or sentences in a story, on your own fingers. In the end it will be up to *you* to take the statistics and draw some conclusions about your style.

As pedestrian as the "Count-the-Peas" process may seem (you can trust Hemingway never tried this), it can give you strong clues about whether or not you're getting enough cadence, rhythm, and clarity into stories to make them distinctive.

Perhaps then, as you continue writing, you can build on the clues.

You will need: two or three copies of a typical story you wrote, say, six months ago (something relatively long); some crayons or pens of different colors; and a couple of hours for counting and thinking.

If you take the time to do it, this exercise has the potential to indicate—

- Whether you've fallen into certain stylistic "ruts" or bad habits over the years;
- Whether you're making frequent enough use of the power of short sentences at critical locations in stories;
- Whether your prose units are varied enough in length to be rhythmic or to be helpful in creating cadence (or, to the contrary, whether they're too frequently falling into monotonous structures of similar lengths);
- Whether you're maximizing the use of emphasis points in key passages;
- And, finally, the degree to which you're taxing your reader's attention span with cluttering left-branching or suspensive mid-branching sentence modifiers that delay your delivery of meaning.

Before you begin the "StyleCheck," *read the story out loud.* That's always the best first test of what you've written.

StyleCheck No. 1: Evaluating Sentence Lengths

To get started, you will need to count all the peas in the pod:

- Count and record the number of *all* the story's WORDS.
- Count and record the number of SENTENCES. (Anything between two periods counts as a "sentence.")
- In vertical columns, make a running list of the WORD COUNTS IN EACH SENTENCE (27, 32, 14, etc.) and in EACH PARAGRAPH.
- Divide the total number of words by the total number of sentences to come up with your AVERAGE NUMBER OF WORDS-PER-SENTENCE.
- Divide the total number of words by the total number of paragraphs to come up with your AVERAGE NUMBER OF WORDS-PER-PARAGRAPH.

Now, take a look to see what these numbers might be telling you about your stylistic *habits.* (Obviously, the more stories you evaluate using these methods, the more valid and revealing your findings will be.)

What Is Your Average Sentence Length? This statistic, in itself, may not tell you much. Some reporters can write long sentences that remain graceful and comprehensible; other writers can muddy up a short one. It depends a lot on how you structure sentences, and where you place sentence modifiers. (More about that shortly.)

But . . . if you find you're averaging, say, twenty-five or more words per sentence, you definitely need to consider whether you're packing too much into sentences for typical newspaper readers.

Are You Manipulating Sentence Lengths Enough to Achieve Variety, Rhythm, and Cadence? Examine the *range* of your sentence lengths: How far above and below your average sentence length do you venture? (Do the same exercise with your paragraphs.)

What *percentage* of your sentences fall outside the range of, say, seventeen to thirty-two words? How many fall *below* seventeen or *above* thirty-two words?

The answers here may suggest that your sentences (and paragraphs) are falling too frequently inside a certain limited range of words. If that's so, then your writing may be on (or over) the edge of monotony, with little or no chance for generating rhythm or cadence.

In his useful handbook on *Revising Prose,* Richard Lanham declares:

> Obviously, no absolute quantitative standards exist for how much variety is good, how little bad, but the principle couldn't be easier. Vary your sentence lengths. Naturally enough, complex patterns will fall into long sentences and emphatic conclusions work well when short. But no rules prevail except to avoid monotony.[2]

The question is, simply, are you *manipulating* sentence lengths to stress your main points and to give variety and voice to your writing?

Are you, indeed, avoiding monotony?

The cold numbers should provide hints.

Does Your Story Feature at Least One "Jesus Wept" Sentence? The
Bible's shortest sentence dramatically expresses Jesus's reaction on learning that his friend Lazarus has died:

"Jesus wept."

Short sentences can pack extraordinary power into your writing.

Examine your own story. With a red pen *circle* any short sentences (ten words or under) that you've used in one of the story's key spots (when the robber pulled the gun and fired; when the bus ran the red light and crashed; when the bank examiner discovered the missing numbers; when the researchers realized the new drug was working; when the PTA meeting erupted into a shouting match; when the mayor first learned he had prostate cancer). Was there at least one impressively short sentence that you used to deliver *special meaning?* If not, go back now and search for a place where you could have or should have used one.

Next, look at *where* and *how* you employed all the short sentences in the story, keeping in mind how (1) a short sentence gains power if it's placed at the end of a paragraph; and (2) it acquires even more force if it's isolated in its own paragraph.

---

2. Richard Lanham, *Revising Prose* (New York: Scribner's, 1979), pp. 25–26.

StyleCheck No. 2: Testing "Emphasis" Positions

You have two methods for creating emphasis within a sentence:

1. *Grammatical emphasis* (where you work to get key words into subject and verb positions)
2. *Positional emphasis* (where you strive to save a memorable word or phrase for the sentence's end)

Are You Making Maximum Use of Grammatical Emphasis? Go through your story with a colored pen, underlining the *subject words* and *verbs* in the base clauses of each sentence.

Then, go back and read all these underlined words out loud, consecutively. Ask yourself: Are you *telling your story* through these subjects and verbs?

A better test: Read that list of words out loud to a friend, and then request, "Based on what you've just heard, tell this story back to me." See what you get back. Would most readers be able to discern at least the larger dimensions of your story through just the subjects and verbs of your base clauses? Do you tend too often to fill these key grammatical positions with abstractions—rather than concrete words or proper nouns—and with "to be" verb forms?

Using a yellow highlighter or other such marker, isolate your story's most crucial half-dozen sentences. Then, do an especially close scrutiny of how you're using the subject and verb in those most critical sentences. The question: Are the subject and verb of the base clauses of these crucial sentences among the *key words* in your story? They should be.

Are You Creating Cadences through Use of Positional Emphasis? Newsroom writing coaches encourage reporters to put important words where they count the most: at a sentence's end. It's particularly valuable to remember to do this at the end of *paragraphs*. Words placed there tend to resonate and linger longer in the reader's mind. If you place rhetorically salient words in that end spot, readers will feel the energy in your prose, and they will better sense your writing voice.

You can easily evaluate how effectively you're using this terminal emphasis position:

Using some sort of color code, mark the last six or so words of all your story's paragraphs. Do you manage to get memorable words or phrases into those "end stress" positions? Or do your sentences tend just to dwin-

dle, dribbling out insignificant information at the ends of too many paragraphs? Are you using that terminal emphasis position to create cadences
that underscore your story's major moments of drama or action? Or, do
you muffle many cadences by repeatedly placing attributive tags at the ends
of paragraphs?

It is there—at the ends of paragraphs—that you're most likely to create
any *emotions* the reader will feel.

Here's a dumb trick that might work. I call it the "Thumper Rabbit
Cadence Test for Prose." It's suggested by Joseph Williams in his book
Style as a way of determining the *intensity* of your cadences:

Read your story out loud, he urges, "thumping your finger on the last
few words of every sentence. Do the words you thump feel like the words
that should be thumped? If not, revise the sentence so that you do thump
on the words that should receive the most emphasis."[3]

What you're trying to determine, with all this thumping, is this: How
much difference is there between your most emphasized and your least
emphasized words? Are you clearly enough signaling *significance* to readers, by placing especially meaningful words in the end spots?

StyleCheck No. 3: Assessing How You "Branch" Sentences

This final "StyleCheck" focuses on how you tend to use what are known as
free modifiers (see pages 200–01). The issues are (1) *where* you tend to put
them and (2) *how long* you tend to extend them.

We have three *directions* for modifying sentences: toward the front; in
the interior; or at the end. Here's a sentence that begins with a "left-branching" free modifier (in italics)—

> *Fearful that the new gang member might be a public informer,*
> Brown hired a private detective to do a background check on
> Stevens.

—and another sentence that's interrupted by a "mid-branching" free
modifier—

---

3. Joseph M. Williams, *Style: Ten Lessons in Clarity and Grace,* 5th Ed. (New York:
Longman, 1997), p. 154.

> Then President Bush, *encouraged by the latest poll that showed him with a 78 percent approval rating,* called Atty. Gen. John Ashcroft and told him to launch the investigation.

—and, finally, one that ends with a "right-branching" free modifier—

> Hurricane Dennis moved along the coast toward the Carolinas on Sunday, *prompting evacuation orders for the fragile Outer Banks barrier islands.*

Using a color code for each type of branch, go through the story and underline all the free modifiers. (Some sentences may include more than one type.) Then, count the number of left branches in the story, and do the same for mid branches and right branches What *percentage* of your sentences includes left branches? Mid branches? Right branches?

Now, count all the words in each left-branching modifier, and total these numbers. Do the same for mid branches and right branches. Divide the total number of words in all the left branches by the total number of left-branching sentences so that you can see how long these front-loaded modifiers tend to be, when you use them. Do the same for mid-branching and right-branching structures.

Take the total number of words in your story, and divide that figure into the total number of words in all your left branches. What percentage of your total word count is left-branching? And do the same for mid-branching structures and right-branching.

These figures could point to some of your *tendencies* when it comes to how you branch modification structures. You might discover consequential habits in your writing that you aren't conscious of (and some that you badly need to change).

Left-Branching Modifiers. What percentage of your sentences branch to the left? More significantly, *how long* on average is that branch? Those numbers can be critical. When you branch modification to the left of a sentence (like this one), you *delay* the announcement of its topic. Challenged by a sentence that begins (like this one does) with a long left-branching free modifier, a reader may struggle to find your meaning. And if many sentences in your story begin that way, the reader may flip pages to seek easier fare. It thus makes sense for a reporter to be *sparing* in the frequency and length of left-branching constructions.

Mid-Branching Modifiers. How many of your sentences include suspensive, mid-branching constructions? More importantly, how *long* are these constructions? How long, on average, do you *delay* the mating of subject and verb in the base clause of sentences where you deploy mid-branching modifiers? The writer, faced with the choice of whether or not to insert a mid-branching modifier like this one you're reading, must decide how much the construction will test the reader's attention span or patience. (Did it cost you extra energy to fathom that last sentence? Could a different structure have made it easier to read?)

Mid-branching and left-branching free modifiers are not in themselves damnable. Each can be effectively used in journalistic writing—so long as you remain aware that you're holding readers in syntactic suspension, and so long as you know *why* you're doing that.

Right-Branching Modifiers. The greater beauty of right branches is that they appear *after* your base clause has declared your subject and verb, allowing you to get away with writing much *longer* modifiers that will likely remain impressively clear.

The clarity of your writing depends significantly on how you begin sentences; but the way you end them more often determines your writing's vigor, voice, and emphasis. A right-branching sentence allows you to express your topic at the front and then to focus the rest of the sentence on elaborating and refining your meaning. If you can save evocative words for the end, that gives your right-branching sentence all the more power and cadence.

—

This "Count-the-Peas" approach to examining style is mathematical, but, ultimately, it's entirely subjective. *You* have to interpret what the numbers suggest. The potential is there for this tedious finger counting and underlining to yield a telling X-ray of your writing.

What you see may benefit your effort to create stories that are more accessible, rhythmical, and forceful.

Meanwhile, we'll await the delivery of those upgraded software media, those "writing partners" capable of revealing more than just the difference between our *burros* and *burrows.*

Most items in this list of our favorite books about writing were published recently. Thanks to the expansion of the Internet to include Web sites selling used books, even the older titles can usually be obtained easily.

A few books on our list were written by novelists, others by English teachers or grammarians, but most are by journalists who learned the fundamentals of their craft through years of long days—and sometimes longer nights—toiling over stories in newsrooms.

All provide insight into what writers do as they search for stories, for structures, for sentences, and for words that will attract readers and compel them to continue reading. —DENNIS JACKSON AND JOHN SWEENEY

The Writing Life

Becoming a Writer, by Dorothea Brande (1934/Macmillan, 1996).

This 1934 classic about writers and the creative process has been reissued. Brande's chapters on "Harnessing the Unconscious" and "Learning to See Again" and her observations about writers' work habits still inspire.

Bird by Bird: Some Instructions on Writing and Life, by Anne Lamott (Doubleday, 1994).

Lamott never bores and often delights with her offbeat views on life and art. The talented author of novels and nonfiction books here conducts a lengthy workshop, and nearly everything she says about creative writing can be applied daily by newsroom writers.

How Reading Changed My Life, by Anna Quindlen (Ballantine, 1998).

This engaging little book by novelist and Pulitzer-winning columnist Quindlen reminds us that "there are only two ways, really, to become a writer. One is to write. The other is to read." Her short paean on the joys of reading concludes with her listing scores of books she loves and recommends.

Wild Mind: Living the Writer's Life, by Natalie Goldberg (Bantam, 1990).

Here and in *Writing Down the Bones* (1986) and *Thunder and Lightning* (2000), Goldberg suggests how writers can escape "monkey mind" (the conscious self) to enter the unconscious realm of "wild mind." She translates her idiosyncratic ideas into practical instructions that can help writers both free their imagination and discover discipline in their work.

The Writing Life, by Annie Dillard (Harper, 1989).

This short volume takes a comparatively highbrow approach to the Art of writing. But Dillard interestingly recounts "what the actual process of writing feels like . . . inside the mind at work," and provides technical information that holds value for journalists.

Finding Good *Stories*

The Art and Craft of Feature Writing, by William E. Blundell (Plume, 1988).

A former top writer and editor at the *Wall Street Journal* offers the lowdown on how the *Journal* staff comes up with those marvelous front-page features. Blundell is especially good on ways to frame a story. He covers the entire process, from a story's conception to the reporter's final act of self-editing and revision.

Intimate Journalism: The Art and Craft of Reporting Everyday Life,
by Walt Harrington (1997/Sage Publications, 2000).

> A solid collection of stories about real people. Harrington, in his excellent "Prologue" and "A Writer's Essay: Seeking the Extraordinary in the Ordinary," spells out what it takes to make readers care.

Writing Nonfiction Narrative

The Art of Fiction: Notes on Craft for Young Writers, **by John Gardner (1984/Vintage, 1991).**

> Gardner, a poet and novelist, taught fiction writing for many years before his death. This book is based on his notes from those classes. Whether you are a young writer or old, if you try the exercises, you will learn a thing or two about the power of observation.

Follow the Story: How to Write Successful Nonfiction,
by James B. Stewart (Touchstone, 1998).

> Clear, convincing advice from a former *Wall Street Journal* editor, Pulitzer-winning reporter, and author of best-selling nonfiction books. Stewart teaches and demonstrates narrative writing techniques, devoting chapters to topics such as leads, transitions, structure, description, dialogue, anecdotes, and endings.

Writing Creative Nonfiction: How to Use Fiction Techniques to Make Your Nonfiction More Interesting, Dramatic, and Vivid,
by Theodore A. Rees Cheney (Ten Speed Press, 1991).

> A readable explanation of how to alternate scenes and summary, with helpful observations on handling dialogue.

Writing for Story: Craft Secrets of Dramatic Nonfiction by a Two-Time Pulitzer Prize Winner, **by Jon Franklin (1986/Plume, 1994).**

> Franklin advises feature writers to get back to old-fashioned storytelling. His chapter on how to organize material is worth the price of the book. He also includes two examples of his own writing, so you see a master at work.

Developing Your Craft

The Art of Readable Writing, **by Rudolf Flesch (1949/Macmillan, 1994).**

> Flesch's "Readability Formula" is based on statistics that now seem dated. But his argument in favor of "plain talk" in newspapers—concise, uncomplicated declarative sentences, written in familiar words—has as much resonance and meaning for journalists today as it did in 1949. Flesch's book remains in print, and for good reasons.

Best Newspaper Writing, **edited by Christopher Scanlan (Poynter, 2000).**

> Since 1979, the annual volumes of *Best Newspaper Writing* have reprinted winning stories from the American Society of Newspaper Editors Distinguished Writing Awards. The books also feature informative interviews with the winning reporters, their comments often centering on *how* they write and revise stories.

Coaching Writers: The Essential Guide for Editors and Reporters,
by Roy Peter Clark and Don Fry (St. Martin's, 1992).

> Clark and Fry are leaders of the good-writing movement at newspapers. They offer tips on how editors and reporters can work together. They also give examples of how writers benefit from knowing how the writing process works.

Editing for Today's Newsroom, by Carl Sessions Stepp (Lawrence Erlbaum Associates, 1989).

See chapter 7 for ways editors can help writers find the real story. And see sidebar 6 for how *not* to edit copy.

Good Advice on Writing: Great Quotations from Writers Past and Present on How to Write Well, edited by William Safire and Leonard Safir (Fireside, 1993).

Compendium of treasurable statements about writing—hundreds of them, alphabetized by subject (accuracy, adjectives, brainstorming, clarity, clichés, etc.). Inspiration, insight, and frequent laughs can be gained from this and similar compilations—such as Donald Murray's *Shoptalk* (1990), George Plimpton's *The Writer's Chapbook* (1989), or Jon Winokur's *Advice to Writers* (1999).

Newsthinking: The Secret of Making Your Facts Fall into Place, by Bob Baker (1981/ revised edition, Allyn & Bacon, 2002).

A book devoted to mental organization. Baker, a *Los Angeles Times* editor and freelance writing coach, constructs a model of how a skilled reporter uses the moments between the last scrawl in a notebook and the first stroke at the keyboard.

One Writer's Beginnings, by Eudora Welty (1984/Harvard, 1995).

Little gem of a book by one of America's master storytellers. It features three sections: "Listening," "Learning to See," and "Finding a Voice"—titles that reflect the book's relevance for newsroom writers.

Revising Prose, by Richard A. Lanham (1979/Allyn and Bacon, 2000).

Frequently reprinted, this is perhaps the best book on revision techniques. Lanham provides a "cure" for what he derides as "The Official Style"—be it "bureaucratic, social-scientific, [or] computer-engineering-military"—and underscores the need for translating all writing "into plain English." Especially good: chapter 3 on "Sentence Length, Rhythm, and Sound."

Style: Writing and Reading as the Discovery of Outlook, by Richard M. Eastman (1970/Oxford, 1984).

One of the classic writing textbooks used in American colleges in the 1970s and 1980s. Reporters of any generation can learn from its chapters on "The Vocabulary of Detail," "The Vocabulary of Feeling," and "The Vocabulary of Intensification." Eastman also thoroughly explains the techniques of effective sentence building.

Writing and Reporting News: A Coaching Method, by Carole Rich (1994/Wadsworth, 2000).

Perhaps the best of recent print journalism textbooks. It includes seven chapters on "Constructing Stories" that can be useful not only for novices but as well for veterans seeking to learn imaginative new ways to approach the old art of storytelling in newspapers.

Writing to Deadline: The Journalist at Work, by Donald M. Murray (Heinemann, 2000).

Expands Murray's small but worthy volume *Writing for Your Readers* (now out of print). The Pulitzer-winning columnist and acknowledged dean of newsroom writing coaches attempts to "demystify" journalism by breaking it down into a *process*, a "logical series of language acts that anyone who can write . . . can perform." Especially good on story organization, leads, style, and editing.

Writing with Power, by Peter Elbow (1981/Oxford, 1998).

Written by one of the most respected writing teachers in U.S. colleges, this volume is long (384 pages) but rewarding. Elbow stresses writing as a *process.* His five chapters on revision—"the hardest task of all"—provide valuable tips on how to get more "power" into a final draft.

Working with Words

Associated Press Guide to News Writing, by Rene J. Cappon (1982/Prentice Hall, 1991).

See Cappon's chapter on clichés for an idea of the kinds of sins we commit every day.

The Careful Writer: A Modern Guide to English Usage, by Theodore Bernstein (1965/Free Press, 1998).

A little dated (but still in print), Bernstein's book is based on his years as an in-house critic at the *New York Times.* See his section titled "One idea to a sentence." Also see his *Watch Your Language* (1958), particularly chapter 2, "Storytelling," for sound advice on writing leads.

Modern American Usage, by Wilson Follett, edited by Jacques Barzun (1966/Hill & Wang, 1998).

Barzun completed Follett's work after the author died. Barzun is a conservative on many points of usage, but you may find him persuasive. Read the section on "journalese."

The New Fowler's Modern English Usage, by Henry Fowler, 3rd Ed., edited by R. W. Burchfield (1926/Oxford, 1998).

Often revised—and updated as recently as 1998—this is the classic for purists. If you want to be a language maven, this is the book you have to own, read, and use.

The Suspended Sentence: A Guide for Writers, by Roscoe C. Born (1986/Iowa State, 1993).

A longtime reporter and editor for publications such as the *Wall Street Journal,* Born offers a useful series of memos on errors frequently committed by writers. See chapter 5 on "who" and "whom"—it's the best explanation around.

The Transitive Vampire: A Handbook of Grammar for the Innocent, the Eager, and the Doomed, by Karen Elizabeth Gordon (Times Books, 1984).

A good-humored look at how sentences work and why. Despite the light touch, it gives you the basics of grammar in a clear, concise way. Pantheon books published an enlarged edition in 1993, titled *The Deluxe Transitive Vampire.*

Words on Words, by John B. Bremner (1980/MJF Books, 1998).

Interesting facts on the origins and usage of words. Bremner picks up where Theodore Bernstein left off. The book is authoritative and entertaining.

RICHARD AREGOOD won the Pulitzer Prize for commentary in 1985, for his *Philadelphia Daily News* editorials. His editorials have also brought him a Walker Stone Award and an unprecedented three Distinguished Writing Awards from the American Society of Newspaper Editors. He joined the *Daily News* in 1966, subsequently working as a news reporter, assistant city editor, features editor, deputy sports editor, news editor, and editorial writer before becoming editorial page editor in 1980. A native of New Jersey, he moved to the *Newark Star-Ledger* in 1995 to become editorial page editor there.

AMANDA BENNETT was part of a team of *Wall Street Journal* reporters who won a Pulitzer Prize in 1997 for articles chronicling the development of AIDS therapies. She had a long, distinguished career as a *Wall Street Journal* reporter and served for a time as its Atlanta bureau chief. In 1998 she joined the Portland *Oregonian* as managing editor in charge of investigative and long-range projects, and she was a leader of an editorial team there that won the 2001 Pulitzer Prize for public service. In summer 2001 she was named editor and senior vice president of the *Lexington Herald-Leader* in Kentucky. She is the author of *The Death of the Organization Man* (1990) and coauthor of *The Man Who Stayed Behind* (1993) and *The Quiet Room* (1994).

MARK BOWDEN was a National Book Award Finalist for his best-selling *Black Hawk Down* (1999), which recounts the 1993 Battle of Mogadishu in Somalia. Portions of that tale first appeared as a twenty-nine-part serial in the *Philadelphia Inquirer,* and the stories received the Overseas Press Club's 1998 Boyle Award for Best Foreign Reporting. Bowden helped adapt *Black Hawk Down* into a screenplay for a major motion picture. That film, produced by Jerry Bruckheimer and directed by Ridley Scott, opened nationwide in January 2002. Bowden's more recent thirty-eight-part *Inquirer* series, "Killing Pablo," revealed the secret ways the United States funded and participated in the deadly manhunt for Columbian drug lord Pablo Escobar. The stories provided the basis for an hour-long CNN documentary aired in 2000, and an expanded version of the *Inquirer* series was published as *Killing Pablo: The Hunt for the World's Greatest Outlaw* (2001). Simon and Schuster simultaneously released *Killing Pablo* as the first-ever enhanced CD audiobook. An earlier *Inquirer* story by Bowden—about an unemployed Philadelphia dockworker who found $1.2 million—was made into the 1991 feature film *Money for Nothing.* His stories have appeared in *Playboy, Sports Illustrated, Men's Journal, Rolling Stone, Creative Nonfiction,* and *Readers Digest.* He has written two other books, *Doctor Dealer* (1987) and *Bringing the Heat* (1994). He is currently writing a screen adaptation of *Killing Pablo,* and continues to work, as he has since 1979, as a reporter for the *Philadelphia Inquirer.*

J. TAYLOR BUCKLEY is a long-time reporter and writing coach for *USA Today.* He began there in 1982 as founding managing editor of the "Money" section, and he later became the paper's first and only full-time in-house critic, writing daily critiques and a training journal for the staff. He still travels to Gannett Company newsrooms to teach writing and reporting techniques. At *USA Today* he has also worked as a sports columnist and as the paper's first full-time Moscow correspondent. In four decades as a print journalist, he has also been a city hall reporter, city editor, news editor, business editor, and editor-in-chief, and was the first managing editor in Wilmington, Delaware, to be in charge of both the *Morning News* and *Evening Journal.*

LUCILLE S. DEVIEW is writing coach at the *Orange County Register* in California and has coached editors and reporters at the *Christian Science Monitor,* at *Florida Today,* and at numerous media writing workshops around the country. Earlier, she was associate editor of fifteen weeklies in the Detroit area and an award-winning staff writer at the *Detroit News.* Her collection of essays, *Up North: A Contemporary Woman's Walden,* was published in 1977. One of her plays, "A Summer with Hemingway's Twin," won the 1997 National Play Award from the National Repertory Theatre Foundation in Hollywood. It was included in the Festival of New American Plays at the Charlotte Repertory Theatre and received a full performance at the Alternative Repertory Theatre in Santa Ana, California, in 1999. Born in 1920, deView continued through 2001 writing "Retrospective," her weekly column on aging that is syndicated by Knight-Ridder/Tribune News.

DONALD DRAKE works on special projects and coaches narrative writing at the *Philadelphia Inquirer,* where he has been a reporter and editor since 1966. He is the author of *Medical School* (1978), which follows students from their first day in medical school through their residencies; *Hard Choices: Health Care at What Cost?* (1993); and *Making Medicine, Making Money* (1993). He began his career as a copy boy for the *New York Herald Tribune* in 1954 and subsequently worked as a reporter at a medical magazine and five newspapers. Drake was *Newsday's* first science and medicine writer. His stories have won numerous awards from media and medical groups, and in 1982 he received a Robert F. Kennedy Journalism Award that annually honors outstanding reporting on problems of the disadvantaged.

JON FRANKLIN won the first Pulitzer Prizes ever awarded in the categories of feature writing (1979) and explanatory journalism (1985). He won his Pulitzers while working for Baltimore's *Evening Sun* and subsequently spent nine years as a creative writing teacher at the University of Oregon. His books include *Shocktrauma* (with Alan Doelp, 1980), *Not Quite a Miracle: Brain Surgeons and Their Patients on the Frontier of Medicine* (with Doelp, 1983), *Guinea Pig Doctors* (with John Sutherland, 1984), *Writing for Story: Craft Secrets of Dramatic Nonfiction* (1986), and *The Molecules of the Mind* (1987). After a recent stint as a science writer, special assignments editor, and writing coach at the Raleigh, North Carolina, *News & Observer,* Franklin now holds the Merrill Chair in Journalism at the University of Maryland.

LYNN FRANKLIN is editor of WriterL, an e-mail writing workshop. With her husband Jon Franklin she cofounded *bylines*, an online publisher of literary nonfiction. Her nonfiction novella *Comfort Me with Apples*—about the recovery of heritage varieties of fruit—appeared on *bylines* in 1997. She lives in Maryland and is working on a book about literary theft.

KEN FUSON won the 1998 American Society of Newspaper Editors Distinguished Writing Award for non-deadline writing. His winning entry was a six-story series he wrote for the *Baltimore Sun* about the backstage preparations for a high school musical. On three previous occasions he had been a finalist for that ASNE award. After a two-year stint in Baltimore, he has returned to work as a general assignment reporter for the *Des Moines Register,* where he has spent most of his career. Fuson also won the 1996 National Headliner Award in feature writing and the 1998 gold medal in the International Regional Magazine

Association's annual competition for best personality feature, for a story he wrote for the *Iowan Magazine*.

DENNIS JACKSON served as editor of the *D. H. Lawrence Review* (1984–94), as managing editor of the *Irish Renaissance Annual* (1980–83), and as guest editor of a special issue of *Style* titled *Newspaper Writing as Art* (1982). He co-edited essay collections titled *D. H. Lawrence's "Lady"* (1985), *Critical Essays on D. H. Lawrence* (1988), *D. H. Lawrence's Literary Inheritors* (1991), and *Editing D. H. Lawrence* (1995), and is the author of *A Programmed Study of Accelerated Reading Skills* (1975). He spent a decade covering sports for newspapers in Mississippi and Arkansas. In 1994 he was Seminar Director for the United States Information Agency's "Bulgarian Mass Media Development Program" in Sofia. He has worked often as a writing coach for East Coast newspapers and media groups. His most recent articles appeared in *Etudes Lawrenciennes, The Black Scholar,* and *Men's Health,* reflecting what he calls his "pathologically eclectic" range of interests. He received a Senior Fellowship from the National Endowment for the Humanities in 1999 to work on a biography of the African-American journalist and political activist Chuck Stone. At the University of Delaware, Jackson is professor of English and Director of Journalism.

HUGH A. MULLIGAN worked as a Special Correspondent for the Associated Press from the 1960s until his retirement in 2001. His assignments carried him to 142 countries; wars in Vietnam, Cambodia, Biafra, Cyprus, and the Middle East; various space shots and presidential campaigns; and on virtually every major trip taken by Pope John Paul II. Mulligan was one of the few reporters present in both St. Paul's Cathedral when Princess Diana married Prince Charles and in Westminster Abbey for her funeral. He covered the rise and fall of the Berlin Wall, President Nixon's trips to China and Russia, and the conclaves that elected the last three popes. He had exclusive interviews with Margaret Thatcher, Ronald Reagan, Bob Dole, the Shah of Iran, Gen. William Westmoreland, South Vietnam Premier Nguyen Cao Ky, Casey Stengel, Bob Hope, and Marilyn Monroe, among many others. For ten years his column "Mulligan's Stew" appeared in more than four hundred papers. His books include *No Place to Die: The Agony of Vietnam* (1966) and *The Torch Is Passed* (1964), the latter an account of President Kennedy's assassination. He has a master's degree in English from Harvard University and in journalism from Boston University. Before joining the AP in 1951, he taught high school Greek and Latin. He won major honors for his reporting from Vietnam and Cambodia, and in 1972 and 1978 he received the prestigious Associated Press Managing Editors Award for outstanding reporting. Between trips, Mulligan has lived for years in Ridgefield, Connecticut.

JIM NAUGHTON has been President of the Poynter Institute for Media Studies since 1996. Previously, he served as executive editor of the *Philadelphia Inquirer* and was widely recognized as one of the driving forces that led to that paper's receipt of more than a dozen Pulitzer Prizes for reporting during the 1980s. After starting as a reporter at the *Cleveland Plain Dealer,* he moved to the *New York Times* in 1969 and acquired a national reputation for his coverage of the 1972 presidential campaign, the downfall of Vice President Spiro Agnew, the Nixon White House, and the Congressional Watergate hearings. He joined the *Inquirer* in 1977 as its national/foreign news editor and remained with the paper until late 1995.

TOM SILVESTRI is vice president in charge of Media General Inc. community newspapers in Alabama, South Carolina, northern Virginia, and northern Florida. Before joining the Richmond-based parent company as director of news synergy and editor of Media General News Bank in 1998, he worked as deputy managing editor at the Richmond, Virginia, *Times-Dispatch*. He directed weekend operations, training, and staff development. Earlier, while he was senior editor for business news, the *Times-Dispatch*'s business section was judged best in the state by the Virginia Press Association (VPA) and one of the best sections in the nation by the Society of American Business Editors and Writers and the National Association of Real Estate Editors. Silvestri had previously worked as a reporter and editor for Gannett Westchester (N.Y.) Newspapers. He frequently leads workshops for media groups and helped found the Virginia Writers' Workshop, sponsored by the VPA. He has a master's degree in business administration from Virginia Commonwealth University.

CARL SESSIONS STEPP is senior editor of the *American Journalism Review* and the author of *Editing for Today's Newsroom* (1989) and *Writing as Craft and Magic* (2000). He has published scores of articles on writing and editing and has served as a writing and editing coach at more than thirty newspapers, including *USA Today* and the *Washington Post*. He worked as a reporter and editor at the *St. Petersburg Times, Charlotte Observer,* and *USA Today* before 1983, when he moved to his present job as a journalism professor at the University of Maryland.

JOHN SWEENEY is public editor and newsroom writing coach for the *News Journal* in Wilmington, Delaware. He has worked with the Wilmington Writers' Workshop since its beginning in 1992, and he currently directs the annual program. He joined the *News Journal* in 1983 and has worked as a copyeditor, city editor, and weekend editor. Earlier, he had been assistant news editor for the Jacksonville, Florida, *Times-Union* and a news reporter at the *Bucks County Courier-Times* in Levittown, Pennsylvania. Sweeney is a former president of the international Organization of News Ombudsmen.

JEANNE MURRAY WALKER has written five volumes of poetry, including *Nailing Up the Home Sweet Home* (1980), *Coming Into History* (1990), and *Gaining Time* (1997). Her poetry regularly appears in periodicals such as *Poetry, American Poetry Review, The Nation,* and *Image.* Among her numerous awards are a National Endowment for the Arts Fellowship, the Calladay Award, and the Prairie-Schooner/Strousse Award. In 1998 she was named a Pew Fellow in Poetry and received a $50,000 stipend. In 1990 she wrote her first play, "Stories from the National Enquirer," and it won the Washington National Theater Competition. Her plays subsequently have been performed in Boston, Chicago, London, and various other cities. Her most recent work, "Inventing Montana," was performed at the Centenary Stage in Hackettstown, New Jersey, in March 2000. She travels frequently in America and abroad to read her work and to teach writing workshops. She lives in Philadelphia and teaches at the University of Delaware.

Books from Allworth Press

Making Crime Pay: The Writer's Guide to Criminal Law, Evidence, and Procedure by Andrea Campbell (paperback, 6 × 9, 320 pages, $19.95)

The Writer's Guide to Queries, Pitches & Proposals by Moira Anderson Allen (paperback, 6 × 9, 288 pages, $16.95)

writing.com: Creative Internet Strategies to Advance Your Writing Career by Moira Anderson Allen (paperback, 6 × 9, 256 pages, $16.95)

The Writer's Legal Guide, Second Edition by Tad Crawford and Tony Lyons (paperback, 6 × 9, 320 pages, $19.95)

Marketing Strategies for Writers by Michael Sedge (paperback, 6 × 9, 224 pages, $16.95)

Writing for Interactive Media: The Complete Guide by Jon Samsel and Darryl Wimberly (paperback, 6 × 9, 320 pages, $19.95)

Business and Legal Forms for Authors and Self-Publishers, Revised Edition by Tad Crawford (paperback (with CD-ROM), 8½ × 11, 192 pages, $22.95)

The Writer's Guide to Corporate Communications by Mary Moreno (paperback, 6 × 9, 192 pages, $19.95)

How to Write Articles That Sell, Second Edition by L. Perry Wilbur and Jon Samsel (hardcover, 6 × 9, 224 pages, $19.95)

How to Write Books That Sell, Second Edition by L. Perry Wilbur and Jon Samsel (hardcover, 6 × 9, 224 pages, $19.95)

Writing Scripts Hollywood Will Love, Revised Edition by Katherine Atwell Herbert (paperback, 6 × 9, 160 pages, $14.95)

So You Want to Be a Screenwriter: How to Face the Fears and Take the Risks by Sara Caldwell and Marie-Eve Kielson (paperback, 6 × 9, 224 pages, $14.95)

The Screenwriter's Guide to Agents and Managers by John Scott Lewinski (paperback, 6 × 9, 256 pages, $18.95)

The Screenwriter's Legal Guide, Second Edition by Stephen F. Breimer (paperback, 6 × 9, 320 pages, $19.95)

Please write to request our free catalog. To order by credit card, call 1-800-491-2808 or send a check or money order to Allworth Press, 10 East 23rd Street, Suite 510, New York, NY 10010. Include $5 for shipping and handling for the first book ordered and $1 for each additional book. Ten dollars plus $1 for each additional book if ordering from Canada. New York State residents must add sales tax.

To see our complete catalog on the World Wide Web, or to order online, you can find us at *www.allworth.com*.